WORLDS WOVEN TOGETHER

Literature Now

Literature Now
Matthew Hart, David James, and Rebecca L. Walkowitz, Series Editors

Literature Now offers a distinct vision of late-twentieth- and early-twenty-first-century literary culture. Addressing contemporary literature and the ways we understand its meaning, the series includes books that are comparative and transnational in scope as well as those that focus on national and regional literary cultures.

Caren Irr, *Toward the Geopolitical Novel: U.S. Fiction in the Twenty-First Century*
Heather Houser, *Ecosickness in Contemporary U.S. Fiction: Environment and Affect*
Mrinalini Chakravorty, *In Stereotype: South Asia in the Global Literary Imaginary*
Héctor Hoyos, *Beyond Bolaño: The Global Latin American Novel*
Rebecca L. Walkowitz, *Born Translated: The Contemporary Novel in an Age of World Literature*
Carol Jacobs, *Sebald's Vision*
Sarah Phillips Casteel, *Calypso Jews: Jewishness in the Caribbean Literary Imagination*
Jeremy Rosen, *Minor Characters Have Their Day: Genre and the Contemporary Literary Marketplace*
Jesse Matz, *Lasting Impressions: The Legacies of Impressionism in Contemporary Culture*
Ashley T. Shelden, *Unmaking Love: The Contemporary Novel and the Impossibility of Union*
Theodore Martin, *Contemporary Drift: Genre, Historicism, and the Problem of the Present*
Zara Dinnen, *The Digital Banal: New Media and American Literature and Culture*
Gloria Fisk, *Orhan Pamuk and the Good of World Literature*
Peter Morey, *Islamophobia and the Novel*
Sarah Chihaya, Merve Emre, Katherine Hill, and Jill Richards, *The Ferrante Letters: An Experiment in Collective Criticism*
Christy Wampole, *Degenerative Realism: Novel and Nation in Twenty-First-Century France*
Heather Houser, *Infowhelm: Environmental Art and Literature in an Age of Data*
Jessica Pressman, *Bookishness: Loving Books in a Digital Age*
Sunny Xiang, *Tonal Intelligence: The Aesthetics of Asian Inscrutability During the Long Cold War*
Thomas Heise, *The Gentrification Plot: New York and the Postindustrial Crime Novel*
Ellen C. Jones, *Literature in Motion: Translating Multilingualism Across the Americas*

WORLDS WOVEN TOGETHER

ESSAYS ON POETRY AND POETICS

VIDYAN RAVINTHIRAN

COLUMBIA UNIVERSITY PRESS   New York

COLUMBIA UNIVERSITY PRESS
Publishers Since 1893
NEW YORK   CHICHESTER, WEST SUSSEX
cup.columbia.edu

Copyright © 2022 Columbia University Press
All rights reserved

Library of Congress Cataloging-in-Publication Data
Names: Ravinthiran, Vidyan, author.
Title: Worlds woven together : essays on poetry and poetics / Vidyan Ravinthiran.
Description: New York : Columbia University Press, 2022. | Series: Literature now |
Includes bibliographical references and index.
Identifiers: LCCN 2021048834 (print) | LCCN 2021048835 (ebook) |
ISBN 9780231202749 (hardback) | ISBN 9780231202756 (trade paperback) |
ISBN 9780231554695 (ebook)
Subjects: LCSH: Poetry—History and criticism. | Poetics. | LCGFT: Literary criticism. | Essays.
Classification: LCC PN1136 .R38 2022 (print) | LCC PN1136 (ebook) |
DDC 808.1—dc23/eng/20220225
LC record available at https://lccn.loc.gov/2021048834
LC ebook record available at https://lccn.loc.gov/2021048835

Cover design: Chang Jae Lee
Cover image: © Mark Fiennes Archive / Bridgeman Images

for Arvind

The special contribution of literature is its vision, its intuitive grasp of structure, its perspective; not the facts themselves so viewed, but the facts as seen by the imaginative accuracy of a mind that is not merely factual. Therefore, any use of literary examples to illustrate simply, say, overcrowding in cities or the slum problem or modernisation is no use at all, for we bring our categories to it and take them out again, with no new insights gained from the give-and-take. . . . Literature provides patterns and hypotheses directly relevant to social science. It provides a repertoire of perceptions otherwise not available, or perceptions that social-scientists reach only after infinite pains and fact-finding. William Blake said, "Whatever is proven today was once imagined."
—A. K. Ramanujan, *"Towards an Anthology of City Images"* (1970)

Contents

Acknowledgments xi

Introduction 1

"A slave and worshiper at love's doorstep": Mir Taqi Mir 21

Censorship and the Role of the Poet in the Work of Ana Blandiana 30

At Home or Nowhere: A. K. Ramanujan 40

Your Thorns Are the Best Part of You: Marianne Moore and Stevie Smith 55

Eunice de Souza and Indian Speech 77

"Emmental freedom": Czesław Miłosz 90

"There must be something to say": On Verse Sound 100

Elizabeth Bishop, Robert Penn Warren, Cleanth Brooks, Communication, and Other People 111

Ted Hughes, Keith Sagar, and the Poetics of Letter Prose 129

Rae Armantrout's Lonely Dream 141

Dreaming the World: Vinod Kumar Shukla's Extraordinary Sentences 154

Srinivas Rayaprol and Gāmini Salgādo 168

You Can't Close Your Eyes for a Sec: Arvind Krishna Mehrotra 184

Thom Gunn's Shadows Hard as Board   194

Galway Kinnell, Trying to Become Winged   206

A. R. Ammons and "the political (read, human) world"   218

Postlyric and the Already Known: Dawn Lundy Martin   228

"I am not speaking of or as myself or for any/one":
Vahni (Anthony) Capildeo   243

Bibliography   259
Permissions   263
Index   265

Acknowledgments

First, my wife Jenny and my son Frank. Then my parents: Aruljothy and Thirunavukkarasu Ravinthiran. For the books on the shelves—still more for your personal, inimitable, talk styles and gestures. The microculture you recreated in the North of England: a little piece of Sri Lanka. Thank you for your effervescent, unkillable alternative—a demandingly joyous moral and spiritual and aesthetic alternative—to the voices of academia and book talk and popular culture where people resembling us are thin on the ground.

Sometimes, having surfeited on journal articles or book reviews, I feel there's but one route to go. Speaking with you—dextrous migrants, fearlessly jocose Tamils (survivors free of self-pity's emotional clichés)—always sets me right.

Professors Jahan Ramazani, Laetitia Zecchini, Peter D. McDonald, Arvind Krishna Mehrotra, Stephanie Burt, Sandeep Parmar, and Maureen N. McLane read these essays carefully and helped improve them. So did Philip Leventhal and Susan Pensak at Columbia University Press and the editors of the Literature Now series: in particular, I'm grateful to David James. Also to the mentors and mentees and organizers of Ledbury Emerging Critics—both past and present, including those who've left the program—for challenging me to think feelingly and feel thoughtfully. Vikrant Dadawalla helped my essay on Shukla: thank you, Vikrant.

Most of these essays wouldn't exist but for their commissioning editors: Don Share at *Poetry*, Michael Schmidt at *PN Review*, Alan Gillis at the *Edinburgh Review*, Emily Berry at the *Poetry Review*, Meghan O'Rourke at the *Yale Review*, Anjum Hasan at the *Caravan*, Gerald Maa and

Caroline Jean Bartunek at the *Georgia Review*, and Clare Pollard at *Modern Poetry in Translation*, who let me turn in a piece on Mir Taqi Mir four times longer than requested. Thank you for letting me write weird and sometimes wild sentences about the books I love.

WORLDS WOVEN TOGETHER

Introduction

In 1998, Oxford University Press published *Grub Street and the Ivory Tower*, a book of essays contending that "there has rarely been as sharp a distinction" between literary journalism and academic scholarship "as has often been supposed (or wished by some people on both sides)." Big names from both sides contribute essays, with a decent mix of men and women, though everyone appears to be white. The best is Marjorie Perloff's: while the *Times Literary Supplement* brings in specialists for other subjects, she adds this isn't so for poetry—all you need to review for them is to be a well-connected (read male, metropolitan) "certified poet." She excoriates the entitled for dismissing offhandedly swathes of literature they haven't the tools to grasp—reviewers who, above all else, "know what they like."

A smug knowingness is a terrible place to start—as a critic, a poet, or a scholar. It's really closed-mindedness. Certainly, reviewers shouldn't ditch their standards, but in a (poetic) multiculture rife with conscious and unconscious biases, the line dividing aesthetic, from other forms, of discrimination is thinner than we'd like. Our tastes are shaped by our milieu. This is tough to admit, and variegation is to some a fearful thing. We've seen in politics the resurgence of the grumpy plainspeaker, the populist who won't hesitate before declaring his whim law, and some critics—whatever their espoused values—embrace this persona. We struggle with his brusque charms (perhaps he lives inside you as inside me, straining and yapping like a dog at its chain).

At large in the literary world, he has, still, too much power—he's boring—continually being found out, then going on his way quite untouched. He is immortal. Keats met him and saw through him at once, the "man who cannot feel he has a personal identity unless he has made up his mind about everything. . . . Dilke will never come at a truth as long as he lives; because he is always trying at it." In fact, we owe to Charles Wentworth Dilke, editor and author and Navy bureaucrat, one of Keats's great ideas—"I had not a dispute but a disquisition with Dilke, on various subjects; several things dovetailed in my mind, & at once it struck me . . . I mean Negative Capability, that is when man is capable of being in uncertainties, Mysteries, doubts, without any irritable reaching after fact & reason"—and with him I hold no grudge. For Dilke was merely an avatar, of that transnational and transperiodic god of complacency, the Great Mansplainer in the Sky: allergic to uncertainty, always sure who's in and who's out (and pleased as punch to play bouncer). A figure—an aspect of ourselves—to resist. I help organize the Ledbury Emerging Critics scheme, which, founded and overseen by Sandeep Parmar and Sarah Howe, aims to racially diversify literary journalism. Many of our mentees reject the categorical, ipse-dixitish, *de haut en bas* style Perloff laments. Should they arrive at the center of literary power, they won't resemble their peers—they won't *pass*—and so they, mostly women, refuse, some of them, to "write white." Not that they've always the option. Qualities praised in others may be editorially suppressed in their writing (anger, for instance, reads in white men as righteous indignation: among people of color, as among women more generally, it is stigmatized as hysteria and delusion). And Ledbury Critics Stephanie Sy-Quia and Nasser Hussain have also critiqued (in *Tank* magazine) such "shallowly racialist" reviews as poets of color often receive, when reviewers who "know what they like" are stymied by work shaped by pressures they don't immediately understand and are disinclined to research.

I start with Keats because, although these essays were written over many years, and without the anticipation of one day conjoining and cohering, going back to edit and revise and, in some cases, thoroughly rewrite them, I discovered that Romantic poet popping up all over the place. Negative capability is one cure for facilely fizzy journalism; the overly systematizing nature of some academic discourse; and for the tendency to camouflage provincialism as a sensitivity to forms of difference one finds ways of neglecting (by, perhaps, announcing its absolute otherness, fetishizing it, or asking "as a white person can I really teach or write about this material?," hiding the real motivations behind "staying in your lane").

Let's consider poets of color in the UK and the U.S., and those resident in the Global South. Journalism often treats their work blithely, biographically, and in terms of a notional "authenticity" it remains in the metropolitan reviewer's power to confer or deny. But academia has the opposite tendency, of tiptoeing conceptually around the work, never getting to grips with it, or being challenged out of its own complacency: the *other*, it seems, is ultimately unknowable, and so no encounter is possible. Nods to countless Anglo-American professors, and their conceptual terms—their brand—are required before one is permitted to analyze an actual, for example, Indian poem. It's a philosophical problem of long standing—here's David Hume: "Let us chace our imagination to the heavens, or to the utmost limits of the universe; we never really advance a step beyond ourselves, nor can conceive any kind of existence, but those perceptions, which have appeared in that narrow compass." Which means—Frances Ferguson steps into the fray—that "a reader can only read the texts that say what he already knows." Or—put another way, by Jarad Zimbler, and with reference to world literature (Ferguson was talking about Coleridge): "Can we experience a text as properly inventive without any familiarity with the worlds in which it originates?" When academics worry infinitely about this, developing methodologies upon methodologies, deferring forever an account of what happens as we read, criticism becomes all retch and no vomit.

But the reviewers Perloff criticizes don't worry enough about such things.

These essays are for readers (and writers) of poetry inside and outside the academy, especially those fascinated by the mechanics of poems—with *how they work*. Politics isn't extraneous to literary form but vitally inherent: fascinated by the relation of the creative consciousness to the violence of history, I write against echo chambers and for those open to multiple kinds of both lyric and nonlyric verse, placing modern poetry in conversation with works written elsewhere and elsewhen. (The twentieth- and twenty-first-century Anglo-American focus of many literature and creative writing programs isn't as "diverse" as it pretends.) I write for those curious about "world poetry"—beyond Derek Walcott!—who despair of finding a place to start or a route through the thickets of theory: my essays on South Asian poems (and prose) scrutinize artworks that give pleasure and don't need always to be read in a downright theorized or historicist or postcolonialist way. Rather than periodize or slot my essays into neatly constrictive subcategories of race, gender, and nationality, they're aligned by other means: I'm curious about the serendipitous possible connections you, reader, might make.

Since I feel that poets, especially from minoritized subject positions, are read reductively, in terms of where they were born rather than the shaped expressiveness of their writing, I don't (this has meant some skirmishes with magazine editors) front-load these essays with oodles of context. My preference is to plunge into literary experience—moving *from* there toward biographical and literary backgrounds. This tallies with how in these essays I present and absent myself—as an England-raised Sri Lankan Tamil, part of a diaspora subjected to what Barack Obama called "ethnic slaughter." I'm aware, my sentences and paragraphs and argumentative arcs are aware, that essays on poetry aren't usually written by people who look like me or who have had the experiences I've had. But if the demand placed on the writer of color, and those rooted in the Global South, is so often to self-express in a saleable way (blood oozing photogenically from an exposed wound), I prefer to show that the marginal migrant perspective isn't a matter purely of feeling but also of cerebration: to stand outside the canon is to *know* something about it. Since these aren't essays about me but about other people—writers fascinatingly different from me, who do things with language I never could—sidestepping the confessional quagmire, I parcel out strategically (like Alfred Hitchcock) the cameo appearances my brown face (as round as his, though thankfully with more hair left me) makes in the pieces collected here.

Taking literary thinking into areas as yet unannexed by the media or the academy (poems cognize our realities, they are ways of reconsidering how we live), these are, I suppose, experiments in postcriticism (in Rita Felski's phrase) or "creative criticism" (Peter D. McDonald's, in a wonderfully provocative essay) that don't gloss over mishearings and disquiet and are impatient with ready-made observations and overused scripts. They are experimental wagers—*essais* in the French sense—in a phrase suggested to me by Laetitia Zecchini, they are *affective chronicles* of reader-author encounters, more exploratory than explanatory: subjective, experiential, undecided. Modern poems wonder to what extent in a multiculture experiences are either siloed or shareable—I wish to provoke the reader into new forms of attention, to have you give time to these texts, in the hope that, as they did for me, they'll both strengthen and subvert the person you think you are.

Here, then, is a summary of two existing types of writing about poetry—styles these essays don't so much reconcile as journey between restively, in a to-and-fro that (in my career as both an academic and a journalist) has resembled the code-switching between communities experienced by a person of color. (Some) academics feel I'm colloquially overexpressive; editors at magazines (sometimes) feel my writing's too densely focused, on, say, patterns of sound. Yet to be challenged by the expectations of contrary audiences has enriched my work in ways I could not have foreseen.

Peer-reviewed academic criticism is published in monographs, as chapters in essay collections released by academic presses, and as journal articles. Metaphor when it appears manifests typically as an argument-coordinating concept. Poems are often approached through a theoretical lens or a historicist framework—which can cause problems, as Jahan Ramazani observes, because of the linguistic density of verse, which means it doesn't provide a clear window on reality. If verse is lingered over in its rich weave, it's typically to further an argument that rarely terminates in appreciation. The critic's personality may be expunged from a style disdainful of the first person, one that's wary of relapsing into the belle-lettristic excesses preceding academic specialization, and sometimes (not always!) targets (it relates to a crisis of value in the humanities) the objectivity-sound of the social sciences. The idea of "lyric" taken for granted in book-reviewing may be critiqued (as by the "New Lyric Studies") or defended (Jonathan Culler) at a remove from the praxis of contemporary poets; yet are minoritized poets more likely to be read seriously in academic articles than in review pages that are reductive and even prejudiced?

Literary journalism is often reviewery—focusing the contemporary at the expense of works from the past. It's introductory, effervescent, and its imagery is local and provisional, with coordinating concepts replaced by so many metaphorical tries at lassoing literary experience. Journalism foregrounds the personality of the critic, who writes in a style close to speech. Value judgments are essential, a type of pure responsiveness is more often assumed than examined, and reviews can tend toward either outright praise (reviewers and poets often know each other) or clickbait hatchet jobs (reviewers and poets often know each other). (The use of review space to further private vendettas has for decades compromised UK book talk and is often accepted as a given.) The endeavor feels imperiled, as critics horrified by the diversification of poetry react with unthinking apologias for "quality" and "craft," and—looking beyond verse—fraught think pieces: Christian Lorentzen's "Like This or Die," for one, considers in *Harper's* "the fate of the book review in the age of the algorithm." We increasingly mistrust the authoritativeness of commentary emanating from metropolitan centers, which are also hubs of privilege: the Internet, after all, enables anyone with a connection (and I don't mean, of the lit-schmoozy kind) to publish their opinion widely and instantaneously.

The division of writing-about-reading into two camps bespeaks an epistemological crisis. A fear that what used to be called knowledge was in fact, all along, only entrenched privilege, a self-replicating culture function. (There existed once a species of assurance, in themselves and their impulses, which some possessed, but is now recognized to be self-interested and exclusionary.) Our anxieties around subjective knowledge—an idea essential to the humanities but under attack—shape academic and journalistic criticism differently within the context of internetified opinionation. Felski's call for "postcriticism" mentions a reinfusion of personality and passion into scholarly writing. If peer-reviewed articles on poetry protect themselves against any hint of impressionistic bloviation, and historicisms may be motivated by the desire to get away from such personal responses as poetry—to the everyday reader—might seem designed to elicit, then could verse criticism envision a rapprochement between academic writing and literary journalism, where some of what Felski asks for already happens?

Besides the work done by my fellow organizers and tutors and mentees on the Ledbury program, I admire peers who've pressed back against, deformed and deflated, the subjective/objective, journalism/academia binary or—this applies to many though not all the names which follow—found other ways of describing a minoritized aesthetics (discussing race and poetry vividly and sometimes personally). Of many, I'll mention Paisley Rekdal, Walton Muyumba, Kamran Javadizadeh, Dorothy Wang, Sumana Roy, Kayombo Chingonyi, Ralph E. Rodriguez, Nick Makoha—on "metic" experience—as well as Will Harris (who *is* linked to Ledbury but whose provocation regarding a UK poetry scene once, not so long ago, as "white as a ski-slope" deserves quoting here); also Timothy Yu, Namwali Serpell, Cathy Park Hong, Merve Emre, Joseph North, Parul Sehgal, Kei Miller, Jesse McCarthy, Ben Etherington, Declan Ryan, and Anahid Nersessian. And let's not forget forerunners within, especially, feminist writing: Felski builds on Eve Kosofsky Sedgwick's rejoinder to "paranoid criticism," and, in the nineties, Elizabeth Hirsh identified a widespread "personal turn."

Writing to and for academics, Felski acknowledges "an understandable wariness of being tarred with the brush of subjective or emotional response."

Ted Hughes mentions "the Englishman's ultimate social skull-crusher: 'Lick of the tar-brush?'—a phrase from colonial days meaning 'tainted with native (Indian or African) blood.'" I place these observations side by side to connect "subjective or emotional response" with the demands of minoritized thought. We're seeing now a *racialized* style of personal criticism, befitting those of us who feel theorization must proceed from lived, discrepant, previously ignored or outright erased vantages. That this links to the slowly increasing presence of people of color within both literary and academic subcultures is illustrated by—I'm impatient to get to, traverse, analyse, delight in, a poem!—the work of Vahni (Anthony) Capildeo. I also discuss this poem in prose, "The Critic in His Natural Habitat," briefly in my essay on Capildeo, but a really good poem can be read over and over (Keats, again: when we've arrived "a certain ripeness in intellect any one grand and spiritual passage serves . . . as a starting-post towards all 'the two-and-thirty Palaces.'") The "habitat" appears an Oxbridge college: the poem's a joke at the expense of a white scholar snugly and smugly enclosed in a white environment, a joke made by a woman of color who, having felt—and I empathize—marginalized there, now turns the tables. Capildeo mocks the Critic by borrowing, burrowing into, his browbeating voice:

"You seem to be serious about literature. Have you ever considered writing up some of these thoughts of yours? A poet like you could bring a fresh perspective to criticism. People would appreciate that. You needn't worry: they wouldn't expect scholarship. My book came out last year. You don't want me to bore you with that. It's just an in-depth study of darkness and the imagination in the seventeenth century. The seventeenth century might not be your cup of tea. Oh, is that your book? I'm afraid I don't read much contemporary poetry. Will you give me a copy? Only if you have one spare, of course. Sultry photo! I'm never sure about books-with-author photos. The rail station photobooth? Really? You don't write for The Times Literary Supplement, do you? Dorina recently did a brilliant review of Tricia's edition of Gussie's translations of Brazilian slum poetry composed in Spanish by a French guy who taught on an art history course here, oh, donkeys' years ago.

I don't remember his name."

In my essay on Capildeo, I give the U.S. reader as a point of reference the work of Claudia Rankine. This is a poem about such microaggressions as Rankine analyzes: the Critic's sexist toward Capildeo, or whomever the woman he addresses turns out to be, but the racial undertow's more elusive. "A poet like you could bring a fresh perspective to criticism." Much pivots on what Robert Frost named sentence sound or "the sound of sense." Which words are vocally spotlighted? Is it a sentence about how a *poet* brings a "fresh perspective"—what a moribund phrase that is—"to criticism," or about how a poet *"like you"* could do so—a dark-skinned woman the Critic exoticizes?

It's a moment (in a dramatic monologue, but in prose) liable to divide readers. To some, it may sound innocuous, to others racist: in other words, the personal dimension to reading, which I've emphasized, is integral. The sentence may have a *darker* meaning, pertaining to the woman's complexion—the Critic is, Capildeo notes mischievously, a scholar of "darkness and the imagination in the seventeenth century." Academic self-categorizations align with identity boxes: Capildeo probes the relation of creativeness to scholarship. Often minorities enter English departments as creative writers, not academics: the criticism they do write is published in public-facing, literary-journalistic, venues (in, say, *Granta*, rather than *PMLA*). The danger is if we don't consider journalism or magazine-writing a knowledge-producing endeavor—cognitively habile along, even, routes impossible within academia—we may come to occupy the Critic's patronizing perspective. In his "habitat," people of color are grudgingly billeted as voices expressing their experiences, so long as their writing is distinguished from true "scholarship." Long-standing racisms resurface: people of color are emotional, "sultry," insufficiently "serious" about literature. They (we) are creatures who feel and suffer but who don't think.

Samuel Johnson said the task of criticism was to "improve opinion into knowledge." For the scholar, it's a given that value judgments are partial and prejudiced. The word *beautiful* won't survive peer review. Academics read historically, theoretically, archivally. Yet I suspect this voice—its presumed neutrality, its jargon, emulous of the social, or even the hard, sciences, which can never arrive at its longed-for destination, for books are written and read by people, not machines, people whose experiences mustn't be disclaimed. So my essays try for a tonally various prose that, drawing on both academic and journalistic moves (inducements, suscitations, claims and qualms, the hither and yon of averment and doubt) consciously enacts, and makes available to the reader—inviting them to disagree—the very traversal of opinion toward knowledge that makes the humanities anxious. I'm not calling for a return to soupy essays in appreciation: I *am* saying the return of personality to poetry criticism may be at this point not a lotus-eating extravagance but a cognitive must, a long-required vetoing of untrue neutralities. Here's an alternative description of the critic, borrowed from Maureen N. McLane, who, in turn, rejigs a Wallace Stevens poem:

> The susceptible being arrived, a far-fetched creature, speaking
> in its own accent of deviation.

It's possible to accept our placement within culture without disowning our subjectivity. Better to write, when possible, out of that voice arising sometimes without our explicit control, out of the sentences that—encountering a poem—become alluringly available to us. Our tastes, shaped by our parish, should remain susceptible of alteration, but they still deserve to be articulated (humans are evaluative creatures). Moment-by-moment accounts, phenomenological readings, of poems, following the trajectory of one's shifting response, rather than beginning with a mind (thronged with biases) already made up, might probe in our dealings with literature the role played by culturalist presuppositions. If we've conscientiously expunged pleasure, repulsion, a panoply of affective disturbances to do with reading, from our academic prose; and if this silencing also plays out in the public sphere, as a denial of the very existence of subjective knowledge, then what form might the return of the repressed take, now poetries tied to subcultures of race, gender, class, and sexuality demand serious consideration?

Our exaggerations, in journalism (redescribing books physically, as rollercoaster rides, for instance, out of the fear they, and it, will be found boring) and in academic prose (positioning itself as a radical, world-changing intervention, insisting the politics of poems inheres in their supposedly *forcing* readers to do things, like confront their assumptions, recognize their privilege, clean their bathroom sink . . .)—it all exposes ourselves. That is: we don't know to what extent experiences can be shared (including, across dividing lines of race, class, and gender), nor can we adequately connect with a world whose exploitations and evils we despair of remedying. Could it be that it's because we don't know how to do politics, that we have such violent opinions? Pressed as to the sources of our knowledge, we hide within a performed individualism or the appearance of an impossibly learned, and therefore bulletproofed, rigor.

On this note: might I inform the U.S. academic reader that "lyricization," which presently dominates their conversation, simply isn't mentioned in many UK articles or monographs, and that poets themselves from all over the world are baffled when the idea is mentioned? If we've misread, for generations, all sorts of poems as lyrics, and the solution is to be found in the writing of those U.S. academics who have shaped the "New Lyric Studies," this is both a crisis and a response to a crisis of which a large poetry-reading and poetry-writing public remains completely unaware. I meet poets from the Maghreb, on a British Council project, and our conversation—translating each other's work—concerns such minutiae as are rarely mentioned by academics, even those who vaunt a "return to form." I pick up the latest issue of the UK magazine *PN Review*, and in it Sinéad Morrissey, the much-awarded Northern Irish poet, writes intelligently, and, to me, persuasively, about the lyric and pronouns in it without becoming entrapped by the U.S. debate at all.

It isn't surprising that not everyone is familiar with every school of criticism; the disjunction occurs when ideas are positioned as effecting a seismic shift. It can then be disorienting to find—stepping outside subcultures—that, for many, poetry continues much as before (or is being transformed in alternative ways). For those of us who do interact, face-to-face, with several communities of interpretation, and of creation—including those in the Global South—this feeling of existing between conversations, between (Seamus Heaney) "diamond absolutes" that never touch, can become estranging.

Yet it can also be exhilarating to exist between worlds—rather than trying to fuse the claims of far-spaced coteries (say, those of journalism and academia), to keep journeying between such clear-cut worlds, tracing one's own path.

I want critics of different stripes to talk to each other. I'm also fascinated by the idea of poems talking to each other across divides. Criticism is written within multiple contexts, one of which must be, as I've said, the transformation occasioned by the Internet in our styles of argument. My essays, several of which originally appeared online, embrace a certain volatility, undecidedness, and openness to criticism. If we felt able in our writing to acknowledge what we *don't* know, what we look forward to finding out from others, this would expand the precincts of our assertiveness, freeing us to step outside our comfort zones to burst, even, the Anglo-American bubble, and discuss a wealth of world literatures. As Rajagopalan Radhakrishnan insists, "there is nothing to be gained by freezing or exoticizing 'alterity' and 'difference' into a mystique"—we need to actually read and analyse the works of people distant from us, even if it means we sometimes get things wrong or even embarrass ourselves. In fact, the gaps in our knowledge may themselves be revelatory, of flows of global power and the current parameters of critical reading and critical persuasion. "If comparative studies are to result in the production of new and destabilizing knowledges, then apples and oranges do need to be compared," says Rajagopalan, "audaciously and precariously." What would this look like?

Here's the Indian Guyanese poet Mahadai Das:

> A tiny ant walked on my book's side as
> I struggled to read one page.
> With my big human mouth, I blew it away,
> or tried to.
> Hurtly, it swaggered. Then,
> I was remorseful.
> I let it come and read my page.
> After all, it had known the book-tree millions
> of years before my birth.

Reading this first section of "Ant and Eternity," I'm reminded of a poem by Thomas Hardy—might these works speak to each other? I believe so: quoting them side by side needn't flatten their differences or—as long as we remain conscious of such things—erase those power dynamics (of global conquest as well as literary canonicity), which mean you're less likely to have met with Das's poem than with Hardy's "An August Midnight":

> I
>
> A shaded lamp and a waving blind,
> And the beat of a clock from a distant floor:

> On this scene enter—winged, horned, and spined—
> A longlegs, a moth, and a dumbledore;
> While 'mid my page there idly stands
> A sleepy fly, that rubs its hands . . .
>
> *II*
>
> Thus meet we five, in this still place,
> At this point of time, at this point in space.
> —My guests besmear my new-penned line,
> Or bang at the lamp and fall supine.
> "God's humblest, they!" I muse. Yet why?
> They know Earth-secrets that know not I.

Hardy's poem, also in sections (which the numbering makes discrete, even as "Thus" sutures them in one thought movement), suggests an event better understood as multiple events, with, in them, multiple actors (human and insect). With ruffled meter and rhyme, he presents an ordered domesticity still mysteriously resonant; the room he depicts is part of a larger ecological continuum. "On this scene enter . . ."—a stage direction. The poem's funny in the disparity between great and small, its juxtaposition of the human who speaks with the nonhuman "guests" at whom he seems—initially—to poke fun.

Hardy's poem is about writing; Das's is about reading, or struggling to read. What is it, we wonder, keeping the speaker from understanding her "page?" It's this challenge to the flow of her concentration, as much as the ant's arrival, that generates a multipart poem Das segments, like Hardy, with Roman numerals. She uses this device in only one other poem: the nine-part sequence "For Maria de Borges," which presents within an equivalently heterotemporal malaise (the sections, their varying time signatures), a personality pictured, matching the poem's scissions, as dismembered into a half-human, half-animal predicament:

> From whence has this traveller come
> with his long hair, his lost eyes?
> I am a pair of hands.
> A pair of feet.

> . . .
> Tomorrow, I rise
> between dead thighs of another day.
> To be bridled like a horse between the hours,
> a bit between my teeth, a bruising saddle
> on my back.

Postcolonial time doesn't river organically: one examines its glittering flow only to find that what one took for water is in fact shards of broken glass. "Ant and Eternity" is an uncollected poem Das didn't revise before her death at forty-nine from heart problems. So its second part, reiterating the word "house," may be unfinished rather than purposefully spalled. But having said there could be more room in analysis for admissions of unknowing, let me concede that in this instance I don't know what's going on. Certainly, themes of belonging and rejection, related to domesticity and its boundaries, continue to predominate; the speaker becomes like the houseless ant and also morphs into "boarish" water plants; the rubber factory may gloss the mass production of natural latex within Guyana and even Forbes Burnham's takeover of big industry when he came to power. But we can't be sure of much more than that the transformation of "a tiny ant" into "a lone ant" occurs here and continues into the third section:

> I saw a lone ant
> and I wondered whither were its companions.
> Where was the battalion? Under the earth?
> Suddenly, three ants appealed to me,
> on my tabletop with clasped hands, bodies straight up.

The ants with their "clasped hands" are personified—Hardy too has his "sleepy fly, that rubs its hands"—as supplicants. The archaism, "whither"—akin to "whence" in "For Maria de Borges"—suggests a lapsed language style and lifestyle; linking this with the solder-ants separated from their "battalion," we might consider Das's shift from activism to a poetics of reticence. Denise DeCaires Narain Gurnah explains that "the trajectory her work charts from nationalism to disillusionment is not uncommon amongst Caribbean poets; what is distinctive about Das's oeuvre is that this shift is so dramatically and decisively mapped"; early poems that "assume an active, visionary role for the poet as well as a clear sense of the constituency being addressed," and in which "the labour provided by enslaved and indentured people, so violently misused in the past, is recognized as a powerful resource," are succeeded by "knotty, secretive and introspective" works addressing no one in particular.

The ants are soldiers. The ants are workers. But they're divided, solitary, and appeal to the poem's speaker for help. She, with her "big human mouth," might blow them away—a phrase from action films, with violence in it. But the ant hangs on, and, appearing human in its response, is rewarded: "Hurtly, it swaggered. Then, / I was remorseful. / I let it come and read my page." The line break after "then" is subtle: it critiques the speaker's shift toward a spurious guilt. She, like the speaker of Hardy's poem, self-admires (her ecological sensitivity glances at itself in the mirror): "God's humblest, they!' I muse. Yet why? / They know Earth-secrets that know not I."

Hardy shatters his poem's humor with that couplet whose chiastic syntax—"They know . . . know . . . I"—makes it curiously *voulu*. It probably means insects know secrets about the earth that we don't, though other readings loiter. Speaking a language at a remove from mine—and yours—these poems have us consider their distance from us in place and time. Part 4 of "Ant and Eternity": "Had the blue god and his wife sent them to me? / Will loneliness be the land of my sojourn? / And, having done their job, the three ants disappeared." I've mentioned the history behind Das's poem, the end to an unrealizable dream of the nation (harnessed to a vision of working the land). Here the ants seem emissaries—from Krishna and his consort?—reminding the poet of an irrecoverable past. Hardy, too, would like to believe God sent these creatures to him, that their jay-walk across his page is no accident. The Victorian-Edwardian poet worries nature is so much unfeeling matter adrift without meaning or purpose. The dream *he* has lost is not a politics but a theology.

Ankhi Mukherjee argues that "the overdeterminations of race, class and gender are too real, and they persist but indeed they should not lead to dubious negotiations between aesthetic standards and social engineering. Neither should texts be read and canonized for the politics of blame they embody. It is equally absurd, however, to deny the cultural embeddedness of aesthetic standards." So: two poems meet "at this point of time, at this point in space." And not, I hope, in the fashion of the iceberg and the Titanic, in Hardy's "Convergence of the Twain." Instead, I hope these poems illuminate each other, and to this end I'll cite Foucault: "We are in the epoch of simultaneity; we are in the epoch of juxtaposition, the epoch of near and far, of the side-by-side, of the dispersed. We are at a moment, I believe, when our experience of the world is less that of a long life developing through time than that of a network that connects points and intersects with its own skein."

Now, why don't you order a copy of Das's poems from Peepal Tree before reading on?

Would this be "close reading," as maligned by both Franco Moretti (who calls for its opposite, "distant reading"), and the Warwick Research Collective, for whom formalism entails an "abstraction from . . . social determinants and structuring conditions of existence?" Yes and no. A type of close reading I do admire—practiced, for instance, by Helen Vendler—may overstate and overrate the deliberation of the poet: she sees Keats's odes, for example, as experiments in disallowing, each time, a different sense— sight, touch, smell, hearing—and concentrating on others, while for me the element of calculation is less, and that of spontaneity more. Which for Vendler would devalue the work. But to me, Keats's creativeness is finer for its contradictions, its patchwork, the humane fusion in it of marmoreal permanence (that which he called, in Milton, "stationing") with that classbound, insecure, all-in-the-moment fervor motivating him always to turn nothing into something, conjuring riches out of the air:

> O Moon! old boughs lisp forth a holier din
> The while they feel thine airy fellowship.
> Thou dost bless everywhere, with silver lip
> Kissing dead things to life.

Do you agree with me (as I tell my students, you don't have to!) of these lines from *Endymion*, that naff, waffly verse suddenly releases, with that last line, something extraordinary?

It's only human of a poem to be inconstant, to contain fluctuations of energy such as we experience in daily life. Keats knew his immature long poem was mawkish, saying as much in his introduction. But in these lines describing transformation a transformation occurs, and in verse of great power. Here is the Romantic fear—which Hardy inherits and heightens— that the world's no longer legend laden, that it has been made spiritless both by industrialization and by a chasm erupting between subject and object, perceiver and perceived. Nature is "dead things"—until kissed to life—two *i* sounds, short and long, cognitively intertwine from line to line. If it is a joy (forever) to track Keats as he discovers the image, as sound connects with sound, and "silver lip" leads, over the line break, directly into another stress ("kissing" comes, too, out of "bless"), all of this is worth noticing, and feeling over again, not only as a technical feat but also as a window on his concerns and the concerns of his age.

Is criticism, then, like moonlight—falling on poems, restoring them to life? No. Or not often. The power is in the poems themselves, waiting to be recognized.

But would I have learned to love the verse of Rae Armantrout—experimental, post-L=A=N=G=U=A=G=E, U.S. feminist, in so many ways distanced from my own concerns—if it hadn't been for an essay by Stephanie Burt showing the way?

I don't think I would.

Still, it's worth asking: why read criticism at all? I teach a course on South Asian poetry. In preparation, going back to—the first poet in my list, the inaugurator of a pared, post-Independence style—Nissim Ezekiel, I found one day the surfaces of his poems (and the subject matter, which can be, writes Arvind Mehrotra, "priapic") profoundly offputting. I wasn't sure if I still *liked* the poet, if I wanted to read him or teach him.

Then I returned to an essay by Amit Chaudhuri, who—comparing apples to oranges—shows how Ezekiel, *like the English poet Philip Larkin,* is fascinated by the category of the "minor" poet. (You can find this essay in Rosinka Chaudhuri's *A History of Indian Poetry in English.*) Ezekiel practices "an aesthetic of intelligent curtailment" rather than "explosive dissolution; a strategy, then, for long-term survival." He turns smallness of scope and curbed ambition into a poetics that's pungent and—despite everything—profound.

Reading Chaudhuri, and remembering Larkin, I rediscovered Ezekiel. The poems came alive once more; or I felt more alive, reading them. A transfusion of sensibility had occurred.

Here's another example of what literary criticism has meant to me, from Tom Paulin's book on Hardy:

> The spray sprang up across the cusps of the moon,
>   And all its light loomed green
>   As a witch-flame's weirdsome sheen
> At the minute of an incantation scene;
> And it greened our gaze—that night at demilune.
>
> Roaring high and roaring low was the sea
>   Behind the headland shores;
>   It symbolled the slamming of doors,
> Or a regiment hurrying over a hollow floors. . . .
> And there we two stood, hands clasped; I and she!

The comparisons are unsatisfactory and while their sinister, ominous qualities are meant to hint the lovers' destiny—the shadow of their future in the present moment—it's clear that what Hardy really values is the unusual visual effect of green moonlight through blown spray. The rest of the poem is an unconvincing gesture towards significance.

I've complained about snark. But this is more than a hack's sideswipe. Someone who dearly loves a poet's work, who has immersed themselves in it, speaks out with such intimate impatience, almost, as we apply to the foibles of friends and family. Paulin writes as if he knew what Hardy was thinking, feeling, trying to do: and this experiment seems to me noble, not appropriative, because it isn't motivated by takeover but generated out of a try at understanding. Nor does the value judgment terminate with a smug nod of the knowing head, for it was indeed Hardy's gift to wonder out loud, in verse of variable inventiveness, where "significance" could be discovered or asserted in, as I've mentioned, a newly spiritless world.

Paulin, a poet-critic himself, bring us back to the situation of which Perloff complains. I'm a poet as well as a reviewer as well as a scholar of post-Romantic poetics (including in prose): I am, like Paulin, a poet-critic, though the problem with this label is its claim of a special access to verse's inner workings (in this respect, the poet-critic writing about poems comes to resemble the person of color writing about the experiences of people of color). In fact, I admire critics who write this way *without* being poets themselves—Vendler would be one example, or Barbara Everett.

Reading is about recognizing difference, without evoking it as an insuperable barrier to understanding. Reading a critic, we track the arc of their assertiveness without necessarily seeing eye to eye. Their prose may comment on from a distance, or participate in (denying the division between subject and object), a poem's verbal energies. It provides a point of entry, but also something more. When someone shows you what they care about, what they find—returning to Hardy—of *significance*, one meets the object anew. Seeing what others think (and how they think, the shapes their thinking makes), I begin to work out what I think, in the gauzily shifting space between identification and opposition. It's mysterious, and any discussion concerning the authority of the critic has to be pervaded by that mystery. It isn't, for me, about judgments to agree or disagree with, but *styles* of attention we find congenial.

So—here are some poets who fascinate me, and about whom I was granted the license to write freely, or freeishly, showing my feelings as I wouldn't in my academic writing. I wrote to discover what I felt about them; only occasionally, as with the poetry of Arvind Krishna Mehrotra, did I desperately put the word out in the hope of getting them more readers. So I haven't always written *clearly*. I try out adjectives, for the handle they provide on the literary experience—reading poems (I'd like to think) in a way that encompasses deflection, so an essay, less confirmed than diverted by its moments of contact with poems, may be surprised down another route.

For critics with their own untraditional routes toward publication, those who've truly shaped our thinking may be less likely cited in the introduction to a book than in the acknowledgments. My parents refused to teach me or my sister Tamil—drawing a line (if such a thing could ever be possible) under their damaged past. That language-absence, the rescinded gift of their tongue—partnered with the helpless transmission to me, of intonation contours, and thought styles, that *do* spring from, in Derek Attridge's word, their Tamil *idioculture*—operates as a revenant pressure on my prose as on my poetry. And it's in this book of essays, rather than my more staidly academic monographs, that I cease to purge my sentences of those racialized, uninsured, velocities.

My epigraph quotes A. K. Ramanujan, the great poet, translator, and scholar of Indian folklore in multiple languages—a poet who, having moved to Chicago, identified as neither Indian nor American, nor even "Indian-American," but as the *hyphen* in that label. My essay on him, included here, reads him as a forerunner of today's hybridized (in terms of both the poet's identity and the forms they use) poetries; but to discuss not poetry but *poetics*, let me linger on his claim that

> the special contribution of literature is its vision, its intuitive grasp of structure, its perspective; not the facts themselves so viewed, but the facts as seen by the imaginative accuracy of a mind that is not merely factual. . . . It provides a repertoire of perceptions otherwise not available, or perceptions that social-scientists reach only after infinite pains and fact-finding. William Blake said, "Whatever is proven today was once imagined."

This is a Romantic perspective, for which the imagination is a kind of thinking about reality—a claim essential to those of us who believe that poetry isn't just expressive but also cognitive: that it is, itself, critique or philosophy by other (sensuous, enthralling) means. Ramanujan also published a book of poems called *Second Sight*, and with that title, as in the metaphor of "vision" he invokes here—linking literal seeing to Blakean "vision" in the dreamier, epiphanic sense—he's poking fun at Orientalist ideas of Indian mysticism, the third eye in the forehead, etc. He makes, that is, large claims for what literature can do, but with humor and tact. He was an Indian Tamil and I'm a Sri Lankan Tamil—for whom it's hard (but worth doing) to conceive of poetry as possessing political force (both poets and academics make this claim too readily, sometimes in bad faith). My problem is that I keep testing that claim against family experiences, almost obsessively, as one might continue, though it hurts, to touch with one's tongue in one's mouth a bad, painful tooth. I do think verse possesses such power, though it doesn't inhere in hot takes extractable from a poem (the opinions for which some would either champion or "cancel" a writer), but belongs instead to a thought process that, melodically alive in the work, is unpredictable and must remain so in its, in Édouard Glissant's phrase, "meanders of relation," and is finally inseparable from the verse textures it both produces and is produced by.

I'm grateful to the reader of this page: the person picking up a book of essays about poems when there's much else to worry about and hope one can in some small way change for the better. The first two essays concern foreign voices: verse in translation and postcolonial Anglophone verse attuned to Indian speech tones. I wished to begin here, trying for a balance between granting the uniqueness of cultures and establishing conversations across national, racial, and temporal boundaries—such conversations as we stand in desperate need of today.

"A slave and worshiper at love's doorstep"
Mir Taqi Mir

Mir Muhammad Taqi "Mir"—his pen-name, or *takhallus*, appearing in the last couplet of each *ghazal* (pronounced *guzzle*)—was "the most important Urdu poet of the eighteenth century . . . also the most prolific writer of his generation"; born in 1723, he shaped Urdu as Shakespeare shaped English. Introducing *Remembrances*, C. M. Naim explains that autobiography is rare in Persian literature, and that Mir's strategic: he exalts his ancestors, positioning his father as a Shia-sayyid mystic of some renown. He also writes vividly of the fall of Delhi (politicking, coups, gruesome battles). But his own life is given through a Vaselined lens, and the book ends with pages of unrelated smutty jokes. "These eyes have seen everything," he boasts; yet the man who sees and describes proves elusive. We have Mir's elegant querulousness; his both low- and high-toned loathing, passing into calumny, of his uncle Arzu—"chasing in the desert of greed . . . he received nothing but a fistful of air and, kicked around by Time, died"—but the feeling for what an autobiography could and should be is frustrated. Especially since Naim's translation, as that sentence suggests (its quirky syntax) has a vigor to it suggestive of someone we'd like to know better. With Mir, we're talking, after all, about one of the world's greatest love poets in any language. What kind of person was he?

Mir's verse has been used as a window on his life. There are myths of the often brilliant and occasionally obtuse genius of erotic-mystic passion, writing feverishly to either a lover or a God who refuses to respond and toppling into madness as a result (Mir evokes a fit of lunacy, actually by moonlight, in *Remembrances*). He's also been labeled a pederast: "When they're together one or the other is on top, or under, always, night and day. / Like velvet with two-sided pile are these soft-shouldered boys." We can't help but fantasize an author behind poems, especially love lyrics; but there's another problem, to do with verse in translation, and indeed world poetry in English. The verse of other times and places is often read touristically, for a bird's-eye view of those elsewhere. This can be patronizing and reductive, should it assume within texts a core of exotic otherness it becomes their task to transmit. The challenge is to read with a sense of literature's emplacement—while remaining sensitive to a creativeness that less reflects than refracts the circumstances out of which it sprang. And it seems right to concede, in meeting with the other (in poetry as in life), moments of resistance: if it's wrong to judge poems for leaving unconsummated our parochial criteria, it remains counterproductive to pretend to a purified cosmopolitanism and act as if, reading translated works, we're never wrongfooted.

So, to begin with the historical or historicist take on Mir: discussing his love verse, Khurshidal Islam and Ralph Russell argue the pressures exerted by a purdah society with barriers to erotic consummation, "in which there is drastic segregation of the sexes and a marked difference between the cultural level of men and that of women." This would be why his speaker-lover is perpetually frustrated and why his utterances occur in the aching space between desire and its impossible fulfillment. Mir refers closely to the terms of that society, as it was transformed by large events. Working from earlier translations—"My heart, like Delhi city, lies in ruins now"—Islam and Russell add many of his "images are drawn from the experiences of invasion, pillage, and destruction, and to a Delhi audience he could have used none more meaningful."

What this risks excluding is the stylistic accomplishment—the glittering kinesics, the stippled tensions, of Mir's verse. Shamsur Rahman Faruqi's translations, both idiomatic and musical, delight. But a pause is often required, a squint or refocusing, for Mir's verse siphons an immense expressive repertoire—a network of recognitions that once linked the poet with his Urdu reader or listener (ghazals were performed at *mushairas* in call-and-response fashion, with the audience oohing and aahing at the rhymes). This flitting, as one reads, between undeniable oomph and the feeling of missing out, the aura of a skipped hint, occurs (as I read the poems, anyway) in the longer satires, or *masnavis*, too, like Mir's "Account of a Journey to Tisang":

> Can I ever describe the height of the slapping waves, the depth
>   from which they arose,

the surge rising high as if going to have a word with the sky,
and the river's expanse? One would say it was the hem of the
   cloud's skirt
tied with a twist, billowing and swollen.

The topos of inexpressibility occurs in many literatures: the author protests that an experience is beyond his powers of description, then goes on to evoke it anyway. Mir, and Faruqi, skilfully bridle their picture of chaos. Sounds pleach, internal rhyme—"the surge rising *high* as if going to have a word with the *sky*"—provides in English a ripple of the original music. Yet the skirt comparison, with its scrupulous preamble, has to be explained (Faruqi does this often, and conscientiously) with endnotes.

To provide another example: if I find Mir's grotesquely unvisual metaphors challenging—"Each hair of my body is a tongue giving thanks for my broken legs"—it's to my discredit, not his, but such micro-alienations are part and parcel of reading poetry in translation. Academic writing skips such disquiet; (some) journalists assert their instantaneous reactions to poems as categorical judgments, and this can become intolerance of poetry from other cultures. So what I'm trying to do—returning to this paragraph as I edit this essay, rewriting it, at the risk of digression—is examine my impulses. I'm shaped by a strand of modern Anglo-American verse that prefers its metaphors pictorial, or even cinematic (dominant media forms condition how we read); I love, for instance, the poetry of Elizabeth Bishop, who chid Jane Shore in a writing class: "I'd said that a 'ribbon of traffic unraveled into the winter morning' and Elizabeth vehemently (for her) took exception . . . she just couldn't *see* it." I just can't *see* Mir's follicles, on broken legs, giving thanks, or if I can, it reminds me of the computer imagery in an advertisement for a depilatory cream. But reading poetry can be like meeting a person different from ourselves (in all sorts of ways, including race, class, gender, sexuality, and the rest). It's possible to recognize our first response as insufficient (though I feel there's a place for it in critical prose) and reconnect the pleasures as well as the disturbances of poetry to factors impinging without our knowing. And if this is especially true of the poetries of other cultures and other times, and verse in translation, I think it's relevant to all our dealings with literature. The essays in this collection are, in many cases, experiments in writing through my mixed and uncertain feelings toward poems, and in some cases, prose, rather than exalting these feelings into certainties. If the poetic dimension of writing challenges our deepest sense of who we are, we need to get something of this experience back into our writing *about* poetry.

Mir's verse dramatizes this problem in a special way, seeming to record intense unedited emotions, while in fact activating a keyboard of culture-specific metaphors. Seeming up close and personal, it's anything but (we're reminded of this by the cruces touched on in Faruqi's notes). Flipping to the end of the book and back again becomes a salutary reminder of the distance between Mir's time and place and one's own. He, for instance, writes poignantly of animals (remarkable, since they were thought soulless mechanisms), yet what he says of a cat lost me at first:

> Her destiny was to die in that place.
> She was less like a cat than a painted cat, always still;
> her fur had the color of the time of the wolf and lamb:
> there was more red in her color than black.

As the verse glissades from description into periphrasis, many will need Faruqi's gloss: "the time of the wolf and the lamb" refers, apparently, to "twilight before the dawn. This is because the gray of the wolf (the receding night) and the reddish brown of the lamb (the coming dawn) become indistinguishable when the wolf leaps upon the lamb." A knot of predigested animal imagery, lovely and grisly, is encompassed here.

We should resist, then, the interpretation of Mir's poems which sees them as episodes in his own life. Instead, let's say: the distance segregating, in the ghazals themselves, the speaker from his beloved, reoccurs between the poet and the reader (in translation). Just when you think you know him, he darts away. For Mir, like other ghazal writers, isn't a Romantic, let alone a confessional poet. The feelings he depicts are enduring motifs: these statements of adoration, despair, even resentment, aren't original to him. What he provides is perception processed, enriched, transmogrified (lotioned, made pulverous, turned into something both soothingly familiar and tantalizingly *unheimlich*) by a depth, not of conviction, but convention. Reading him, we don't access the feelings of a particular individual so much as enjoy variations on an established theme. The invitation is to a purposively intricate performance, saturated by the rich long history of the ghazal (generations of symbols, conceits, ferocities of tone, and the best phrases).

Frances Pritchett details "a system of conventions," in which "images of longing, pain, loss, and separation clearly predominate. . . . The beloved is an ideal image of beauty rather than a particular, recognisable, beautiful individual"; she cites a "triangular pattern" that "seems to consist of a desirer, an object of desire, and an obstacle or threat to the fulfillment of desire," and suggests a parallel with European courtly love:

> The moth's suicidal love for the candle-flame, the nightingale's worship of the rose, and the caged bird's yearning for the garden directly express the longing of the suffering lover for an inaccessible beloved. The garden's death in autumn, the bird's nest struck by lightning, the candle burnt out overnight, and the withering of the rose are images of ultimate separation and loss. Human figures—Laila and Majnun, Shirin and Farhad, Yusuf and Zulaikha—are those of suffering lovers who endured lifelong separation and even died of love.

Out of desperation (a creative opportunity) the speaker innovates, placing himself in a series of lovers stretching backward in time, while asserting the peculiar magnificence of his own hot-bloodedness:

> I learnt about the rose's cruelties, and observed the fidelity of the bulbul too.
> A handful of feathers is all that is left in the garden in place of the bulbul.
>
> . . .
>
> The bulbul died traveling the path of single-minded fidelity.
> Those are not veins on the rose-petals, they are the claw prints of the bulbul.

Reclaiming the ghazal from its stateside appropriators—"a woman kept saying to me, 'Oh, I just love guh-*zaals*, I'm going write a lot of g'*zaaals*,' and I said to her, in utter pain, 'OH, PLEASE DON'T!'"—Agha Shahid Ali says the form goes back to seventh-century Arabia and consists of "couplets, each autonomous, thematically and emotionally complete in itself. . . . The opening couplet (called *matla*) sets up a scheme (of rhyme—called *qafia*; and refrain—called *radif*) by having it occur in both lines—the rhyme immediately preceding the refrain—and then this scheme occurs only in the second line of each succeeding couplet." Each pairing's isolable, end-stopped, a microcosm, but this "disconnectedness must not be mistaken for fragmentariness," but "actually underscores a profound cultural connectedness."

The rose, the garden, and the bulbul are traditional, as is the experience of suffering and fidelity they symbolize, by standing in for the lover and his beloved:

> Heartsick I passed through a garden yesterday.
> The roses were about to say, "So, how are you?" but I didn't even
>   look at them.

There's a fine-grained impatience to this stuff, a tissue of provocative vocal tones, which may excite the reader jaded by English equivalents. Tennyson, for instance, in *Maud*, has both his passages of spleen and his soft-focus set pieces, where the red rose cries, "She is near, she is near," but these are hygienically compartmentalized. Mir, contrarily, exclaims: "I really can't tell you how much the anger and passion of love irritate me at times." Which is a variation on that inexpressibility topos and an instance of the doublings of Urdu poetics ("anger and passion"), but, also, in this translation, sounds convincingly aggrieved. Mir presses the discourse toward a world-without-end fieriness: passionate feeling is housed within abiding structures, even as the verse asserts that to be in love is to be a slave, a madman, outside and beyond ordinary codes of behavior.

This is self-conscious poetry that accentuates its artfulness, rather than pretending—as a modern, Anglo-American poem might—to be a whisper in your ear or face-to-face speech. "Let my friends and rivals soar high in thought and compose a ghazal like this one," boasts Mir! And there's this gorgeous couplet:

> The beauty mark between your brows
>   is rather like a selection dot between the two lines of a verse.

The beloved's beauty melts into artifice: there exists no love situation separable from the greenhouse of the ghazal itself. (Ghazals, explains Faruqi, are written in Urdu "with two lines of a verse opposite each other in the same line. The reader customarily put a dot between the two lines of a verse to indicate approval, sometimes with the view of compiling a selection.") Mir's speaker vogues, promenades, lays it on thick: blood flows from him, he claims, in "stripes not entirely devoid of artistic pleasure." He's self-consciously purple, a bodybuilder of love-hurt, watching, even as he sobs and beats his breast, his form in the mirror:

> My broken heart is not without its subtle delights.
> Come and stay here a bit in this ruined house.

"Not without," and "a bit," are master touches from Faruqi, and (with apologies to Agha Shahid Ali!) I found the unrhymed translations especially stirring in their brusquerie, the affronted plangency of each jump cut. This applies to the masnavis too: "Love sets water on fire. / Love inspires connection between the sword and the neck." The longeurs of masochism joust with a scintillating decisiveness.

I find one allusion to Shakespeare ("the rain—it raineth every day") in the English version of "Scolding the Rain"—this is a bilingual edition, with Urdu on the facing page—and Mir's self-awareness concerning love's rhetoric (and his lust for both women, it seems, and boys) also suggests the Bard:

> It's just a nice conceit to say her lips are rubies.
> Everyone has concocted this fiction.

Faruqi's shift, from "conceit," with its soft *c*, to "concocted," with its three hard ones, is delicious. In Sonnet 130, Shakespeare refuses to compare the eyes of his mistress to the sun, her lips to coral, for it's been done; and we see in Cordelia's refusal to one-up her sisters in *King Lear* a rejection of rhetoric that may commence as metarhetoric (the pretense of transcending convention, in truth a deepening of it) but turns earnest. The ghazal's well-worn (to a shine; it isn't threadbare) maneuvers—hearts, and livers, compared to roasted kebabs; the "counsellor" figure, who can't dissuade the lover from his course—suggest artistry, not honesty. But since love is of the essence, feelings central to our lives are investigated and agilely inflamed rather than hollowed out by the poet's formulae: I wonder if it is possible to read the poems entirely in a spirit of connoisseurship. Maybe some of the ghazals resemble self-set philosophical problems, or the automatism of a songwriter rhyming "desire" once again with "fire;" but others are more than this. I don't know. The problem has, I feel, to be recognized as a real one and as ineliminable from the experience of reading Mir; we can't side for good either with Islam and Russell (authentic feeling, canalized by a restrictive society) or Pritchett (a fabulous jazz, riffing on conventions). The problem could be that love is always already "love": the myth of it runs ahead of the actuality, a melange of set pieces from literature and cinema impossible to outspeed, a script inherited from one's parents, peers, and popular culture. Our emotions, even when we're honestly anguished, follow that script. So it could be that the ghazal, affianced to convention, doesn't represent love unreally but with the only honesty possible—our own romances are just as stylized, orchestrated, narrativized. Consider the insights of Erving Goffman's *The Presentation of Self in Everyday Life* or the poetry of A. E. Housman or John Betjeman, which is both hyperconventional *and* deeply felt. Mir's ghazals, emerging from a very specific, even superheated cultural moment, can be read more universally.

There is also in Mir, as in John Donne, a dizzying interpenetration of love language with prayer language:

Love courses through earth and sky, love fills all four directions.
I am a slave and worshiper at love's doorstep. For me, love is God.

Apparent or unapparent, first or last, below or above all is love.
Light and darkness, appearance and reality, love has become all
    this by itself.

The next ghazal's warier: "There's no way I could tell you what love is. / It's a disease of the soul, a calamitous, destructive thing." The lover's capricious, he says one thing and then another, uttering no guaranteeable cosmology; yet there are parallels with Mir's father in *Remembrances*:

My father remained busy day and night in the remembrance of God, and God too did not forsake him. When my father would come out of that state of absorption, he would say to me: "Son, practice love, for it is love that holds sway over everything. Nothing would have taken shape here but for love. Without love, life is a burden. To give one's heart to love, that is perfection. Love creates and love consumes. Whatever exists in the world is a manifestation of love. Fire is love's ardor; wind is love's agitation. Water is the flow of love; earth is the repose of love. Death is love's inebriated state; life is love's sober state. Night is the sleep of love. Day is the wakefulness of love. The Muslim is love's comforting beauty, the infidel its awesomeness. Virtue lies in love's proximity; sin arises from its separation. Paradise is having a fondness for love; hell is to have a true taste for it. The state of love is above the states of worship, gnostic knowing, asceticism, companionship, sincerity, desirousness, and friendship—above even the state of being loved. All agree that the movement of the heavens is caused by love—they never reach what they desire and so keep going round and round.

This isn't a sermon explaining a fixed concept, but an act of poesis in its own right. Aphoristic closure gives way to intoxicated accretiveness; "the state of love" is stylistically exalted, though with no steady outline. The conclusion doesn't limn a crystalline heaven but a less reconciled, and more itchily mobile, desire-powered cosmos, ghazal-resembling in its unsatisfied ardors.

"Long before the Urdu poets adopted the ghazal form from the Persian," write Islam and Russell, it "was moving simultaneously on two levels, so that almost any line might be interpreted as an expression either of a man's love for his mistress or, in the mystic sense, of the worshipper's love for his God." Since "the starting point of mysticism is that true religion is inconceivable without a direct and intimate relationship between man and his God," in "both loves there is the same yearning for union with the beloved," such as the ghazal negotiates. Trying to establish through his father a Sayyid inheritance, Mir opposes to sober orthodoxy an intoxicated mysticism that (Islam and Russell) "has its own commandments"; overlapping, then, with the conventions of the ghazal. So, as well as seeing the verse as symptomatic of gender relations in Mughal India, we may find in it a music of philosophico-religious fervor; a grounding of belief in physical, even painful, revelations, occurring in saint narratives the world over, in the writing of Richard Rolle, for instance, or a hymning of life itself, conceived of, psychoanalytically, as desire. The longing to spire onward and upward, toward a consummation projected with such vim precisely because it can never be achieved—a failure that is no failure, for it means that writing, loving, living, need never end.

Censorship and the Role of the Poet in the Work of Ana Blandiana

My brother-in-law got married in Romania. The bride's family, Orthodox Christian—other faiths, especially Greek Catholicism, were stamped on, if not out, by the Communists—live in Cluj-Napoca, a city whose chaotic wiring against the sky compares with the strands of a spider's web, or the radial cracks in a smashed windscreen. Near big cobbled courtyards, peach-colored churches, ornate, not finicky, began to glow in the dusk. My brown face was stared at, not hostilely. We dined with the parents. Romanians are tremendous hosts—superattentive, ritualistic yet uncramped by niceties. Much wine and clear plum liqueur was consumed, and Tony (his wife, Olimpia, speaks little English, and Romanian men are the heads of their families, or think they are) remarked on the humiliations of life under Communism that we couldn't possibly understand. Except he didn't say *couldn't* or *possibly* (that's how an English person—my parents, never—would talk). I don't remember exactly what he said, but it was explosive. He was angry, and not at us. Then he grinned as the bride and groom practiced their wedding waltz around the living room.

A day or two before the ceremony, we drove to a hilltop monastery whose buildings had pointed little wooden steeples like witches' hats, and then to the Memorial of the Victims of Communism and of the Resistance at Sziget. This 150-mile drive neared the Ukrainian border. We saw the horse-drawn carts familiar in England from hysterical news reports on immigration, handmade bales of hay in different shapes and even colors, small platforms fixed to telephone poles for storks to nest on. Tony pointed out with delight the glimmer of pots and pans on a wooden stoop, a family announcement to the community of a daughter reaching marriageable age.

It was late when we reached Sziget, and Tony had to cajole to get us in. By this point his determination was quietly obvious. The building used to be a prison. You move from room to room learning of one atrocity after another. On the ground floor, Iuliu Maniu, a former prime minister of Romania and supporter of the Allies during the war years, was incarcerated following a show trial and died in 1953; another room discusses the operations of the Securitate, or Communist Secret Police, between 1948 and the revolution of 1989 which saw off Ceaușescu. Both the paper guide and the legends on the walls were hard for an English speaker to follow, especially when hurried. But a sentence stuck with me, following a furious paragraph on the Securitate's "methodical programme of mass indoctrination and manipulation," its strategies of public humiliation and stirring up of "conflicts between the different segments" of the populace, the repression of even "the smallest gesture of independence by intellectuals." We're then told—the syntax contorts like a face wincing—that "despite these draconian measures, the end of the Ceaușescu regime could not be avoided, but the traces of this violation of national consciousness persist even today in the mentality of many members of the public."

We never reached room 51, containing the verse of political prisoners. For Romanians under Communism, poetry was sempiternally dissident, a longed-for sunrise, an underground river and railroad in one. One thinks of the Czech poet Miroslav Holub and of the many Poles—Czesław Miłosz, Tadeusz Różewicz, Zbigniew Herbert, Wisława Szymborska—who've become icons of twentieth-century verse. They are, in translation, our classics. The same can't yet be said for Ana Blandiana, who helped found the memorial at Sziget and many of whose books of verse and prose have at one time been banned in her country. Persecuted ("Ana Blandiana" is a pseudonym) for her opposition to the Romanian Communist Party, she received in 2009 the Legion of Honor. Yet prior to the publication by Bloodaxe of *My Native Land A4* (the meaning is that the blank page is her true homeland), English readers made do with a slender selected works, *The Hour of Sand*. This book, translated by Peter Jay and Anca Cristofovici, was published by Anvil Press and, now out of print, expresses in its editorial structure the tensions of its moment.

This has to do with writing in code—to evade the censor. I'll explain, but let's explore first the sensorium of a single shrewdly animated poem, "You Never See the Butterflies." It could be read different ways, and this is characteristic of Blandiana, as is the unprepossessing nontitle. At one with the poem's originating perception, it appears nothing but the husk of its first sentence, the cocoon the butterfly leaves behind. Her poems are impulsive; they take off from an initial confusion or conceit and resemble the bright unanswerable query of a child:

> You never see
> The butterflies, how they look at each other above us?
> Nor the signs that the wind
> Makes to the grass as we walk by?
> If I suddenly turn,
> The branches are struck dumb
> And wait for us to move on.
> Haven't you noticed the birds are setting
> Haven't you noticed the leaves are going out?
> Haven't you noticed the whispers
> Growing on our backs,
> Like moss on the side of tree-trunks facing north?

The speaker's impatient with her listener; she says—"don't you get it, yet?" Out of this a code emerges: pastoral allegory. I'm reminded of that sentence at Sziget about a mutilation of the national consciousness. A bad, clamped feeling, not without lyrical content, a little movement upward out of the dirt. Blandiana reuses natural props, but deceptively. Birds, unlike the sun, don't set, and leaves, unlike fires, don't go out, so even before the outright metaphor of whispers growing on people as moss does on tree trunks, we're in a strange place where nothing works quite as it should. Not chaos but a new set of rules. As she writes elsewhere, the "sunset is rancid / And the sunrise faked."

Reading *The Hour of Sand* from cover to cover, I was confused by Jay and Cristofovici's apolitical, rather hedged introduction, calling this poem "visionary" and "worthy of Samuel Palmer," authored by a "convinced Romantic who feels that fundamental values are under direct threat" and whose "strong religious or spiritual impulse" draws primarily on "the animistic world of Romanian folk poetry and fairy tale." True, Blandiana is a Romantic, a tetchily dilapidated visionary: she returns over and over again to the interaction between the self and a natural world she still believes enchanted. The butterflies, the wind, the branches—the world responds to us; it isn't dead matter. Yet there's another reading. This is a poem about being spied on. *Et in Arcadia ego*: like death itself, the secret police lurk in paradise. The poet defends against surveillance by writing in code. The butterflies, you never see them coming.

The distance between this reading and the translators' reveals the bind one finds oneself in with poets like Blandiana. We seek from the poets of Eastern Europe a licensed transcendence and earned gravitas, deliverance once and for all from our fear that poetry's a self-regarding middle-class hobby. In their world (we visit it, reading their poems, breathe in its air) poets remain unacknowledged legislators and speak truth to power. The amplitude of atrocity enters these works as a form of chiaroscuro, a halo of shadow, an explicit holiness or an oblique thrill. The structure of *The Hour of Sand* resonates for this reason. Its afterword contradicts the introduction. It doesn't come at the end of the book, but precedes a handful of explicitly political poems ("Everything," or "Totul," parodies one of Ceauşescu's vocal tics and "I believe" describes Romanians as a "vegetal people"). Now the editors come clean. These poems are

> a product of the age of the dictatorship and the long arm of Ceauşescu's repression and censorship. The December uprising took place between the printing of the first edition's cover and of its text. For fear of making Ana Blandiana's life in Bucharest more difficult than it had been, our Introduction could only hint at the nature of the "direct threat" to her country's fabric and values, or at the "circumstances beyond her control" which caused her third banning in autumn 1988. But we decided not to change it, since it focuses on values rather than on circumstances, which are likely to be unsettled for some time.

So reading the book from beginning to end—being puzzled by the introduction, beginning to see through the code, and then coming to a realization of a historical moment, crystallized in the book's very structure, almost as in the plot of a novel—it's an experience I'm grateful for, as when one manages to see a film at the cinema without having it spoiled by the trailer. The final sentence puzzles me, though the focus on values rather than circumstances continues Blandiana's project: the individual isn't simply a product of history but a reality beyond authoritarian distortion. These poems, Jay and Cristofovici suggest, can be read in nonpolitical or even suprapolitical ways, and—a plot twist—perhaps this is in fact their secret, delayed, true meaning.

What I'm saying is that, though the structure of *The Hour of Sand*, with its cloudy intro and demisting afterword, was necessitous, it has also the side effect of letting the work breathe—making, as one reads, the ticklish claim that Blandiana's spirituality is as gruellingly and valuably present in the poems as the politics we might foreground. That said, there are, here, poems impossible to see as unmoored thought experiments untouched by Romanian history. "Perhaps Someone Is Dreaming Me," for one, is not simply a Borgesian conceit, but evokes what it's like to try and locate, and understand, oneself within a mutilated national history:

> That's why my gestures
> Are so soft
> And unfinished,
> With their aim forgotten
> Half-way,
> Grotesquely,
> That's why my outlines get blurred
> Second by second
> And my deeds melt . . .

The speaker arraigns her locale, stating sharply to the reader (I want to say listener; these poems are energetically *spoken*) the nature of the problem. Blandiana's poems remind me of paper airplanes. She folds her perceptions into a metaphor, lets it fly, watches the poem rise, dip, swoop curvilinearly out of view, or crash into a wall. Each conceit's a try at understanding, exposed in a matter of seconds as only provisionally sufficient. I could also mention the "metamatics" of Jean Tinguely or the *ludic*—but these poems are also prayers. They exist to salve the world-weary and to be activated by the desperate. Each briefly and flimsily alleviates, through a momentary clarification, a vast, implicitly grasped trauma.

The individual I label the "speaker" of these poems could be identified with Blandiana herself: cultural spokesperson, an oracle, a voice whose vulnerability rhymes with and expresses that of millions. In the afterword to *My Native Land A4*, she writes:

> Maybe I should be offended by this total dependence on forces that I cannot even minimally influence, but I feel happy and as proud as a lady in waiting that the king has chosen to bear his child. This is an

odd combination of humility and pride that can only result in a special form of liberation. I was convinced until recently that I write because someone inside of me dictates, word for word, something that I have to hurriedly write down, and that I only have to create the necessary conditions for this inner voice to speak, and not stop speaking.

It's like one of those apps that mashes up your face with that of a celebrity—in Blandiana's case, Elizabeth I. She takes the stereotype of the passive woman and reimagines it as a source of power. ("I have never been able to say 'we poets' without embarrassment," she remarks, "just as I have never been able to say 'we women' without blushing.") Those "forces" she depends on aren't governmental or military; Blandiana speaks of "moments of grace," transgressive inspirations as beyond a poet's control as the weather. Yet it does sound as if she's discussing state control—as if her language has once again become encoded—it isn't an allegory in this case, but the rhetoric contains a political valence in how it turns necessity into freedom. If the poet is put upon, harassed, dominated—in other words, a Romanian citizen, prior to the revolution—she can at least append to the forces to which she cedes control whatever description she wishes, emulating in the realm of literary style the freedom of a democratic voter to choose her leaders. The laws that ultimately compel, terrify and liberate, are, she avers (makes us feel, from poem to poem), less those of rotten tyrants than truths elemental, religious, creative. The restless urgencies of the spirit.

"The Owner of the Mill," published in the new book, describes a figure who is to God what Blandiana's infamous satirical tomcat—in a banned children's poem—was to Ceaușescu. That is: as precise a portrait as may be allowed, as will outrun the red pencil of the censor. But in this case the censor is the internalized, historically dejected voice of secular realism:

> What is it made of,
> That dust that he leaves over things,
> So fine (it's almost invisible)
> It only duplicates their contours with a halo of shadow?
> Where is the mill that grinds down everything that disappears
> And produces this sawdust of non-being?
> Like a powder that sticks to your fingers
> When you want to caress something out of the past.
> Or maybe he's the one who's been ground up,

> So that no one will notice when he disappears
> And no one will remember
> The difference between
> The finite cold
> And burning eternity.
> But in that case, who is the owner of that mill where
> Death is nothing but a pale manipulation?

Earlier I applied a phrase from this poem, "halo of shadow," to Blandiana's political verse. Here that extra dimension of significance is religious. Yet there is, again, overlap: we don't know who or what the poet's thinking of—a dethroned being, whose absence is as powerful, shaping lives, as his lost presence. (That the mills of the gods grind slow is an ancient, much-quoted allusion to powers of divine vengeance yet to be activated.) We don't remember the story, our responses are insufficient, but the responses remain nonetheless, keyed to events unlisted in any textbook. Questions are asked, as in "You Never See the Butterflies," but are outfaced by the impossible desire to take something airy and invisible and admire its texture between one's fingers.

The poem's sounds tingle: each l and t, how "duplicates" links up with "halo" (the intonational contour of the line alights on one word and then the other, like a butterfly self-poised upon one flower and landing its weight softly, after an airy hop, on another) and also how the vowel sound of "halo" resurfaces in "manipulation" (not, here, that of the Securitate). These are strange compliments to pay translated verse. One doesn't know who to applaud or even if the felicities are accidental. But the new translators, Paul Scott Derrick and Viorica Patea, must be praised, for the many tiny evidences of an ear sensitive to microeffects of word placement and lineation. "Where" comes trippingly off the penultimate line instead of making the last too portentous; the rhythm of the first four lines, in particular, is brilliantly fluid—even the double "that" sandwiching "dust" seems to work (you come down harder on the first than the second), although the deixis does appear many times in the book and could be trimmed. But perhaps the optional "that" expresses something of Romanian diction? (There's a similar effect in "Stele," describing of the symbol above a child's gravestone "the fingers spread out / As though to ward off something, / That something that cannot be detained by empty hands.") Certainly the effect of precision is essential to Blandiana—the making-sense-of-things, the cautious open-endedness.

"Caress," which the translators tether to "past," also appears in "On Tiptoe":

> I have tiptoed
> Up to the line,
> I only wanted to touch it
>   With the tip of my naked foot,
> Like in summer, when I caress the line
>   Between the land and the sea.
> But the boundary drew back
> As though it wanted to protect itself from me—
> I keep going forward
> Over this sand moistened by death,
> Alive and proud
> That I can push that frontier back
> Or, perhaps, just step over it
>   Unawares.

About a self-aware poem there are clear-cut remarks to be made about the poetic "foot" and "line," and Blandiana's afterword does describe "the work of art itself" as "that tenuous and imprecise boundary between existence and non-existence." This modest poem's one salient line—I'm gawking at the "sand moistened by death"—reveals that ability crucial to the philosophical poet of fusing sensuous detail with a description of reality.

Touch matters to Blandiana. The present moment obtrudes its sensuousness, as if to ask: why fly off into the past and dilemmas of the spirit? Isn't this, aren't I, enough? And there's a beautiful elegy in this book for the poet's mother. But still Blandiana resists merely personal subject matter, and with it idiosyncrasies of style: "related more with the desire to cause sensation than to be, the pursuit of originality seems to me frivolous." What isn't frivolous is what connects one spirit to another, as the poet, touching the ley lines of being, speaks to and for all. Everyone who has been to the sea has played with the tide, with icy feet—we know what this is like.

Blandiana's longing, both nostalgic and utopian, for an organic community healed of modern schisms, is common to many twentieth-century poets. But it's especially pertinent to a country whose economic and technological development has been, is, bitty, deflected, partial. That Romania went industrial only in the middle of the twentieth century is relevant to the yearning, in "Agglomeration," for a vanished world of enchanted ritual in which "every square inch of ground was inhabited / By endless hierarchies of invisible beings." Yet this desire is ironized—"How marvellous to walk around among them / And not to bother anyone"—as the poem evinces complicated feelings about the more actual and dangerously recent past:

> What an exciting life! What tumultuous emotions,
> When even the smallest event was shepherded by a god
> That had to be prayed to, begged and adored—
> A god that extorted sacrifices—i.e., metaphysical bribes—
> In order to carry out his appointed duties.

"Agglomeration" records the caprice of deities in terms recalling a poisoned bureaucracy. Blandiana's nostalgia is self-critical—it can't help but turn into caustic allegory. It is as if, wishing for a world of unpredictable and irrational magic, charged with constant meaning, it hits her suddenly that she's bigging up life in the Socialist Republic.

The risk for a political poet who has accomplished her goal in one sense—the destruction of Communism—but not another (Blandiana is unthrilled by the corruption and ahistorical consumerism of present-day Romania) is of subsiding into either pseudosophisticated resignation or reactionary bitterness. "On Roller Skates" approaches a rant about a youth with "earphones droning in their ears / and their eyes glued to monitors"; "Season's End" describes a universe filled with "dust forgotten in the corners / And empty warehouses / Where meaningless poems are declaimed." Lines reminiscent of *The Waste Land* ask where things went wrong while suggesting of civilization itself an underlying spiritual principle:

> Athens, Carthage, Rome,
> Byzantium, Constantinople, Istanbul,
> Waves of rubble,
> Stair steps
> To the doorway
> (That doesn't, in fact, exist)
> Of eternity.

"Stair Steps," the poem's called, not "Waves of Rubble:" Blandiana is mordant about, she doesn't wholly reject, the aspirations of perishable cultures. A grain of the unearthly is no bad thing; this is where humans start out from, rather than self-interest and a tyrannous expansionism. That the doorway between eternity and the earthly polis doesn't exist doesn't mean we shouldn't build the stairs. A postmodern theology: one believes in God precisely because God doesn't exist.

On leaving the prison museum at Sziget, we were led (hurriedly, well after closing hours) into a darkened chamber with a water basin. A small fee buys a candle whose reflected flame joins the others. "You don't have to," said our hosts, kindly; afterward, Olimpia bought us ice cream down the road. Since we can only begin to understand others using what's presently available, accessible, to us, I thought then—having not yet read Blandiana—of Michael Longley's "All of These People:"

> Who was it who suggested that the opposite of war
> Is not so much peace as civilisation? He knew
> Our assassinated Catholic greengrocer who died
> At Christmas in the arms of our Methodist minister,
> And our ice-cream man whose continuing requiem
> Is the twenty-one flavours children have by heart.
> Our cobbler mends shoes for everyone; our butcher
> Blends into his best sausages leeks, garlic, honey;
> Our cornershop sells everything from bread to kindling.
> Who can bring peace to people who are not civilised?
> All of these people, alive or dead, are civilised.

At Home or Nowhere
A. K. Ramanujan

> What we seek, we must find at home or nowhere.
> —William Hazlitt

Attipat Krishnaswami Ramanujan was born ninety years ago in Mysore—1929—and moved to the U.S. three decades on, in 1959. He was, in Jahan Ramazani's parlance, a *transnational* scholar-poet, whose verse and criticism (on the folklore of India and classical literature in Kannada, Tamil, and Sanskrit) was plurally informed and enriched; and so both of these anniversaries deserve to be celebrated. Ramanujan joked of being the hyphen in "Indo-American"—belonging, then, to two countries, and also to neither. Wendy Doniger, his colleague at the University of Chicago, explains:

> His sadness was that while he was in India, he missed America, and in America, he missed India. He was never really complete in any one place, but that also is why he was so wonderful.
>
> He always was on the side of the angels when it came to human values, never "politically correct" but he had a feeling for the underdog, for people of color, for women, for the poor, and he didn't have to work at it. There was always a lot of heart in it—he was sharp as a tack and very critical, an interesting combination—he didn't just love everything but he loved the right things.

We find this "sadness" in Ramanujan's most-anthologized poem, "Self-Portrait," a brief masterpiece:

> I resemble everyone
> but myself, and sometimes see
> in shop-windows,
> > despite the well-known laws
> > of optics,
> the portrait of a stranger,
> date unknown,
> often signed in a corner
> by my father.

It's one of the best first lines, and line breaks, in twentieth-century verse. Keats praised the "camelion poet," who "has no Identity—he is continually in for—and filling some other Body"; this poem's speaker isn't so transparently empowered. Trying to fit in, the immigrant may forget who he really is. Subject to other "laws" than those of optics, and commerce-surrounded (those "shop-windows" slant-rhyme with "laws" to spotlight both line endings), where he should contemplate his reflection, he discovers only "the portrait of a stranger."

Another Indian poet, Dom Moraes, performs an equivalent trick, calling his autobiography *My Son's Father*; probing the Oedipus myth, Ramanujan says in Indian lore the son rarely kills the father, and the pressure is to deny one's instinct toward independence from one's family (where, in the West, or some of it, we might, contrarily, deny our dependence on others). He published a sequence of "Images," which aren't strictly imagist; they've family in them and, rather than iconic instantaneousness, the leavings (pun intended) of a muddled inheritance:

> *Farewell*
>
> Mother's farewell had no words,
> no tears, only a long look
> that moved on your body
> from top to toe
> with the advice that you should
> not forget your oil bath
> every tuesday
> when you go to America

Tooth

The large tooth in my left jaw
aches: it's mother again
complaining of the large tooth
in her left jaw
the week before she died

The Hindu idea of reincarnation is sullied: the poet's "mother" returns as a physical sensation only, though Ramanujan's line breaks pressurize the sound running through "ache," "again," and "complaining," as if trying to extract from pain an actual presence. (As Simone Weil says of grief, "the presence of the dead person is imaginary, but his absence is very real: henceforward it is his way of appearing.") Memory, as we'll see, is central to Ramanujan's poetics ("amnesia is a curse," he says, "a form of alienation from one's self, for one's self is largely constituted by memory") and vital to the first poem too, which relates not a farewell but—look closely—the lack of one. Although "mother" says nothing concerning the departure, her "look" silently tattoos her child with obligations.

If the speaker, or speakers, of Ramanujan's poems feel they're the creation of their parents—who transmit a history impermissive of newness—we must grasp the (it's his word, quoted later in this essay) "nuances." In "Self-Portrait," the ingenious, poem-defining words are "sometimes" and "often." When we qualify ourselves, it may be through lack of confidence, but since the poem is so laser-exact, this can't be the case for its speaker—he details an experience that (rather than defining him) comes and goes. So there's time, and space, for him to be someone else, to explore other possibilities: a view of the immigrant, and by extension anyone, is advanced in which instability and ability are one and the same thing. "Identify yourself," says the lawman, and we're encouraged, by the spirit of the age, to market ourselves through categorization (consider those "shop-windows" again), as cleaving to a particular community; to have opinions, and become identical with them.

It isn't only on the Internet that we praise or damn people based on their claims about the world, and themselves; what would it mean to think otherwise? For "opinions," says Ramanujan—in another interview—are "only a small expression of one's attitudes. They are an uncertain, often rigid expression. One is more, and often less, than one's opinions. And they don't often match other things in oneself. So please read them as gestures." Writing in his diary on October 12, 1976, "I've never made my opinions very clear, because I distrust opinions, and value doubt," he revisits the idea but a month later:

> I dislike having sweeping opinions, but "ifs" and "buts" and "perhapses" are tedious—people think you're being pedantic, picayune. But there's no way out of dogmatism and stereotyping except through nuance, reservations. Opinions harden one's heart. W. B. Yeats disliked women with opinions—but men with opinions are no better. They're bearable, and even lovable, because they're more than their opinions. The "if and but and perhaps" style may be deadly, tedious, but sweeping opinions are dangerous: "Now we have a principle, we can kill."

As this suggests, Ramanujan—though we may praise him as the poet of race, nationhood, identity, gender, for whom we have been waiting—prefers to topple our beloved presumptions. He wouldn't fit into today's media and Twitter culture, for he refuses to take a person as being identical with the things they say. What the diaries agonize about is how to attain to, and maintain, an experience of genuine mental freedom out of which real thinking, about oneself, and those we love, and our histories, might commence.

The "sadness" Doniger cites, eventuating in "Self-Portrait," could be construed—unfixed in time and place, the immigrant goes on their nerve—as anticipatory of such a real, if comfortless, freedom. Ramanujan disdained the notional "exile" often imposed, as a guarantee of pathos and significance and a critical template, on the writers we call (at risk of walling readers out) postcolonial. "I have come to this country voluntarily," he explained—in a 1989 interview with A. L. Becker and Keith Taylor—"I don't even call myself an expatriate, because I've done a lot of work on India . . . more comfortably here than I could even have done it in India. For instance, in the Chicago Regenstein Library, there are books on Kannada and Tamil which probably only I will read." It was at Chicago that Ramanujan rediscovered (that may be too large a word) the classical literatures of India; he recognized that "the English language, English-educated Indians . . . and English people are important forces in the rediscovery of the Indian past." Attentive, as Doniger explains, to injustice, he refused a Manichaean view—Empire bad, pure indigenousness good—favoring, alternatively, the impure hybridity of (it's Wordsworth) "the very world, which is the world / Of all of us,—the place where, in the end, / we find our happiness, or not at all!"

Ramanujan's unearthing of seemingly lost literatures is enlivened by his quirk of relating the close-at-hand to the far-off, in often nonplussing ways, as when, mooting the blend in classical Tamil verse of "the vivid particulars of bird, beast, insect, drum-beat and falling water" with a "highly formal scheme of idealised landscapes," he says these works "seem to anticipate Marianne Moore who suggested that poets ought to be "literalists of the imagination" and that poems ought to be 'imaginary gardens with real toads in them.'" This isn't a naive flattening of dissimilarities: the comparison is truly, bidirectionally, illuminating. It arises of his own creativeness, for as Arvind Krishna Mehrotra notes, "if the ancient Tamils are among Miss Moore's Borgesian precursors, Ramanujan is among those who learnt from her example: his five-toed lizards, salamanders, quartz clocks, and poem titles that double also as first lines can be traced to her." Ramanujan was forthright about his Anglo-American influences: "that's part of my expressive means. I've read Pound, and I've read Indian things. I think with them. Why shouldn't I use what I have?" The Ezra Pound reference appears in "The Striders," the title poem of Ramanujan's 1966 debut, named for the New England water insect:

> No, not only prophets
> walk on water. This bug sits
> on a landslide of lights
> and drowns eye-
> deep
> into its tiny strip
> of sky.

The "bug"—Ramanujan enjoys that U.S. word, its monosyllabic grunt—walks on water, like Jesus, yet is fragilely self-enclosed in its own "tiny" region. The poem's rhymes mime its conscientiousness of movement, evoking both Coleridge, who compares "the mind's self-experience in the act of thinking" to a water insect working "by alternative pulses of active and passive motion," and Yeats, glorying in thoughts of the great acting "upon silence" as does "a long-legged fly upon the stream" (these *l* sounds pass into Ramanujan's "landslide of lights").

It's with Pound's arrival in the poem—"Hugh Selwyn Mauberley" evokes the soldiers of World War I walking "eye-deep in hell / believing in old men's lies"—that Ramanujan shifts to seeing the insect as, it would appear, drowning. Like the speaker, or addressee, of "Chicago Zen":

> Watch your step. Sight may strike you
> blind in unexpected places.
>
> The traffic light turns orange
> on 57th and Dorchester, and you stumble,
>
> you fall into a vision of forest fires,
> enter a frothing Himalayan river,
>
> rapid, silent.
>
>   On the 14th floor,
> Lake Michigan crawls and crawls
>
> in the window. Your thumbnail
> cracks a lobster louse on the windowpane
>
> from your daughter's hair
> and you drown, eyes open,
>
> towards the Indies, the antipodes.
> And you, always so perfectly sane.

Published in *Second Sight* in 1986, this poem renews the vision trope (in both senses, seeing and imagining) of "The Striders;" movement, or its defeat (the "stumble") returns; the ripples of Lake Michigan morph eerily into another insect. Whose death by squashing—the "thumbnail" seems to do it instinctively—is one of those tiny, eddying actions that neuroscientists explain may activate prior to our conscious decisions. Guillermo Rodríguez observes that "in the subtropical climate of south India, insects and reptiles dwell year around in houses, and larger animals live on the streets and always close to humans. Even in many larger cities, houses do not cut off the inside from the outside, and there is no real divide between nature and the cultured, technological world of humans. This environmental feature may denote a psychological and cultural trait in India." This feeling of unboundaried space begins to shape, in that critic's terms, the "eco-aesthetic consciousness" Ramanujan also derived from the ancient Tamil poems he translated. Taken further, the idea of overlapping realms turns postcolonial:

> When I was in India I studied English Literature and thought about Shakespeare and T. S. Eliot and quoted them. I still remember evenings when, two or three friends, we would walk around in the markets of a town in South India where the women from which we bought the bitter leaves, the mango or the bananas did not know even one word of English and we would go and buy all sorts of things in a totally Indian environment and talk about Proust, Plato and Shakespeare. So, it seems to me, the world in which we live is not one world only. Worlds are woven together and interpenetrate, creating the world we know.

In this snippet for a 1990 brochure for the Jerusalem Poetry Festival, a long, happily lax sentence appears idyllic (the poverty of the market women isn't dwelt on) and, as often in Ramanujan's prose, stakes his own experience as an alternative to Anglo-American intellectual categories. "So, it seems to me" hesitates phrasally on the borderline between apology ("because of my unique experience, I can't help thinking this way") and scholarly assertion ("logically, therefore, I can deduce").

But in "Chicago Zen," this sense of the uncontainable, and walls broken down or melted in the blink of an eye to nothing, becomes a terror. I don't think either vision contradicts the other: Ramanujan's prose isn't in denial, nor is his poem melodramatic. We must look to the verbal details. There's something murky about the repeated verb "crawls," which its decisive, agential successor, "cracks," can't airily dismiss. Because it also appears in Ramanujan's diary entry of July 6, 1959, describing his sea journey from Bombay to New York—"The sea is a bright blue, with little crawls of foam on it. . . . The sun makes the water-face mercurial, like silver blocks continually chipped by the wind"—I wonder if he's thinking, both here and there, of John Ruskin's famous example of the pathetic fallacy in the verse of Alton Locke: "They rowed her in across the rolling foam— / The cruel, crawling foam."

"The foam is not cruel, neither does it crawl," says Ruskin: "the state of mind which attributes to it these characters of a living creature is one in which the reason is unhinged by grief. All violent feelings have the same effect." Ramanujan's poem vibrates with such feelings: violent, but also complex. It's reminiscent of a dream he jotted down, although his son Krishna Ramanujan and Rodríguez, editing the diaries, date that dream two years after the poem's publication: "Mysore with coconut palms. An apartment like mine here in Ann Arbor on the 13th or so floor, high up with large windows. Veda and Saroja have come home from their work, walking a stretched double tightrope from their office to my window. I'm anxious they should fall, but they walk fast and enter through the window." This shows that Ramanujan's spliced or doubled locations aren't only a feat of technique but express life-defining forebodings. In his poem, the role played by his daughter is paramount: family plunges him once again into the past. Nor should we miss the pronoun stratagem, where the speaker reprimands himself, but in doing so brings in the reader (as in, I see now, "Farewell"). Poets of counterpublics may be drawn to the "indeterminate potential," in Jonathan Culler's phrase, of boat-rockingly porous pronouns: one thinks of Claudia Rankine's use of the second person in her prose poems, or lyrical essays, on the aggressions faced by African Americans, or another gifted Indian poet, Arun Kolatkar, toying with that pronoun in *Jejuri*.

"Middle Age" also depicts an alarmingly at-once transit between nations: "Vietnam eyes my children in the sandbox / . . . while Biafra gives me // potbellied babies with copper-red / hungry hair." But while that poem objects to the denial by the U.S. bourgeois of suffering overseas, the associativeness of "Chicago Zen"—despite the title—is more rampant. Its speaker bounces like a trauma survivor between past and present: like, in fact, a veteran of Vietnam, shell-shocked and given to flashbacks. The flip is also between continents, a compelled and compulsive migration of the mind. Ramanujan would have sympathized with Elizabeth Bishop, transplanted from Canada to the U.S. to South America: "It is funny to come to Brazil to experience total recall about Nova Scotia—geography must be more mysterious than we realize, even." He resembles a chaos theorist, concerned that the flap of a butterfly's wings in Brazil may provoke a tornado in Texas:

> Mother brings me tea again at 6 a.m.
> before she dies in another time zone
> and the calendar
>
> whirls me out into snow flurries
> and fears of market crash
> in another hemisphere

If Ramanujan's concatenations suggest emotional chaos, a chili-spiced confessionalism, this may be due to our unfamiliarity with the classics he studied and translated and took as influences. In Tamil verse, "a kind of syntactic suspense," he explains, can be crucial ("lines are not end-stopped") and, in puṟam poems, "images rush and tumble over one another." These are "poems about good and evil, action, community, kingdom; it is the 'public' poetry of the ancient Tamils," contrasted with akam, or "love poems . . . about experience, not action," and featuring "idealised types, such as chieftains representing clans and classes, rather than historical persons." It is for his translations, collected in *Speaking of Śiva*, *The Interior Landscape*, and *Hymns for the Drowning*, that Ramanujan remains best known:

> Will he not really think of us
> when he passes the clumps of milk-hedge
> with their fragrant trunks
> and hears the redlegged lizard call
> to his mate
> in cluckings that sound like
> the highway robber's fingernail
> testing the point of his iron arrow,
> will he not really think of us, friend?

This poem from *Kuṟuntokai*, an anthology "from the first three centuries AD," is erotically suggestive throughout. The syntax, bookended by near-identical lines, is fizzy with the speaker's excitement (ascribable to her beau), but there is, too, a virtuosity, an originality coextensive with tradition, and a fulfillment of archetypes to the succession of details, which are actually metaphors. A stylishly unflummoxed haste, a savoring of each desire-displacement. Ramanujan translates classical Tamil unfloridly: he admires these poems for being anti-Romantic, spare, controlled, and conventional (in the best, art-deepening sense). We see, hear, the touches of the translator—heedful of what's possible in English, which quiddities can be translinguistically retained—in the unlovely word choices, "clumps" and "clucking," that form a guttural soundscape.

Ramanujan translated many lyrics in a woman's voice, and his thinking about gender emerges in both his verse and scholarship. In "Men, Women and Saints," he considers anthropologically the post-Freudian notion that "each sex envies the other:"

> The conversion and other experiences of the saints often parallel initiatory and other rituals—transvestism, role-reversals, humiliation, nakedness (in both male and female saints), assimilation to ghosts, being made or called crazy till one's normal intelligence and everyday orientation is transmuted. . . . Not only do saints like St John of the Cross, Vidyāpati and Nammālvār go transvestite in poetry, as the paṇḍās of the Puri temple do actually, and write passionate poems from the vantage point of gopīs in love with Kṛṣṇa, suffering and enjoying "symbolic wounds" like the African initiates—in classical Tamil, three-fourths of the dramatic love poems by male poets are put in the mouths of women.
>
> This taking on of a woman's persona by male poets and saints has, thus, multiple meanings: to become bisexual, whole and androgynous like the gods themselves (Puruṣa, Śiva and Viṣṇu); in a male-dominated society, it serves also to abase and reverse oneself, rid oneself of machismo, to enter a liminal confusion, become open and receptive as a woman to god; and it is possibly also a poetic expression of the male envy and admiration of women.

We might question—with the multifarious travails of trans people in mind—the psychoanalytic language of "envy" and of a male annexing of the female, but we glimpse through the screen of Ramanujan's formidable erudition his own concerns. He revisits the idea, adding in "Who Needs Folklore" that "oral and written forms in a culture often wish to be like each other, like the two sexes, male and female. . . . Yet each defines and marries the other." "Love Poem for a Wife and Her Trees" is vivid in its ambivalence, a lyric of devotion that gets embattled, almost whines, before recovering its goodwill toward a "foreign body / with a mind // that knows what I'll never know" and its recognition of the role-playing common to marriage:

> Yet I know you'll play at Jewish mama,
> sob-sister, daughter who needs help
> with arithmetic,
>
> even the sexpot nextdoor, topless
> tree spirit on a temple frieze,
> or plain Indian wife
>
> at the village well, so I can play son,
> father, brother, macho lover, gaping
> tourist, and clumsy husband.

This bravely grants the intrusion of culture into even our sexual lives and their power dynamics; within our desire to see, and touch, the essence of the person we love most (in this most basic, cardinal, rendezvous of self and other) there may lurk a contrary longing to dress them up as ghosts from the past and have them talk or act according to scripts our desires can't do without. These facts configure even one-half of an intimate conversation with one's spouse, where the startling line break pinpointing that "gaping / tourist"—a divided self, both Indian and not, lusting, absurdly, after sculpture—cuts deep.

The desire in Ramanujan to cross over to the woman's side, and play her role or roles, unfolds more wholly, shockingly even, in "Highway Stripper." It's a U.S. road poem in which the speaker "on a highway / to Mexico" sees the driver in front ("a woman's hand") chuck out of the window items of clothing: a "white shoe fit / to be a fetish," a skirt, slip, blouse, bra, and underwear. He speeds up, wanting a better view, and I wonder if the poem develops out of Vladimir Nabokov's *Lolita*, which has in it a road trip as Humbert hauls his victim from state to state, and also a prose diorama of grisly self-pleasure and post-orgasmic self-loathing after he loses her:

> I would be misled by a jewel-bright window opposite wherein my lurking eye . . . would make out from afar a half-naked nymphet stilled in the act of combing her Alice-in-Wonderland hair. There was in the fiery phantasm a perfection which made my wild delight also perfect, just because the vision was out of reach, with no possibility of attainment to spoil it. . . . I would crowd all the demons of

my desire against the railing of a throbbing balcony: it would be ready to take off in the apricot and black humid evening; did take off—whereupon the lighted image would move and Eve would revert to a rib, and there would be nothing in the window but an obese partly clad man reading the newspaper.

Humbert's solipsistic fantasy (inspired, no doubt, by Leopold Bloom's in *Ulysses*) reveals a man primally allured by his own imaginative intrigues who flees reality into the unreal embrace of a woman (or, gallingly, a child) he less perceives than creates. As the illusion ends and Eve reverts "to a rib"—how marvellously this evokes the ectoplasmic fabrication of a sex partner out of nothing, of an objectified woman out of the fevered male brain!—the man in the window may as well be his own reflection. Ramanujan's speaker, in "that glimpse and after- / image in this hell / of voyeurs," finds at the wheel of the car in front, a Mustang, only "a man, / about forty, // a spectacled profile," listening to sports on the radio; he overtakes, stares back, but still there remains "only a man";

> had he stripped
> not only hat
> and blouse, shoes
> and panties
> and bra,
> had he shed maybe
> even the woman
> he was wearing,
>
> or was it me
> moulting, shedding
> vestiges,
> old investments,
> rushing forever
> towards a perfect
> coupling
> with naked nothing
> in a world
> without places?

The short, enjambed lines become horribly one-way: the speaker hurtles down the road, unsure who he is and what he's doing. Nabokov harks back to the Bible, and the production of Eve out of Adam's rib; neither appear directly in Ramanujan's poem, but his "perfect / coupling / with naked nothing" could read as a death wish; the desire, akin to that of Joyce's Stephen Dedalus, to fly by the nets of nationality, language, religion; or Edenic longing. Certainly, a snake slithers through the poem—not Satan but the speaker himself—shedding its skin. Yet Ramanujan's poem isn't, like Nabokov's novel, about a predator. There are many ways we could read the man in the car—as an old-style cross-dresser or someone discarding an ex's clothing or maybe jettisoning evidence of an extramarital affair. I think he is a cross-dresser, a figure to sympathize with for the poet curious about the porousness of identity categories.

Ramanujan raises the stakes: we move from sex fantasy into metaphysics, a poetics of world-crossing that melts down all solids into a fluxional plasm. Playing on words, he compares composition (of a poem) to decomposition, worrying the idea in several poems—"I lose, decompose / into my elements, // into other names and forms"—including "Oranges":

> Oranges on the refrigerator
> are covered with the ash of living
> mould that would look like a sci-fi
> undersea forest through a microscope.
>
> . . .
>
> Bacteria thrive in the kissing mouth,
> the dying brain. Just wait,
>
> you too will live again.

The break that simultaneously, or after the most delicate pause, both severs and sutures "living" and "mould"—linked with ash, a holy substance for Hindus, as well as incinerated corpse residue—makes Ramanujan's point succinctly. At the close of the poem there reappears that plaintive assonance from "Tooth"—"brain," "wait," "again"—ending it with, for a punchline, another bathetic reincarnation. In the "Upanishadic cosmo-vision that appealed to Ramanujan," writes Rodríguez, "the idea of art and creation merges with the notion of the composite body and the transformation of matter."

Introducing Ramanujan's poems, Vinay Dharwadker observes that "when composition cannot be separated from decomposition, the self can possess a stable 'centre' or a principle of self-determined identity only in an ironic sense." I've mentioned the syntax Ramanujan takes from classical verse; he also mentions stories in Indian folklore that are "performative," meaning that to recite one can be a drama-producing action within an epic, an act of healing or self-healing—summarizing, with habitual wordplay, the legend of an old woman who "tells her stories, her family secrets, only to lighten herself, not to enlighten anyone." In "Chicago Zen," and poems like it, we might see a trope-swollen cascade as catharsis, an homage to classical poetics, or—combining these ideas—poetic form placed in the service of memory and therefore salvific. The strength of irony wavers, and with it the balance between onrushing feeling and an effort toward self-possession. "Anxiety," writes Ramanujan—the name of a poem, and its presiding antimetaphor—has "loose ends / with a knot at the top / that's me." It's an especially deft and brilliant, because device-undoing, list lyric:

> Flames have only lungs. Water is all eyes.
> The earth has bone for muscle. And the air
> is a flock of invisible pigeons.
>   But anxiety
> can find no metaphor to end it.

"Anxiety" is a medicalized condition; a philosophical concept; and—I'm tempted to say, affixing the postcolonial template—it may express in this poem, and others like it, a corrosive rootlessness: the world traveler's unforgettable recognition that all values are relative, that any structure of feeling or belief can only be provisional and liable to contradiction at whatever moment. (The knot metaphor, which, as Rodríguez observes, occurs in many Ramanujan poems, also brings to mind his lecture notes: "A poet, like a medium, is both born . . . and made. He is, in an old Tamil phrase, a twist in the embryo"; and his diary of July 21, 1983: "I'm afraid one has to be tactful even with oneself—not say, 'produce now!' and tie oneself up in knots.") Though he stressed graciously the opportunities coming his way in the U.S., Ramanujan wasn't a happy man. His diary hums with worries, and worrying about worrying, about sex, work, poetry, countless dreamed-of projects: "Where's the time for it all, how do I get them all done, in this morass of self-pity and chaotic non-directed eddying of days?"

It could be those unfastened to any one locale simply can't live an unexamined, doubt-free life; yet Ramanujan doesn't construe this as purely a grievance. When my wife and I moved to the U.S., I was struck by how, though it saddened all our parents, mine—Sri Lankan Tamils who came to England over forty years ago—were more sanguine. "It's different for us," my mother said, "because we are immigrants"; a remark that cuts both ways, for she didn't mean only that immigrants suffer, that home's indistinct to them, but also that (we're talking about a middle class here, not refugees) the nation-crossing gambits of global modernity suit them better. I've realized in other words that people like me, and my family (and, I'm arguing, Ramanujan) may be—despite their sufferings—in some ways luckier than those locked in place. His magisterial genius reminds people who, of whatever background, sense in some ingrained way that we don't belong, that to feel uprooted, precarious, a skater over the world's deep surfaces, is also to be vouchsafed a glorious doorway to the resources, the unwitherable dream, of world culture.

Your Thorns Are the Best Part of You
Marianne Moore and Stevie Smith

Linda Leavell, whose biography of Marianne Moore was published in 2013, introduces this reissue of the poet's 1924 debut, *Observations*:

> There is no such thing as a definitive edition of Moore's poems, for she revised her work throughout her life, continually asserting her authority in an ongoing dialogue with her reader.... Published on her eightieth birthday, *The Complete Poems* presents her final intentions but not necessarily her most compelling ones. Moore was not the same poet at eighty that she had been at thirty-seven, when *Observations* was published, nor was her readership the same. Twenty-first-century readers deserve to know the innovative poems that so excited H.D., Eliot, Williams, Pound, and Stevens and that were an "eye-opener in more ways than one" to the young Elizabeth Bishop. And they deserve to discover the emotional urgency of this socially engaged poet, whose views about multicultural tolerance, biodiversity, heroic open-mindedness, democracy, and individual liberty we are only now beginning to appreciate.

In Moore's verse, snippets of borrowed speech or writing are recognized as such—they wear, quite without shame, their quotation marks—but her first impulse wasn't to attribute, to include notes directing her readers to the original sources; this happened only at the prompting of Scofield Thayer, editor of the *Dial*. Moore's "Note on the Notes" in the *Complete Poems* acknowledges contrary responses: "some readers suggest that quotation-marks are disruptive of pleasant progress; others, that notes to what should be complete are a pedantry or evidence of an insufficiently realized task." Since she has "not yet been able to outgrow this hybrid method of composition, acknowledgements seem only honest." So we have the poet apologizing to some people for including the voices of other people in her verse, in a possibly distracting way—alliteratively pleading: "Perhaps those who are annoyed by provisos, detainments, and postscripts could be persuaded to take probity on faith and disregard the notes."

As Leavell comes to argue the contemporary relevance of *Observations*, another voice emerges. This isn't the scholar analyzing and explaining the work, or the biographer documenting the life. It's the salesperson talking, and uneasily, because aware always of her script, yet unwilling to entirely commit to its banalities. Academics are leaned on to speak this way, by publishers, funding bodies. Sometimes the voice, unhappily internalized, rises up from within, becomes fused with our real ambitions (having been there, I sympathize). But the strain shows, as "emotional urgency" comes together, earnestly, with "socially engaged"—we couldn't have our poets any other way—and the next clause hesitates as to whether Moore simply has opinions ("views about . . . heroic open-mindedness?") or whether she has, let us say, the right opinions. Do we read poets for their "views," and if we are "beginning to appreciate" Moore's, is this because they agree with ours? I don't mean to harp on about one sentence in a dedicated scholar's introduction — written, no doubt, to time and word limits, as well as responsive to the current publishing (ugh) climate, but I do think the question must be asked, and that in such matters we should express ourselves precisely. For example, racists also have "views about multicultural tolerance," strong ones, which they periodically communicate to me with an unvariegated stridency surely appalling to Moore, typically out of fast-moving cars.

I'm not saying that Moore wasn't forward-looking and sensitive, or that these qualities haven't been neglected, or passed over because camouflaged by the knottiness of her musical meanings, the lovely and tedious divagations resulting from her refusal to ever not nuance. But I am saying that I wouldn't go to Moore to have my "views" confirmed—that's not what she's for—and when she is prissy or illiberal (she worried to Elizabeth Bishop that an unnamed acquaintance was "in the clutches of a sodomite!") her verse remains intimate with me. In fact, the tendentious caviling of her poems around the prospect of intimacy, their concern to assert views that can be shared, and a perpetual spiky awareness of their own off-putting behaviors—this is why I read her. Moore writes about self-protective animals, their often beautiful armor, and her poems don their polished plate, and occasionally take it off, with marvelous ceremony. "Black Earth," excluded from the *Complete Poems* and happily included here, appears to self-describe with unusual openness:

> Openly, yes,
> with the naturalness
> > of the hippopotamus or the alligator
> > when it climbs out on the bank to experience the
>
> sun, I do these
> things which I do, which please
> > no one but myself. Now I breathe and now I am sub-
> > merged; the blemishes stand up and shout when the object
>
> in view was a
> renaissance; shall I say
> > the contrary?

The poet evokes in creatures and landscapes qualities she would like to possess. In this she is rather like the critic in the business of transforming her, Marianne Moore, into an ideal citizen. Yet, as the third stanza reveals, there is always a turn; the recognition of a difficulty, a complication that reveals the power of assertion as proceeding from an injury (those "blemishes stand up and shout"). Is Moore tolerant, open-minded? Sometimes. There are things one shouldn't be tolerant of (she is not afraid, as some are, of the position of judgment, is in no danger of becoming tolerant of intolerance), and openness of mind is periodic—you couldn't live that way all the time; the fontanel must close if we are to survive. (The motives of publishing and publicity are not always good, in turning social injustices, and our injustices to nature, into buzzwords.) And maybe the opening of the mind is not its own achievement but a gift from outside us, unpredictable and to be anticipated, if never presumed.

Moore knows this, and it relates to her alternation between aphorism and incomprehensibility. Between self and other she discerns—can't help but recognize and crabbily adorn—countless barriers. Some of these wink in and out of existence, are playful, like those of a pinball machine or the antic obstacles the player leaps and slides between in a platform video game; others of long standing thaw ominously, like Arctic sea ice decimated by black carbon. So I can't see her as a cultural spokeswoman, not because

Moore doesn't worry where, and how, we worry, but rather because her poems simply don't communicate that way. (Does our insistence on the politics extractable from them manifest a remaining anxiety about the readability of her verse?) In her poems, someone speaks, would assert, and other voices protrude—rarely solely to confirm what has been said or bully the reader. If there is a simple message, it never quite reaches us but is, like Zeno's arrow, paralyzed at every point of its arc through the air.

If Moore's borrowings allow for her characterization as a modern collage artist, a devil-may-care dialogic experimenter, Elizabeth Bishop had quite a different view. Helping Moore with her translations of La Fontaine, she comes to a sadly astonished awareness of her mentor's difference from other people, linked to her inability to hear or write verse in conventional ways. It seems that Moore "was possessed of a unique, involuntary sense of rhythm, therefore of meter"; what else would one expect, given that "she looked like no one else" and "talked like no one else" and that "her poems showed a mind not much like anyone else's?" The younger poet wonders of the older whether her deep-down oddity is helpless or chosen—it could be that her poetry emerged at a modernist threshold, that she was set free to experiment?—and is finally led to "realize more than I ever had the rarity of true originality, and also the sort of alienation it might involve." When Bishop helps her out with simple rhymes or turns her drafts iambic, Moore is astonished by what to others would be quite obvious emendations, or normalizations. It's like those quotations in her verse—someone else arrives to lend a hand, to say what the poet is herself unable to, where she is prevented by abiding and mysterious impediments. Because a lack is remedied by it, a pedestrian encounter takes on the aspect of grace: "Marianne would exclaim, 'E*li*zabeth, thank you, you have saved my life!'"

There are in *Observations* slight poems Moore was right to exclude from the *Complete Poems*, with its mighty epigraph, "Omissions are not accidents." These are short lyrics, stingy rather than pointed—there's a run of several at the start of the book. But we might consider "Reticence and Volubility" a rejoinder to the sales voice looking to package Marianne Moore for the twenty-first century:

> "When I am dead,"
> The wizard said,
>   "I'll look upon the narrow way
>   And this Dante,

> And know that he was right
> And he'll delight
>   In my remorse,
>   Of course."
> "When I am dead,"
> The student said,
>   "I shall have grown so tolerant,
>   I'll find I can't
>   Laugh at your sorry plight
>   Or take delight
>   In your chagrin,
>   Merlin."

This was first published in the May 1915 issue of *Poetry*, as "The Wizard in Words." Tolerance doesn't mean to this poem what it means to us. (Nor does the concept of offensiveness, when it appears in conjunction, in "Injudicious Gardening": "The sense of privacy / In what you did—deflects from your estate / Offending eyes, and will not tolerate / Effrontery.") Matthew 7:14: "Because strait is the gate, and narrow is the way, which leadeth unto life, and few there be that find it." Moore is concerned, like the apostle, and Dante, with ethics, though a coherent theology is replaced by misunderstanding encounters. The wizard and the poet discover a stance toward each other, but the student, "grown so tolerant" — a word placed under ironic scrutiny—can't respond to the wizard either with laughter or approval at the moral "remorse" she understands, instead, as "chagrin." I can't pretend to understand the poem wholly, but I recognize Moore's interest in failed relationships and the limitations of retrospective judgement— the "delights" of moralizing. We wish to draw connections between ourselves and others, but to do so simplistically is a form of arrogance. Moore returns over and over again to this problem, and sometimes her poems don't work because they do no more than utter a stalemate. All the poetry, for instance, of "To Be Liked by You Would Be a Calamity" is in the title. Which can't be said of "Roses Only":

> You would, minus thorns,
> look like a what-is-this, a mere
> peculiarity. They are not proof against a worm, the elements, or
>   mildew

> but what about the predatory hand? What is brilliance without co-ordination? Guarding the
> infinitesimal pieces of your mind, compelling audience to the remark that it is better to be forgotten than to be remembered too violently,
> your thorns are the best part of you.

The reader, the critic, seeking to turn Moore into someone entirely like themselves, will come up against those thorns. Her personality is indelible and refuses "to be remembered too violently." I delight less in the content of her opinions than the scrollwork of their framing; a defensiveness admitting of ebullience, and heartfelt pleasure, as she quests for the large, the livable, statement through fields of digression.

Observations contains several of Moore's large and small masterpieces, unweatherable poems everybody should read. "To a Snail" is here; two versions of "Poetry"—more on this later—as well as "Critics and Connoisseurs," "When I Buy Pictures," "A Grave," "Snakes, Mongooses, Snake-Charmers, and the Like," "Silence," and "Marriage." Those familiar with the *Complete Poems* will notice changes—typically she cuts the flab and swaps in clarifying punctuation; the later versions are the better ones. This is also true when she relineates: "The Fish" is printed here in a six-line stanza, rather than, as eventually transpired, a five; Moore must have realized there was no need for an intervening line containing only one word. *Observations* mentions "chaff" a few times, and separating the wheat from it is precisely what she editorially accomplished. Leavell observes that these changes represent not only a response to free verse, an incorporation of its strategies, but also an assertion of Moore's authority. The changes she makes are part of the difficult conversation this rather bizarre and, as Bishop has it, alienated person is trying to have, throughout her career, with her growing audience. If she moves to accommodate the reader, she also insists on her own predilections—the technical preferences of the poet about the tiniest quirks of sound and meaning. Moore's self-editing extends what's going on in the poems themselves, whose processes of assembly, whether consciously stilted or magically all-at-once and deft, are part of the spectacle.

Leavell describes Moore as a poet of "precision," and it's curious to note that in the original version of "Bowls" a key line reads: "I learn that we are precisians;" Moore's revision was to "precisionists." For her, finding the right word is a moral duty, and "Picking and Choosing," about literature and literary criticism, is improved when she picks and chooses what she wishes to keep in it. Trimming the verbiage, she has her poem speak with the clarity it praises in others. Yet the original does score a couple of points over its superior successor:

> Literature is a phase of life: if
>   one is afraid of it, the situation is irremediable; if
> one approaches it familiarly,
>   what one says of it is worthless. Words are constructive
> when they are true; the opaque allusion—the simulated flight
>
> upward—accomplishes nothing. Why cloud the fact
>   that Shaw is selfconscious in the field of sentiment but is
>   otherwise re-
> warding? that James is all that has been
>   said of him, if feeling is profound?
> — FROM *OBSERVATIONS* (1924)

> Literature is a phase of life. If one is afraid of it,
> the situation is irremediable; if one approaches it familiarly,
> what one says of it is worthless.
> The opaque allusion, the simulated flight upward,
> accomplishes nothing. Why cloud the fact
> that Shaw is self-conscious in the field of sentiment
> but is otherwise rewarding; that James
> is all that has been said of him.
> — FROM *COMPLETE POEMS*

In the later version, Moore is unafraid to speak (relatively) clearly; she removes what "accomplishes nothing" and has learned how not to cloud the facts. The line break has us dwell a moment on the name of Henry James—the shift to free verse has made possible a different inflection, capturing rather than displacing the authority Moore describes and would emulate. Previously, the dead matter about words being "constructive / when they are true" arrived to rhyme with "if"; it's no great loss. Yet the connection between "if" and "life" is more clearly felt in *Observations*. And it is a pity to lose the shift in the first two lines from a colon to a semicolon—Moore's attentiveness to how these gently unlike forms of punctuation, and the repetition, alternatively color that hinging word. Rereading these poems, I was struck by her feeling for the semicolon as the grammar of tact. Moore takes this, I think, from her studies in prose style: "You were the jewelry of sense; / Of sense, not license"; "'I should like to be alone'; / to which the visitor replies, / 'I should like to be alone; / why not be alone together?'" "The deepest feeling always shows itself in silence; / not in silence, but restraint."

"An Octopus," that masterful ecopoem, a gigantically reader-resisting biomass of collateral quotation—evocative of Mount Rainier and its glacier—contains in *Observations* a full page of extra description. I quote some, not all:

> Inimical to "bristling, puny, swearing men
> equipped with saws and axes,"
> this treacherous glass mountain
> admires gentians, ladyslippers, harebells, mountain dryads,
> and "Calypso, the goat flower —
> that greenish orchid fond of snow" —
> anomalously nourished upon shelving glacial ledges
> where climbers have not gone or have gone timidly,
> "the one resting his nerves while the other advanced,"
> on this volcano with the bluejay, her principal companion.

The first quotation is from Clifton Johnson's *What to See in America*, the others from government pamphlets Moore consulted in her research. (Notes on the lines that follow mention a "comment overheard at the circus" and Anthony Trollope.) Mount Rainier's complexity is twinned with its value—this is why the poet must be unobvious in her approach—and she won't have the reader take her word for it, but confects a masala of appreciative utterance. The "treacherous glass mountain" is said, itself, to possess the power of admiring; this is an extension of Moore's own spreading admiration for multiple phenomena, including the orchid. This "anomalously nourished" flower (I love that haughtily appreciative, that scientifically cherishing adverb, it is Moore through and through) is feminized and forms a partnership with the blue jay positioned as male. Rather like the climbers taking it in turns to ascend the mountain, one subject hands on the baton to the next—the glacier gives way to the snow-fed goat flower, which is in turn replaced by the bird.

Moore writes inclusively: she pastes in what others say, how different plants and animals behave. This means she's unavoidably in the business of turning all this otherness into herself or wishing to become closer to it. But these edits reveal the dangers. It was hard to know when to stop, and the question of what or who to mention next, to move the poem on, is one Moore struggled to solve. Leavell includes both the 1924 and the 1925 versions of "Poetry"; a third, radically shortened, appears in the *Complete Poems*. The 1925 poem is only transitional—a genuinely intriguing misstep:

> I too, dislike it:
> there are things that are important beyond all this fiddle.
> The bat, upside down; the elephant pushing,
> a tireless wolf under a tree,
> the base-ball fan, the statistician—
> "business documents and schoolbooks"—
> these phenomena are pleasing,
> but when they have been fashioned
> into that which is unknowable,
> we are not entertained.
> It may be said of all of us
> that we do not admire what we cannot understand;
> enigmas are not poetry.

The list isn't sensuously imagined and contributes only the theme of endurance (the elephant "pushing," the "tireless wolf"). The movement from "I too, dislike it"—is this actually shocking, or only humorous, for the poet to say this about poetry?—to the social hedging of what "may be said of all of us" is, unbelievably for Moore, a smidge cowardly. Yet—to return to Leavell's introduction—if "twenty-first-century readers deserve to *know* the innovative poems" of *Observations* as they originally appeared, Moore does suggest here, contrarily, that in these poems data is "fashioned / into that which is *unknowable.*" There's something to poems that we as readers will never be able to pin down.

What we "know" is not a secure possession in "The Labors of Hercules." Here Moore immortalizes the words of, according to the note, "The Reverend J. W. Darr"—in arguing

> that it is one thing to change one's mind,
> another to eradicate it—that one keeps on knowing
> "that the Negro is not brutal,
> that the Jew is not greedy,
> that the Oriental is not immoral,
> that the German is not a Hun."

Here are the social "views" we are glad to acclaim; but the careful reader will require no such assurance that Moore is on the side of the angels. It's good to have the first line and a half, cut by Moore in the *Complete Poems*, given its acidulous querying of the cliché, to change one's mind: "eradicate" suggests racial cleansing. Moore is alert both to what we can know, and should keep on knowing, and what we can't. Her revisions remind me of Ludwig Wittgenstein: "what we cannot speak about we must pass over in silence." For "unknowable" appears in neither of the other versions of "Poetry." The first, longer, messier, quotes Yeats on poets as "literalists of the imagination" and is famous for going one better and defining poems as "imaginary gardens with real toads in them." But Moore would finally shun all evasive talk and canonize a majestic snippet. In the *Complete Poems*, she states what she believes. She no longer provides evidence to support her case or nervously talks around the subject, for the reader must make up her own mind. About poetry, that is, and about Marianne Moore:

> I, too, dislike it.
>   Reading it, however, with a perfect contempt for it, one
>   discovers in
>   it, after all, a place for the genuine.

*

There is an English poetry, written by women, skeptical about the need of men to take themselves seriously. (Gender is fluid, cultural; yet the target exists, and these poems hit it, they're both funny and clever.) Take

Wendy Cope, who in "A Policeman's Lot" pokes fun at Ted Hughes, who says the "progress of any writer is marked by those moments when he manages to outwit his own inner police system." To be read to the strains of "The Sergeant's Song" from Gilbert and Sullivan's *The Pirates of Penzance*:

> No, the imagination of a writer (of a writer)
> Is not the sort of beat a chap would choose (chap would choose)
> And they've assigned me a prolific blighter ('lific blighter)—
> I'm patrolling the unconscious of Ted Hughes.

Rory Waterman suggests an allusion to Hughes's becoming poet laureate, a role requiring of him further self-policing: "there is, then, a subtle implication, by dint of the poem's placement after Cope's dig at State-sanctioned poetry, that Hughes's 'subconscious' has been rendered a particularly difficult 'beat' due to his willingness to accept the Queen's shilling." In Jo Shapcott's "Religion for Boys," "the little stone figure in the porch" of the temple of Mithras—a goddess in her own right—is amused by the devotees entering where no women are allowed to go:

> She chuckles. These boys do such hard graft,
> big tests where they're sat hard against the fire
> torturing themselves through seven grades towards
>   perfection.

Shapcott's isn't "light verse," but Cope has been labeled this way, and then we have Stevie Smith. Her poems (despite an excellent monograph by Will May, the editor of this collection, and essays by Christopher Ricks and Philip Larkin, among others) still, perhaps, haven't been appreciated in all their fine, textured seriousness. This may be because they poke fun at the kinds of seriousness we've inherited—and would suggest something better.

I say "we": do I mean men, again? "Thoughts About the Person from Porlock" may have been the model for Cope's poem, for it confronts the Major Male Poet, specifically Samuel Taylor Coleridge, who famously blamed the incompletion of "Kubla Khan" on a visitor. Though isn't Smith more alive than Cope to the motivations behind the poet's language of (self-)confrontation? Pomposity is not so much deflated, here, as psychologically reexplained:

> Coleridge received the Person from Porlock
> And ever after called him a curse
> Then why did he hurry to let him in?—
> He could have hid in the house.
>
> It was not right of Coleridge in fact it was wrong
> (But often we all do wrong)
> As the truth is I think he was already stuck
> With Kubla Khan.

Smith's perceptiveness, her generosity (that parenthesis), requires of the reader more than a second glance. The "Person from Porlock" was, it turns out, crucial to Coleridge as both an excuse and an escape; for "he was already stuck"—with his poem? He had writer's block?—no, he was "stuck / With Kubla Khan," a personified aspect of himself he'd rather elude.

Smith is especially unsparing of bullying men, like the eponymous "Major Macroo," who lords it over the wife he neglects:

> Such men as these, such selfish cruel men
> Hurting what most they love what most loves them,
> Never make a mistake when it comes to choosing a woman
> To cherish them and be neglected and not think it inhuman.

Yet once again she doesn't terminate with blame, but presses beyond, to explanations. Macroo and his wife are perfectly suited—in a bad way. A dysfunctional society produced the pair of them, even if the power is entirely in his hands. "How Cruel Is the Story of Eve," says Smith, designed to "give blame to women most / And most punishment"; this "is the meaning of a legend that colours / All human thought; it is not found among animals." (Just one smack, of many, at repressive Christianity.) For Smith, as for D. H. Lawrence—or Hughes—animals, when they aren't abominably tamed, provide an alternative to a sick culture; it's good to see this discourse strapped to a feminist argument instead of boosting a male writer's self-esteem. But in both of these poems Smith goes a little further, in asking what we really mean by "human"; and the slant rhyme linking this word, or its negative, with "woman" (one of Smith's best) reappears in "Girls!" from *Mother, What Is Man?*:

> Girls! although I am a woman
> I always try to appear human
>
> Unlike Miss So-and-So whose greatest pride
> Is to remain always in the VI Form and not let down the side
>
> Do not sell the pass dear, don't let down the side
> This is what this woman said and a lot of balsy stuff beside
> (Oh the awful balsy nonsense that this woman cried.)

"Balsy," not *ballsy*. But we shouldn't reduce this poem to a joke—at least, not before it does this to itself. Smith's rhymes, and slant rhymes, are analytic, exhortatory, they sing with corrective spite. In the space between "girl" and "woman" she locates a deep uncertainty, and while she is evidently scornful of those, like Macroo, who consider women less than "human," she is also alert to the need to keep up appearances, how tough it is "to appear," to oneself and to the world, as a being coherent and complete. How miserably inevitable it is that valuing oneself (as a woman, a particularly "human" woman) is accomplished at the expense of someone else—who must be judged wanting if one is to be found, in contrast, acceptable.

"Miss So-and-So" corresponds to Major Macroo in her military language—these are the dying strains of the British Empire, reduced to team calls in assemblies for sixth-formers—and we see here how Smith doesn't stop at unworthy men but also gleefully attacks overrefined or vicious or class- or race-conscious women and (it's the title of this next poem) their "Parents:"

> Oh beautiful brave mother, the wife of the colonel,
> How could you allow your young daughter to become aware of the scheming?
> If you had not, it might have stayed a mere dreaming
> Of palaces and princes, girlish at worst.
> Oh to become sensible about social advance at seventeen is to be lost.

If the first couplet of "Girls!" has the punch of a Beyoncé lyric, this is closer to the songs of the Oompa Loompas in *Charlie and the Chocolate Factory*. Smith repeats herself—there are things she cares about, which more than get her goat, she demands change—but she's also capable of many species of poem. Here's a short one—a comic's one-liner, really, though it's a couplet:

> This Englishwoman is so refined
> She has no bosom and no behind.
> — "THIS ENGLISHWOMAN"

May's helpful note directs us to Edmund Waller's poem "On a Girdle": "That which her slender waist confin'd, / Shall now my joyful temples bind," he writes, and also— "A narrow compass, and yet there / Dwelt all that's good, and all that's fair." In Smith's poem, "refined" means—the irony is strong—*sophisticated*, but it also describes the Englishwoman as a creature, like one of the ludicrously effete dogs at Crufts, bred by specialists into what they consider a pure and pleasing shape. She is asexual, the victim of a mutilation—it's as if the toffs, fleeing those urges associating them with animals (and the lower classes), were the subject of Lamarckian evolution. The energies each generation neglects—the life not lived—affect the stature of the next. And misery, as Larkin has it, "deepens like a coastal shelf."

As this poem suggests, Smith's true target is—again, this is one of her titles—"The English":

> Many of the English,
> The intelligent English,
> Of the Arts, the Professions and the Upper Middle Classes,
> Are under-cover men,
> But what is under the cover
> (That was original)
> Died; now they are corpse-carriers.

Her verse comes with pen sketches attached: whimsical, piercing depictions of the characters in the poems, or the speakers of them, vibrating with irregular life. "This Englishwoman" appears wearing a hat with flowers on it, her pointed face the shape of the base of an iron (she's smiling, smugly; the tiny lines of her eyebrows are cruel), protecting herself not from the rain, but the sun, with an umbrella. I'm reminded once more of D. H. Lawrence: "Man fixes some wonderful erection of his own between himself and the wild chaos, and gradually goes bleached and stifled under his parasol. Then comes a poet, enemy of convention, and makes a slit in the umbrella; and lo! the glimpse of chaos is a vision, a window to the sun." Smith, too, is more than—a dead word—unconventional; she is an avowed "enemy of convention," and would let in the sun that her Englishwoman shirks. Like Lawrence, she is a writer who would turn on its head the great English project of disapproval—really turn it against itself: "There is far too much of the suburban classes / Spiritually not geographically speaking. They're asses." She would disapprove of the disapprovers. The snobs, the sexists, the repressed.

Some explanation may be necessary here. Humans are status-conscious: Smith is particularly savvy about literary coteries, "picking inferiorly with grafted eyes," in which "So-and-so must be the driven out one, this the pet"; the familiar tale of "Miss Snooks, Poetess," who never wrote a poem "that was not really awfully nice / And fitted to a woman," and so "made no enemies / And gave no sad surprises / But went on being awfully nice / And took a lot of prizes." Yet to be English is to enter into a special relationship with disapproval, an ineffaceable class-consciousness that persists today (it's not the same as the division between rich and poor), however ironized (a common excuse) or deferred or disguised the compulsion to affront may be. Sometimes this urge to degrade is redirected toward the minorities of the moment—Eastern Europeans, for instance. But the accents of disapproval are the same, they are recognizable. The English, compelled to revisit and renew, in so many details of their private lives, the distinction between working-class and middle-class lifestyles (those who've crossed this border, even a generation back, are petrified of being deported) have found ways of continuing this conversation into the twenty-first century, even while turning it into a joke or changing the terms. The problem is that, as Smith tells us in "The English," these people are infectious. Once you start to disapprove of them, to become intolerant of their intolerance, you're at risk of playing their game. So Lawrence tries to counter the murderous force of class disapproval, taking as the guarantor of his convictions the permanent scandal of our sexuality, which he deploys as a deeper, a more convincing, authority than the snobbishness of the repressive bore. In so doing, he risks becoming a bore himself, a perfervid sermonizer. What Smith does is less obvious and easy to miss. She counteraccuses, but also places the voice of accusation itself under scrutiny.

On first approaching a publisher with her poems, Smith was told to "go away and write a novel." Despite the more announced vitality, the love-addled bursting oomph, of its reader-buttonholing protagonist Pompey Casmilus, *Novel on Yellow Paper* resembles Marianne Moore in its humorous digressive capturing of multiple voices. But Smith quotes, often, as critique. Not to summon viewpoints to her aid, but to shred them irreversibly. Here are some "nice little quotations for your scrap book. Or if you have no scrap book you can shoot them at your friends at your high-class parties":

> Should I Marry a Foreigner? . . . You do not say, dear, if he is a man of colour. Even if it is only a faint tea rose—*don't*. I know what it will mean to you to give him up but funny things happen with colour, it often slips over, and sometimes darkens from year to year and it is so difficult to match up. White always looks well at weddings and will wash and wear and if you like to write to me again, enclosing stamped addressed envelope, I will give you the name of a special soap I always use it myself do not stretch or wring but hang to dry in a cool oven.

Advice from an agony aunt—but the no-color of the newspaper voice has started to run, has become crazily creative in its paranoia about race, decorum, wedding-wear, the housewife's proper domesticities. ("Colours are what drive me most strongly," says Smith; also that there "is no very strong division between what is poetry and what is prose": like Moore, she's intrigued by prose, has an ear for its borrowable forms, and clearly relishes in this passage the sonic bounce from "envelope" to "soap.")

"I cannot play this game of quotations one minute longer. I get bored. But I am far too quickly bored. Reader, are you? Do you know how I think of you? I'll tell you." That's Pompey, breaking off to speak to the reader in a voice that is deliciously vivid. Smith's poems have this quality too, and this is why it's hard to separate them from the institution she has become; the singing "disenchanted gentility" (Seamus Heaney) of her reading voice; the film, *Stevie*, about her life; and even those significant sketches she sticks next to the verse. But what I'd stress is how carefully written, how intelligently stylish, how deep-diving the words on the page can be; for I do think this is the best way to appreciate Smith, as a poet's poet, whose printed voice can be both intimately hers and wryly denatured in its ventriloquisms. Yes, some of her poems are jokes. Others are consciously archaic or exercises; the longer ones can be dull, in which blurting looseness allows for the evaporation of the reader's interest. She is interested in how far her voice, and that of others, can carry—how cogent our utterances really are; her verse is undecided on this subject and so she risks superficiality. But she also writes works of undeniable art. Poems to read, and reread.

We might compare, for example, the woman-on-woman violence of "Girls!," "Parents," and "This Englishwoman" with "Everything Is Swimming," from *The Frog Prince and Other Poems*:

> Everything is swimming in a wonderful wisdom
> She said everything was swimming in a wonderful wisdom
> Silly ass
> What a silly woman
> Perhaps she is drunk
> No I think it is mescalin
> Silly woman
> What a silly woman
> Yes perhaps it is mescalin
> It must be something
> Her father, they say . . .
> And that funny man William . . .
> Silly ass
> What a silly woman
>
> *Elle continua de rire comme une hyène.*

The quotation is from a short story by Jules Barbey d'Aurevilly, whose title in the 1900 translation, *Weird Women*, is "At a Dinner of Atheists." This group "composed exclusively of men" indulges—as the author says every all-male group does—in "abuse" of the opposite sex, being "disgusted with females—as they cynically called women." (More disapproval of disapproval!) The story is told of Major Ydow and his wife Rosalba, who sleeps with the narrator, Mesnilgrand (he mentions "those beautiful arms I had so often bitten"; Smith is much taken with biting; it appears a few times in her verse) and becomes pregnant. The child—Ydow's certain it is his—dies. One day Mesnilgrand must hide when the Major arrives and abuses Rosalba. She says she has never loved him, that the child was not his, but Mesnilgrand's; she is portrayed as "insolent, ironical, laughing with the hysterical laughter of hate, at the most acute paroxysms of his wrath." Ydow responds by smashing the vase in which he has, absurdly, embalmed his son's heart; he attempts to rape her with his sabre-pommel covered in hot wax—with the idea of "sealing his wife" as she had sealed her letters to lovers. Mesnilgrand finally acts. He leaps out, kills Ydow, calls for a surgeon in case "the beautiful mutilated body" is still alive, and visits a church graveyard to bury the heart of the child that might have been his.

This ghastly tale may, d'Aurevilly suggests, have shattered the cynicism of its audience—we return to the hideous metaphor of "sealing": "A silence, more expressive than any words, sealed the mouths of all." I summarize the story to reveal the importance of Smith's allusion. Her poem critiques the misogyny that, beginning with remarks at a party (as hostile in atmosphere as the dinner of atheists), is nevertheless continuous with real violence against women. If other Smith poems accuse other women, intolerant of their intolerance, here that disapproving voice is itself revealed as eventually tyrannous. A woman's effusiveness is mocked by the partygoers, attributed to alcohol, drugs, or a man—the doings of her father or "that funny man William"—while the ellipses catch perfectly the tone of the behind-the-hand-whispered, snide aside. The French, in italics, suggests a superior perspective and confirms Smith's target as the gossipers, not the woman herself. Whose laughter continues—but how impervious is it to humiliation?

The verse shifts, without clarifying quotation marks, from what the woman says—briefly, her voice is that of the poem—to the framing of her remark by an incredulous auditor: "Everything is swimming in a wonderful wisdom / She said everything was swimming in a wonderful wisdom / Silly ass." With that switch from "is" to "was," Smith's apparently immediate, incautious style contrives with intelligence a collision of different voices; a testing, as in Moore, of the power of assertion. I'd never thought about the absence from one of her most famous poems, "Not Waving but Drowning," of what Joyce referred to as "perverted commas"—until I read, in this edition, May's note:

> Nobody heard him, the dead man,
> But still he lay moaning:
> I was much further out than you thought
> And not waving but drowning.
>
> Poor chap, he always loved larking
> And now he's dead
> It must have been too cold for him his heart gave way,
> They said.
>
> Oh, no no no, it was too cold always
> (Still the dead one lay moaning)
> I was much too far out all my life
> And not waving but drowning.

According to May's note, the version published in December 1956, in the essay "Too Tired for Words," places "lines 3–4, 9, 11–12 in speech marks, and reduces second stanza to three lines with breaks after 'dead' and 'way'; the first two lines of this revised stanza are also in speech marks. A typed draft shows an illustration of a man being pulled from the water in place of the deliberately disjunctive female figure in published versions." Smith writes about world-weariness, melancholia, and depression better than anybody, with cauterizing humor and an awareness of how feeling is always, happily and horribly, prior to thought. This is a wonderful example of a masterpiece receiving the editorial attention it deserves—our experience of the poem is enriched by May's intervention. Smith is indeed "deliberately disjunctive," in multiple senses. "Moaning" isn't obviously a speech verb, so, even if the colon is there as a pointer, "I was much further out than you thought" is laid harshly bare. It isn't speech cooled and hardened and situated within a larger utterance—it touches the reader directly. We then have what "they" say—again, the speech isn't framed as speech until revealed as the opinion of the misunderstanding "meelyoo"—Smith's lovely mocking spelling, elsewhere—represented by that cold pronoun. The dead man has passed beyond understanding and must speak from beyond the grave to explain himself to those with no ear for his torment. In "A Dream of Comparison," Eve, who wishes only for a "cessation of consciousness," argues with Mary:

> Mary laughed: "I love Life,
> I would fight to the death for it,
> That's a feeling you say? I will find
> A reason for it."
>
> They walked by the estuary,
> Eve and the Virgin Mary,
> And they talked until nightfall,
> But the difference between them was radical.

Christopher Ricks observes a superbly disjunctive final rhyme. (I think of Moore's "I May, I Might, I Must": "If you will tell me why the fen / appears impassable, I then / will tell you why I think that I / can get across it if I try.") Smith is preoccupied with the incommunicativeness between, as Wittgenstein has it, the world of the happy and the world of the unhappy, and the endlessly, perversely creative ways in which we fail to understand each other, in a war zone of cross talk. Yet she also asserts the possibility of connection and is fascinated in particular by the complexities of friendship.

Two "war poems," the first, again, famous; Smith referred to it as a mere steal from *Still the Joy of It*, by Littleton Powys, although her verse adds a lot—this isn't a found poem:

> It was my bridal night I remember,
> An old man of seventy-three
> I lay with my young bride in my arms,
> A girl with t.b.
> It was wartime, and overhead
> The Germans were making a particularly heavy raid on Hampstead.
> What rendered the confusion worse, perversely
> Our bombers had chosen that moment to set out for Germany.
> Harry, do they ever collide?
> I do not think it has ever happened,
> Oh my bride, my bride.
> — FROM *I REMEMBER*

> Basil never spoke of the trenches, but I
> Saw them always, saw the mud, heard the guns, saw the duckboards,
> Saw the men and the horses slipping in the great mud, saw
> The rain falling and never stop, saw the gaunt
> Trees and the rusty frame
> Of the abandoned gun carriages. Because it was the same
> As the poem "Childe Roland to the Dark Tower Came"
> I was reading at school.
> — FROM *A SOLDIER DEAR TO US*

In the second poem, a child understands more of the sweet-mannered veteran than he knows. In the first, will the old man and his young bride truly coincide or merely "collide," as those bombers don't, in the air? The speech is given, once again, without quotation marks, as if the poem spoke for each, and both; in "A Soldier Dear to Us," there is no need to speak of what is known by other means. In "Dear Karl," written to a German boyfriend, Smith sends him Walt Whitman's poems and seeks to preempt the "indignation" with which we ward off the emotional claims of others—"'How dilettante,' I hear you observe, 'I hate these selections / Arbitrarily made to meet a need that is not mine and a taste / Utterly antagonistic.'" Summoning Yeats as well as the American poet, she insists on spreading the cloths of heaven under her lover's feet:

> For I, I myself, I have no Leaves of Grass
> But only Walt Whitman in a sixpenny book,
> Taste's, blend's, essence's, multum-in-parvo's Walt Whitman.
> And now sending it to you I say:
> Fare out, Karl, on an afternoon's excursion, on a sixpenny unexplored
>   uncharted road.

But Smith does have a joyous expansiveness, her riskily unprotected prolongations of self toward other, to give. What is caustic and comically summative in her verse is countered by this sweetness. I read "How do you see?" where her long-argufying lines quiz, are sardonic and potent:

> Oh Christianity, Christianity,
> That has grown kinder now, as in the political world

The colonial system grows kinder before it vanishes, are you
  vanishing?
Is it not time for you to vanish?

And it seems to me she (not D. H. Lawrence) is that impossibility, not to be predicted (or taken lightly or taken for granted): an English Whitman.

Eunice de Souza and Indian Speech

For many English-language poets of the mid- to late twentieth century, speech surpassed a mere fascination and became instead their *sine qua non*, guaranteeing their writing worldly relevance. The history of modern American poetry is the history of countless attempts at a democratic vernacular: Robert Frost, for one, foregrounded speech sound, or "the sound of sense," wishing to play the rough-hewn tones of homespun voices off the grid of meter. But this idea of national authenticity can get ugly— Elizabeth Bishop spoke critically of something "unturned" to Frost's poetry.

When the "sound of sense" coarsens into the sound of common sense, it shuts down other options; if the voice is what matters, then *which* voices, exactly, do we praise as authentic? It's one thing to rediscover—as in, say, the work of the Romantic peasant-poet John Clare—dialects and accents previously scorned and marginalized. But not all of us speak in voices tied unequivocally to one milieu. Some of us have, for lack of a better word, denatured voices, talk behaviors shaped by power struggles and global transit.

Eunice de Souza was born a Goan Catholic in Poona (or Pune) in 1940. She studied in Wisconsin, taught in Bombay (today's Mumbai), and before her death in 2017 published four collections of poetry, two novels, children's books, and anthologies of Indian women's writing. She's one of a generation of post-Independence poets. In the United States and the United Kingdom, we're beginning to pay more and more attention to poets of color; this is a wonderful thing, but customarily means poets of color living where we do. The suspicion may arise that, in praising these authors, we're in part praising ourselves (for our enlightened diversity, our halo-affixing sponsorship of the cultural melting pot) while overlooking what is cordoned off as "world poetry." This neglect isn't helped by postcolonial studies, which tends to focus not on poems but on novels, whose representations allow for a leap out of the literary toward real-world pain. (The work of Jahan Ramazani, Laetitia Zecchini, Charles Pollard, and others on poetry bucks this trend—but do these interventions reach outside the academy?) When we do speak of poets from the Global South, we rarely discuss them aesthetically.

But Indian poets of this generation were obsessed by aesthetics. They grafted their voices onto poetic structures they admired in Anglo-American poets, exploring the metamorphoses that occurred. They redirected feelings of linguistic otherness to avoid the impasse evoked by A. K. Ramanujan (a poet, translator of ancient Tamil poetry, scholar of Indian folklore, and professor at the University of Chicago who described himself as the hyphen in "Indian-American"): "A great deal of Indian writing is upstairs English, platform English, idiom-book English, newspaper English . . . a formality, a learned posture." Adil Jussawalla (also a poet and a magisterial stylist in journalistic prose) elaborates:

> The voices of those of us who speak English in India aren't the voices which are heard in the poems we write. I put it as bluntly as that.
>
> Every poet has at least two voices: a literary voice, and the one in which he normally speaks.
>
> . . .
>
> Many of us try to write poetry which is colloquial in its thrust, which tries to follow the patterns and nuances of everyday speech. This is a strand in modern British and American (particularly American) poetry. . . . The legitimacy for this colloquial direction in poetry came from abroad, from poets like Whitman, Eliot and Pound who lived in societies which were fully English-speaking, unlike ours. . . . We only have our own colloquial middle-class uses of English as currency and sometimes not even those.
>
> . . .
>
> What's at work here is an overcoming of disjuncture—the kind of disjuncture between the spoken word and the written word that Whitman and Sandburg never had to contend with and never foresaw since it happened and is happening in the colonies.
>
> —"Readings with Parrots and Angels," *Sunday Observer,* August 15, 1999

With their brilliantly idiomatic verse, de Souza's poems grapple with these very issues by exploring disjunctures of literary voicing.

Discussing voice, I should define my terms. De Souza isn't, for instance, a performance poet. While such poetry gives political meaning to the presence of a poet's voice in the room, it's a different kind of voice, stylistically evoked in print, that we get from her (as with Frost). I speak of what the British critic Eric Griffiths called the "printed voice," represented through lineation, punctuation, rhythm, and sound. Consider de Souza's parenthesis in "For S. Who Wonders If I Get Much Joy Out of Life":

> Sometimes I down a Coke
> implacably at the Taj.
> This morning I terrorized
> (successfully)
> the bank manager.
> I look striking in red and black
> and a necklace of skulls.

"Successfully" is the great word—the great line—here. That brief aside turns writing back into pluckily labile speech. The reference to the goddess Kali in the title of de Souza's 2009 collected poems, A *Necklace of Skulls*, sets this poem's final lines in dialogue with Sylvia Plath's "Lady Lazarus": "I rise with my red hair / And I eat men like air."

De Souza also uses parentheses for this purpose—to infuse writing with the momentum of speech—in her prose; in, for instance, *Dangerlok*, her short novel of 2001. Her protagonist Rina resembles her: a poet and teacher battling both conservatives who refuse, for instance, to teach Arundhati Roy, preferring dead white Western men, and radical pseuds on antiliterary hobbyhorses. Here, too, a snippet in parentheses rumples the rhythm and reorients the tone:

> She thinks, this is too easy to parody, and tunes in for a minute while a gay poet who is certainly gay but not a poet talks about (oh dear) subversion. She just wishes he could write. She just wishes he didn't feel he had to be subversive every second of the day. Every conversation she overhears runs like this: We must piss on their ideas, we must shit on their ideas, her ideas come from her vagina, etc. He is miffed too because she does not respond to his performance. After she makes

a few brief points in an In Conversation session, he says loudly to the audience, is that a Goan accent? She ignores him. The alternative would be to kick him. How's that, she thinks, for subversion.

"Oh dear"—that ironized version of a prissy, gendered, exclamation—points to stereotyped behaviors and hollow, overused language. ("Subversion" is much discussed, though rarely enacted, at literary gatherings: de Souza's recognition that participants are often, for personal reasons, "miffed"—an untechnical word they'd never use, for it minimizes their feelings—suggests these debates lack gravity.) And while I wince at Rina's scorn for the gay poet who's "certainly gay but not a poet," seeing the false, self-interested pieties of progressive litterateurs punctured has a tonic effect. Snobbery is ridiculed, sexism skewered. De Souza's prose is keyed to speech rhythms and attentive to the power games played out in speech situations. She analyzes the patterns of egotism reducing literary "conversation" to self-marketing, dramatizing the connection between writing on the page and the will to power of people talking less *with* than *at*, or across, each other, jostling to be heard. But she still summons the idea of the "poet" as someone capable of creating works more resonant than an entirely personal response.

De Souza wrote of Indian voices speaking English in a literary context where poets were attacked for using what nationalists claimed was a colonially imposed language. Amit Chaudhuri (who also observes that memoiristic autofiction may not be a Western invention) contradicts that nativist position: for Indian authors, "the English language was already theirs, linked not so much to the colonizer as to their sense of self and history." De Souza: "No matter that / my name is Greek / my surname Portuguese / my language alien. // There are ways / of belonging." Today, when blood-and-soil rootedness has become tyrannical in India, her objections sound more than frazzled. They sound heroic:

> Really, all this chatter about who is true-blue Indian. . . . Rina's very first memories are of riding on an elephant (her father was posted in the tribal areas of Chhattisgarh at the time), and she hopes that is Indian enough! Anyway, she knows who she is. She is a lapsed Catholic who prays in moments of panic, a vague lefty who likes the occasional good meal in a restaurant and does not feel too much guilt about it, a teacher who likes her students and her work but likes the

occasional day at home alone. Anyway, it's the writers they are really after, those who write in English. Apparently, one cannot capture the soul of a nation in English. Well, she is not a writer but if she were she would not want to capture the soul of a nation. She would just natter, maybe about parrots or people or a stray pup she had taken to. Does anyone know anything with any clarity about souls or nations?

The prose strains with that double "anyway": the division between de Souza herself and Rina breaks down. Free indirect speech grows forced, as when Robert Browning morphs blank verse into a synthetic vernacular. But the theme remains. A writer, Rina thinks, should trade grand, Nehruvian aims concerning the "soul" and the "nation" for "nattering." Talking, that is, about matters of the heart.

I'm thinking—speaking of hearts—of one of my favourite de Souza poems, "Bequest." Her lyrics resist both excerpting and paraphrase: they have a plenary cohesion. This poem takes the form of a speech act dwelling on what others have said. Talking and listening are affirmed as humane realities, even when laced with spite or counteraggression:

> In every Catholic home there's a picture
> of Christ holding his bleeding heart
> in his hand.
> I used to think, ugh.
>
> The only person with whom
> I have not exchanged confidences
> Is my hairdresser.
>
> Some recommend stern standards,
> others say float along.
> He says, take it as it comes,
> meaning, of course, as he hands it out.
>
> I wish I could be a
> Wise Woman
> smiling endlessly, vacuously
> like a plastic flower,
> saying Child, learn from me.

> It's time to perform an act of charity
> to myself,
> bequeath the heart, like a
> spare kidney—
> preferably to an enemy.

Each stanza continues the impulse, but from an unexpected angle, fusing reactive aliveness ("ugh!") with goffered hauteur ("whom," "preferably"). The poem is avulsive, not linear; it doesn't babble onward but materializes in so many separate, chary squirts.

To claim de Souza as a poet of speech (Arvind Krishna Mehrotra, too, praises her "microphoned ear") isn't to say she talks too much: quite the opposite. Minimalism borders on mysticism. Creatively sardonic, ever twitchy, de Souza remains, however faintly, a religious poet, for it is possible to take the ending of "Bequest" at face value, even though the heart to be donated would be a weaponized gift should it ooze poison. (And is "he" a lover, a bully, or Christ as both?) She leaves questions unanswered and feelings suggestively glimpsed: "Even this poem / has forty-eight words too many," she writes in "It's Time to Find a Place," and "Conversation Piece" has only, including the title, twenty-six:

> My Portuguese-bred colleague
> picked up a clay shivalingam
> one day and said:
> Is this an ashtray?
> No, said the salesman,
> this is our god.

He said / he said: perspectives collide. The "salesman" claims the shivalingam (a phallic symbol of Shiva, although it can be nonrepresentational, a gesture toward verticality drawing the eyes upward) is sacred, even though he's put a price on it. The internal rhyme of "clay" and "day," culminating in the long *a* of "salesman," puts that last word up in lights, stressing that in India the sacred and the economic are interwoven. The shivalingam, purchased, could become a "conversation piece" for one's coffee table, but the poem is itself a "conversation piece," depicting a conversation or failed conversation. It's like a joke, with a punchline (imagine, "a Portuguese-bred

Indian walks into a bar . . ."), and reveals, as in de Souza's fiction, her willingness to write from her own life because "colleague," I suspect, doesn't roll off the tongue unless you're an academic like her (or me).

The oppressive Hindu nationalism orchestrated by Narendra Modi, which has made India dangerous for all minorities, and especially Muslims, has turned teaching my course on "South Asian Poetry in English" at Harvard into an exercise in the surreal, even before the coronavirus outbreak. Two hours a week studying the intricacies of de Souza and others might seem obtuse in this world: fiddling while Rome burns. De Souza mentions the harassment of Muslims in *Dangerlok*. That made-up word, which Rina learns from her "bai," or maid, begins as a catch-all term for ruffians of all stripes, then broadens in meaning:

> This must have been the day after Babri and before the bombs. Before the bombs probably. Like so many others, she must have stayed at home, uneasy.
> . . .
> A friend in another part of Bombay rang her. Her in-laws, she said, had heard the Muslims were coming by sea. They and other worthies would be ready for them on the terrace, rocks in hands. She did not ask the friend where the in-laws would find the rocks. Her friend did not like her in-laws. Feed them to the Muslims, she said to her friend.

Again, there are so many speech acts, though you have to look for them in the prose, much as you might sift sand through your fingers, hunting for a rare, unbroken shell. A friend rings the narrator, Rina; this friend reports what her in-laws said, embedding one utterance within another, a matryoshka effect. "Worthies" is a dead-alive English word pursuing a zombie existence in a former colony; it is here as satire. It's a rock in de Souza's hand, pitched at the heads of the intolerant.

For she isn't afraid to go on the attack. Her first book of poems, *Fix*, published in 1979, targets the sexism of her religious education, with its distortion, amounting to erasure, of women's bodies and voices—systematic obfuscation of half the population's creaturely, thinking, feeling, existence:

> Pillar of the Church
> says the parish priest
> Lovely Catholic family

> says Mother Superior
>
> the pillar's wife
> says nothing.
> —FROM "CATHOLIC MOTHER"
>
> Well you can't say
> they didn't try.
> Mamas never mentioned menses.
> A nun screamed: You vulgar girl
> don't say brassières
> say bracelets.
> —FROM "SWEET SIXTEEN"

These poems frame silenced, contradicted, speech acts: "the pillar's wife / says nothing;" "Mamas never mentioned menses," "A nun screamed," "don't say brassières." Some people say nothing because others say crushing things to them. Or they react like a rubber band, snapping into utterance without knowing what they're talking about, simply because the opposite, to not hit back at once, would be submission. From the same poem:

> At sixteen, Phoebe asked me:
> Can it happen when you're in a dance hall
> I mean, you know what,
> getting *preggers* and all that, *when*
> you're dancing?
> I, sixteen, assured her
> you could.

The lack of quotation marks makes for a giddy slide in, through, and out of the voices this poem records. "*When*," at the end of the line, has its querulous vim underscored, avoiding the neat rhyme of "what" and "that." Poetic form is tailored to display one type of Indian (young, female, Goan, mid-century) voice. De Souza isn't (as Frost sneered about free verse) playing tennis with the net down. It's more like squash: she hits each ball of sound, each round molecule of speech, against the wall, and when it hurtles back she knows just what to do.

In both prose and verse, de Souza loves slangy abbreviations because they represent Indians taking charge of English, doing their own thing with it. From *Dev and Simran*, published just two years after *Dangerlok* (these are short novels, matching her short poems) in 2003: "Off we go to a gynaec and I swear, Maya, his prodding and poking wasn't just medical"; "Ye gods! Then Ved got senty and said, 'We really miss Dev,' and I found myself with tears in my eyes"; "there was this guy, some lecturer in philosophy who didn't like to take off his undoos, and when he finally did, he ran away, just about stopping to put on his trousers." These examples concern the sexual war between men and women: *Dev and Simran* is about bereavement (how Simran and her friends cope with her husband Dev's death), and in *Dangerlok* Rina shares letters and calls with a lover who may have discarded her for other women. Yet speech remains central: Rina's communications highlight the intensifications and diminutions of actual and printed voices, and *Dev and Simran* flips, as in Virginia Woolf's *The Waves*, among the voices of different characters as they grieve for their friend.

Simran recounts her marriage tenderly, without idealizing it, in passages so finely microadjusted, exploratory, and pliant that they can be analyzed like poetry:

Love. Had my marriage to Dev been a Grand Passion? Hardly. I didn't really have a checklist for his qualities. He was familiar, comfy to be with most of the time. No, it wasn't a Grand Passion. It hardly ever was. Something more subtle perhaps, more insidious. The way he held his cigarette, a shade of blue against his skin, the talc all over the shower-room floor, the unemphatic voice.

I once saw a painting called "Silence." It was painted white all over and had just one yellow spot in a corner. Taped music had filled the gallery, some inept woman moaning out a raga. I didn't know what to make of it. Now I know, and it's nothing to do with blank whiteness.

Weird to recall the way I would stand at the window and look at the birds Dev called me to see. He never got tired of them, especially golden orioles, but I would be impatient because I was in the middle of whisking an egg for an omelette or some such. Seems ridiculous now, to exchange an omelette for an oriole. But perhaps I'm just getting sentimental in retrospect. Omelettes had to be made, after all. No one lives life as if death is around the corner.

The unemphatic voice is real; the moaned raga isn't. Relationship counselors talk of bids for attention. When one party asks the other to come see, to share an experience, it can be damaging not to pay heed. Simran realizes she rejected Dev, ever so mildly, each time he called her to the window and she said she was busy, turning back to her omelet. "The melodrama of grief," she says elsewhere, "is almost more upsetting than the event itself." In de Souza's poem "Travelling," "a golden oriole chases a crow // Mine host waxeth sentimental. / Not a lover in sight." It's no good to get "senty," for overstrong feeling robs even bereavement of that sting of reality keeping contact with the dead loved one. One has to be realistic: "no one lives life as if death is around the corner." In even the best relationship—I sense this commonplace hovering behind the scenes, but never activated, by this writer so alert to idiom and surgical regarding cliché—you can't make an omelette without breaking some eggs.

De Souza, attuned to the countless tiny hemorrhages of spirit and feeling that can desiccate a life, writes personally, but her poems resist the reductions of confessionalism. The verbal torsion of their closing flourishes remains mysterious: something's been said, and snappily, but the essence is hard to grasp. "The Hills Heal" begins, "The hills heal as no hand does:" does this mean the hills recover as a human being can't or that the sight of hills cures us, beyond the power of anyone else's "hand" to do so? She continues, "The heart is stilled by the blue flash / of a lone jay's wing." Monosyllables sing with internal rhyme and alliteration, but the poem's end suggests closure is an illusion:

> Yet the world will maul again, I know,
> and I'll go gladly for the usual price,
>
> Emerge to flay myself in poems,
>
> The sluiced vein just a formal close.

"There is a charge," writes Plath, "For a word or a touch / Or a bit of blood / Or a piece of my hair or my clothes." De Souza's transaction is less clear. Her speaker can't remain in her serene pastoral, for the "world" barges in and she wishes for connection. But while the poem announces its own "formal close," the meaning of that final line evades us. The vein is "sluiced"—rinsed of debris—rather than, as we might expect, "sliced." Intertwining threads of sound (*know-go-poems-close, again-flay-vein*, and the slant rhyme of *price* and *close*) enkindle a music irreducible—despite that self-sabotaging word *just*—to a simple statement.

This acoustic sensitivity grounds a postcolonial self-consciousness about how Indians talk. "Most of my friends annoy me," thinks Maya in *Dev and Simran*: "Deblina, brought up in Standard, affects a kind of Indian English, coming down hard on her consonants like a hammer on hard wood." But Maya is herself the product of an educational system struggling to articulate ideas of identity in a global multiculture, just like de Souza's own students:

> My students think it funny
> that Daruwallas and de Souzas
> should write poetry.
> Poetry is faery lands forlorn.
> Women writers Miss Austen.
> Only foreign men air their crotches.
> —"MY STUDENTS"

Compression is vital to each of those last three lines, laying out an assumption that canonical British literature is all an Indian student knows or needs to know. "Rina's neighbour on the ground floor was from what a BBC newscaster called Utter Pradesh. It was pretty utter, if you discounted Bihar, which was about as utter as you could get." How can Indians get out from under British texts and British voices? "Poetry is faery lands forlorn": I read that single line and think of Macaulay's notorious pronouncement that "a single shelf of a good European library" is "worth the whole native literature of India and Arabia." But the poem also works by appropriating the weakest line of Keats's nightingale ode (in which he takes his eye off his subject and appears, if you trust his critics, to be thinking about a painting) and forcing its archaism toward a revelatory speech moment.

I don't think de Souza ever quite solves the problem of how personal, or distanced, she'd like poetry to be: "Poems can have order, sanity / aesthetic distance from debris. / All I've learnt from pain / I always knew, / but could not do." If one wanted to place her transnationally within a gendered tradition, there's the caustic humor of Wendy Cope, Stevie Smith, and Selima Hill: women mocking the hubris of the Major Male Poet. But the restive vexatiousness of her poems is unique: their refusal to commit to a solacing narrative or coordinating rhythm or to become one-directional and (in the fashion of a more nakedly activist poetry) predictably devastating.

We find an example of this in "Women in Dutch Painting," a poem easy, I think, to misread without the illumination of *Dangerlok*. For Rina, everyday life provides an antidote to national horrors, if only because the unpredictable offers hope. Watching the news, she

> looks for the people in the background. The woman entering a shop, a young couple holding hands. She likes to know what people are doing when they are not bobbing endlessly in front of the wall, or dying of hunger, or just dying, as they seem to do so insistently and predictably. It seems important that the woman keeps entering that shop; that the vegetable man put up a new board saying LEAKS PARCELY AVACADO when the politician is shown kicking a picture of Rushdie in the face while his followers laugh and applaud.

The woman and avocado both reappear—a sisterhood, domestic yet unreconciled—in de Souza's poem:

> The afternoon sun is on their faces.
> They are calm, not stupid,
> pregnant, not bovine.
> I know women like that
> and not just in paintings—
> an aunt who did not answer her husband back
> not because she was plain
> and Anna who writes poems
> and hopes her avocado stones
> will sprout in the kitchen.
> Her voice is oatmeal and honey.

Were it not for the passage from *Dangerlok*, we could mistake for defeatism the apolitical happiness this poem sponsors. The private self-renewals of these women may seem paltry, but Maya in *Dev and Simran* dismisses her previously "bookish" injunctions to those she works with—the assumption they have concrete life-changing options: "I would tell vacillating women to take a stand. But they couldn't, otherwise they wouldn't have been vacillating in the first place. I would tell women who were being beaten to leave home. What they did was leave the Women's Studies Unit. Where could they go given the price of flats in Bombay?" "Women in Dutch Painting" doesn't *assume* the society it depicts can be changed. It's realist, not utopian, in its smart-casual syntax, which like silk combines delicacy with tensile strength through careful placement of individual words within each sentence.

The strength of these women is expressed in the negative, but a negative (those five instances of the word *not*) gradually moving the idea of resistance toward spontaneous self-expression. The poem's oscillation between art and life respects even quiet and superficially unrebellious existences. It responds to the overemphasis on "subversion" parodied in *Dangerlok*, inquiring into what a genuinely political poetry might look like if we discarded our mythmaking and idealist fantasies, our tendency to drastically overstate the immediate revolutionary power of literature. Doing so, we ignore what poems tell us from line to line about both worldly and personal possibilities. Reading de Souza, we realize that the power of speech depends on the existence of those with ears to hear. But if, as John Stuart Mill believed, "eloquence is *heard*; poetry *over*heard," the speech for which the world is not yet ready may find refuge in poems.

"Emmental freedom"
Czesław Miłosz

Professor Timofey Pnin, the lovably hapless, "ideally bald," comic-heroic émigré protagonist of Nabokov's novel, thinks the unthinkable:

> In order to exist rationally, Pnin had taught himself, during the last ten years, never to remember Mira Belochkin—not because, in itself, the evocation of a youthful love affair, banal and brief, threatened his peace of mind . . . but because, if one were quite sincere with oneself, no conscience, and hence no consciousness, could be expected to subsist in a world where such things as Mira's death were possible. One had to forget—because one could not live with the thought that this graceful, fragile, tender young woman with those eyes, that smile, those gardens and snows in the background, had been brought in a cattle car to an extermination camp and killed by an injection of phenol into the heart, into the gentle heart one had heard beating under one's lips in the dusk of the past.

Vladimir Nabokov and Czesław Miłosz—the Russian novelist and the Lithuanian Polish poet—were, are, secret sharers:

> Here, in this garden I held her hand,
> Her body was like a swallow's body
> Fluttering in my palm. Death.
> And I don't even know whether it could be said,
> That she was taken away into darkness by Charon's boat,
> Because of barbed wire, abomination, blood.
> —"A WARSAW FAUST"

Born into the gentry, both idealized a childhood of innocent sensuous wonder—were forced from their homeland—moved to the States to teach, like Pnin. They write poetry after Auschwitz (Nabokov, and Miłosz, sometimes, in prose) and indulge, periodically, in an immodest clinging to the sovereignty of art over unspeakable realities. Both were taxidermists: their curiosity about nature expressed a longing to invert the values of a Darwinian realm (like politics, like capitalism) where, from one perspective, a perspective neither could get beyond, it would seem that the strong exist to crush the weak.

Neither enjoyed music, describing concerts with self-praise of their *visual* nous: "a strange ritual was being enacted," writes Miłosz, and "sound had value only insofar as it set two fields of bows in motion, like wheat bent in the wind." Resisters of the literature of social protest, whatever the risk, they exalted close observation, fusing, like Pnin, conscience and consciousness. Miłosz: "from the taste and scent of bird-cherry trees above rivers / Consciousness hikes through bay and hibiscus thickets"; "consciousness enclosed in itself every separate birch"; "When gold paint flakes from the arms of sculptures, / When the letter falls out of the book of laws, / Then consciousness is naked as an eye." Milosz and his mother Weronika were fired on by an armored train in 1920: "I was two people at once: along with the rest of the living contents of our wagon, I spilled into the ditch and crouched there in the sticky mud, praying and sobbing; but at the same time, I did not stop being curious, nor did my senses cease to recollect impressions as keenly as ever.... On the bank leading down into the ditch was a tree with protruding roots." As this suggests, like Nabokov, Miłosz really had some ego. He could be too overtly self-admiring—alert to, and keen to describe, the relentlessness that saw him through. Bravura passages in the work of both arrest time, preserving in the amber of style the vanishing nanosecond; the conflict between reality and art, history and the imagination, pressed these writers toward the mystical. However influenced by "the pantheistic strain within Lithuanian folk culture," Miłosz, a friend of Pope John Paul, returned gradually, and idiosyncratically, to Catholicism; Nabokov, like Pnin, appears to have believed, or wanted to, in a "democracy of ghosts"—he hints electricity is made of them. The dead abide, even if it is, to return to Simone Weil, their very absence, our need to think of them, which allows them to return.

Though Miłosz, confirms Andrzej Franaszek, "luckily, never had to experience prison or transportation," he had the worse of it—if such things can be measured. Luck, unstably overhauled as fate, looms large in his life and verse—"A Ninety-year-old Poet Signing His Books" mentions "miraculous events / Like the ones that once saved me / From Auschwitz, and also (there's evidence) / From a gulag miner's fate somewhere in Vorkuta." A grenade lobbed into his manor house failed to explode: he lived through both world wars, the Russian Revolution, and the Nazi occupation. He attempted suicide. When Lithuania was absorbed by the Soviet Union, he tried to escape across the border, was turned in by an informer, struck in the face by the Gestapo, and ate his passport as a precaution. Another was confiscated when Poland rescinded his activities as a diplomat. Separated for years from his family in the States, he felt at odds with Anglo-American social and literary values. Prior to his winning the Nobel Prize, for "almost three decades after his defection from Poland in 1951, Miłosz was a writer who had resigned himself to the fact that he had failed and would be forgotten"—remembered only as the author of *The Captive Mind*, his critique of communism that unfortunately endeared him to the U.S. right wing, and for his translations of Zbigniew Herbert. Translating *The Waste Land* into Polish, he remarks it "made somewhat weird reading as the glow from the burning ghetto illuminated the city skyline" of occupied Warsaw, where samizdat editions of his own poems were produced with a cobbler's needle, chenille thread, and a razor blade to cut the sheets to size. (A deceptively shrewd sentence on Eliot: "his precision also began to appear to be just a structural device concealing his intellectual uncertainty.")

The prose of *Pnin* and the verse of "A Warsaw Faust" touches an incontrovertible disparity. The lives of the oppressed and the comfortable don't brook comparison; this means someone moving from one state to another (in both senses) must splinter. Miłosz loved William Blake and argues a life of "the eternal present" as "the definition of happiness." But the guilt always returns to connect the man seduced by the moment (Miłosz, adrift in sunny California) with history's victim. Nabokov reveals the specificity of trauma giving way to a detail-annihilating sentimentality—a coping mechanism. Within his long, lucidly orotund sentences, soft-focus riffs like "the dusk of the past" wish earnestly to be true, not false; or, true to a required falseness, photographic of one's emotional *kavach*. (Pnin, unaware how Mira died, fantasizes myriad deaths by injection, gas, fire.) The Czech poet Miroslav Holub says poetic language can operate as "cosmetic or a camouflage. I strongly resent lyricism as adhesive tape over the mouth. But there are moments when lyricism still does reach further." Miłosz asserts, or diagrams a craving for, immortal values. But he can also be bare, reportorial. "There is a contradiction," he writes of Weil, "between our longing for the good, and the cold universe absolutely indifferent to any values;" as with her, his efforts are "directed towards making the contradiction as acute as possible."

The art is in the oscillation. Franaszek quotes from the news magazine *Przekrój*—founded in 1945, the year of Miłosz's article—his momentous account of the Warsaw ghetto uprising. It's spring. Standing on the balcony, "on a beautiful quiet night, a country night," Miłosz hears it: "They were the screams of thousands of people being murdered. It travelled through the silent spaces of the city from among a red glow of fires, under indifferent stars, into the benevolent silence of gardens in which plants laboriously emitted oxygen, the air was fragrant, and a man felt that it was good to be alive." He's thinking of Blaise Pascal: *"Le silence eternel des ces espaces infinis m'effraie."* Miłosz desires a form that is neither prose nor verse, neither spiritless journalism nor undue embroidery. It aligns with moral speech and is both primordial and futuristic:

> You asked me what is the good of reading the Gospels in Greek.
> I answer that it is proper that we move our finger
> Along letters more enduring than those carved in stone,
> And that, slowly pronouncing each syllable,
> We discover the true dignity of speech.

This emphasis on pronunciation comes of the childhood evoked in *The Issa Valley*:

> Thomas was very fond of his grandfather. He had a nice smell about him and the gray bristles above his lip tickled his cheek. He lived in a little room where a print showing people tied to stakes, with half-naked men putting torches to the stakes, hung above his bed. One of Thomas's first reading exercises was to read aloud, syllable by syllable, the inscription: *The Torches of Nero*. In this way he came to know the name of that vicious tyrant, the name he later gave to one of the pups when the grownups, after examining the pup's mouth, had said it was bound to be fierce because it had a dark palate.

Once again, historical violence erupts into domestic safety, and the care one takes with words becomes seminal. This semiautobiographical novel-memoir was first published in Polish in 1955, and I wonder if we have here the donnée for Holub's poem "Napoleon," about schoolchildren with no idea who he is: "Our butcher had a dog / called Napoleon, / says Frantisek. / The butcher used to beat him and the dog died / of hunger / a year ago. // And all the children are now sorry / for Napoleon." But the verse of Miłosz isn't as rigidly unclad as Holub's or as that of Zbigniew Herbert. The paradox of an unlying art enthralls him. His *Treatise on Poetry* avers, "one clear stanza can take more weight / Than a whole wagon of elaborate prose"; "I want not poetry, but a new diction, / Because only it might allow us to express / A new tenderness and save us from a law / That is not our law"; and he writes in *"Ars Poetica?"*:

> I have always aspired to a more spacious form
> that would be free from the claims of poetry or prose
> and would let us understand each other without exposing
> the author or reader to sublime agonies.

Planished, shapely, and of an enviable gravitas—an authority which isn't only biographical but is felt along the lines—this is Miłosz in English.

Franaszek doesn't provide much literary analysis, although he does, on page 345, discuss the "condensed" history of the *Treatise* as it progresses through "a series of micro-images":

> Chickens cackle. Geese stretch their necks from baskets.
> In the town, a bullet is carving a dry trace
> In the sidewalk near bags of homegrown tobacco.
> All night long, on the outskirts of the city,
> An old Jew, tossed in a clay pit, has been dying.
> His moans subside only when the sun comes up.
> The Vistula is gray, it washes through osiers
> And fashions fans of gravel in the shallows.

"To remain aware of the weight of fact," writes Miłosz, "without yielding to the temptation to become only a reporter is one of the most difficult puzzles. . . . It calls for a cunning in selecting one's means and a kind of distillation of material to achieve a distance to contemplate the things of this world as they are, without illusion." Stylistically, his solution is a poetics of merged time signatures. The duration of the old Jew's dying is situated among the cackling of chickens, the movement of geese, the lovely detail of the water-patterned gravel. The bullet we see in slow motion, "carving a dry trace"—Miłosz insists "the aesthetic experience" is central, and also beautifies bullets in his account of the Warsaw ghetto uprising. He, his wife Janka, and her mother took refuge in a house previously home to literary gatherings: "From our host's bookcase I dug out a volume of sociological essays about pre-war Poland, *The Young Generation of Peasants*, and plunged into its sorry reckoning of my own and my country's past, from time to time dropping flat on the floor as bullets traced long patterns across the plaster." I wonder if I'm alone in discerning a trace of vanity. Miłosz wishes to both affirm and dispel what we might perceive as an incongruity between atrocity and intellectual analysis of it. In so doing, he casts himself as hero and begins to write poems hard to respond to more than sentimentally.

This is the whole of "In Common," published in the 1991 collection *Provinces*:

What is good? Garlic. A leg of lamb on a spit.
Wine with a view of boats rocking in a cove.
A starry sky in August. A rest on a mountain peak.

What is good? After a long drive water in a pool and a sauna.
Lovemaking and falling asleep, embraced, your legs touching hers.
Mist in the morning, translucent, announcing a sunny day.

I am submerged in everything that is common to us, the living.
Experiencing this earth for them, in my flesh.
Walking past the vague outline of skyscrapers? anti-temples?
In valleys of beautiful, though poisoned, rivers.

The question "What is good?" ripens, becomes substantial—moving from pleasure to morality. But the poem falters, it knows it's inadequate, and there are others like it. Like Seamus Heaney who admired him, Miłosz struggles to reconcile his self-delighting responsiveness with the history, subject matter, diplomatic role he has inherited.

"Them," in the antepenultimate line, appears not to refer to the "living" but the dead. I understand this idea from my own life. My parents, Sri Lankan Tamils, raised me to high-achieve, to aim for extraordinariness always—as if in recompense for what they, and people like them back home, were denied. But they also passed on the requirement not only to thrive but to be *happy* about it—again, as if on behalf of both the living and the dead: "experiencing this earth for them, in my flesh." The original version of this essay wasn't published by the periodical that commissioned it: I wonder if they wanted more of a takedown. Reading Miłosz with a scandalized (no one's ever tried to kill or exile me personally) sense of identification, I could not provide—even a weak poem, like this one, touches me, in its inadequacy and guilt and its shrinking to a gesture.

"Experiencing this earth for them, in my flesh"—I'm trying to make the most of this idea, but one could object to Miłosz's leaping from the sensuous to the sensual to the sexual as an artifact of male privilege. "Although there were misogynistic strains within me, I have almost converted to feminism, so much do I enjoy the company of women, that special aura that comes from talking to them and sharing wine." Reading this biography, one sympathises with Janka—so strong-willed and elusive, succumbing eventually to a tumor of the spine. Miłosz nursed her lovingly; she stuck with him through multiple infidelities, including his "strong compulsion to try to hit on women students." Such was the irrepressible libido that Franaszek, like Milosz, links pretentiously with the poet's supposedly more than usual organic sensibility: "It is possible that she did not realise that these social failings were indicative of a core sensuality within him and a hunger for intense, 'naked' sensations, unrestrained by conventions."

From poem to poem, Milosz apologizes for bouncing back; insists it's OK; tells himself, and us, that to survive is no crime and issues no obligations: "No duties. I don't have to be profound. / I don't have to be artistically perfect. / Or sublime. Or edifying. / I just wander. I say: 'you were running, / That's fine. It was the thing to do.'" But no matter how close a poem gets to the author talking or thinking out loud to himself, we have to consider our response. In short, I wonder if Miłosz's self-reassurances are rather too tempting for those of us who, reading the poems, absorb and reproduce their emotional recoveries without having experienced what he has. Franaszek quotes a letter of September 12, 1931, where Miłosz, following a stay in Switzerland, says that Western Europe experiences "no tensions or struggle—which are a prerequisite for confronting so many crucial issues." This is transparently an exaggeration, and I don't mean to naively identify 2022 with the prewar West. Yet when Miłosz refers to a type of conceptually spiritless, "Emmental freedom," it summarizes a perspective that the Anglo-American reader must struggle with. "Mine . . . is a piety without a home; it survives the obsessive, annihilating image of universal disjointedness and, fortunately, allows me no safe superiority." Does this apply more universally, to those sharing in Milosz's epiphanies with the complacency of a WASP teen identifying with the angers of Black rap?

From the horse's mouth: "People in the West like to live in the heaven of exalted expressions about spirituality and freedom, but hardly ever ask the question as to whether someone has enough money for dinner." Those who've suffered, whom history's done dirt on, may press back against the force of reality with loudness, egotism, ecstasies. These affects, qualities, experiences, then become transferable and even salable. Miłosz begins his Nobel speech: "My presence here, on this platform, should be an argument for all those who praise life's God-given, marvelously complex unpredictability." This leap from presence, personality, to proof of the miraculous is asserted in the verse. Yet for us to readily annex his licensed astonishment is surely bad faith, or *Ketman*, the Islamic term he found for the mind-forged manacles of Polish communism. The poet's life-saving egoism reaches and inhabits us. But he was a drowning man, finally cast ashore and drawing in lungfuls of air—we're tourists at an oxygen bar. Some of us, anyway; not everyone "in the West" lives (and dies) this way; what would it mean to read the poetry of Eastern Europe with reference to the murder of George Floyd?

> Human reason is beautiful and invincible.
> No bars, no barbed wire, no pulping of books,
> No sentence of banishment can prevail against it.
> It establishes the universal ideas in language,
> And guides our hand so we write Truth and Justice
> With capital letters, lie and oppression with small.
> —"INCANTATION"

The irony's squeezed into the title: a rhetorical move also appearing in, among other works, "Preparation" and "What I Learned from Jeanne Hersch." This allows the language of the poem to appear unchallenged—or challenged only by history—unignorably solid and radiant. Milosz's yearning for an ideal assertiveness links with the yearning for his gravitas expressed by Western critics in gushing, even fanboy, terms. Donald Davie wrote of his move beyond the "lyric," revealed as insufficient to the twentieth century; Christopher Ricks objected, saying this was true of many. Helen Vendler affirmed the importance of Miłosz to U.S. poets, but also said they shouldn't, couldn't, copy him: "scenes at which he looked with horror will not be seen that way by a child of a young parochial imperium. Americans do not carry in them a thousand years of history."

W. H. Auden said the crack in the teacup opened a lane to the land of the dead. But what if it doesn't—what if there's no route linking our experiences of domestic happiness with the vast carnages underpinning them? Here's "Song on Porcelain," translated by Robert Pinsky:

> Rose-coloured cup and saucer,
> Flowery demitasses:
> You lie beside the river
> Where an armored column passes.
> Winds from across the meadow
> Sprinkle the banks with down;
> A torn apple tree's shadow
> Falls on the muddy path;
> The ground everywhere is strewn
> With bits of brittle froth—
> Of all things broken and lost
> Porcelain troubles me the most.

Miłosz attempts a poetry of happiness, but can do so only in terms of a deliverance from evil. He hopes his verse reveals the fragility of civilization, but appears to doubt the existence of a reader who could permanently learn this lesson. The "savagery of the struggle for existence is not averted in civilisation," and only for a few moments can we not take porcelain for granted; in fact, taking things for granted—those necessities we affirm as rights and not privileges—makes artistic creation possible. Forgetting is required: "for years I used to think about the indecency of all types of artistry, which, in every country I am familiar with, now or in the past, would have been impossible if the fate of the downtrodden and the humiliated were really felt intensely by others." Poor Timofey Pnin knows that Mira was killed in Buchenwald, only "an hour's stroll from Weimar, where walked Goethe, Herder, Schiller, Wieland, the inimitable Kotzebue and others. 'Aber warum—but why—' Dr. Hagen, the gentlest of souls alive, would wail, 'why had one to put that horrid camp so near!'"

"There must be something to say"
On Verse Sound

The trouble, or perhaps the beauty, of talking about the sounds of verse is that you end up discussing other things as well or you worry that your noticings are idiosyncratic fixations (if a reader will have spotted them before you or will agree to after), and then we may feel that stylistic appreciation must be bolted to an overall interpretation of the poem. The approach remains that in which, to apply Alexander Pope, we find the sound an echo to the sense: generations, now, of schoolchildren and university students have observed that in Wilfred Owen's line, "the stuttering rifles' rapid rattle," the *r* and *t* sounds conventionally emulate (they don't reproduce) the noise of gunfire. How do we move beyond this?

Angela Leighton finds a way, always suggestively, though not always—to my mind—with the power to convince. She examines a range of poets—Christina Rossetti, Alfred Lord Tennyson, William Butler Yeats, Edward Thomas, Robert Frost, Elizabeth Bishop, Les Murray, Alice Oswald, and two Grahams rarely considered together, Jorie and W. S.—as well as prose writers (she continues, for instance, her rivetingly up-close analysis of Walter Pater's prose, a feature of her previous book, *On Form*). She analyzes syntax (Pater's dashes, for example) and scans verse compellingly (a hypermetrical line in Walter de la Mare's "The Listeners"). I don't always agree with her—the idea, for instance, that in Rossetti's line "my heart is like a singing bird" one might stress the adjective rather than the noun—but it's good to know of her hearing things differently. This is subjective literary criticism, which mentions the author's uninterest in pursuing a "logically deductive argument" (though the suggestion that de la Mare is as strong an influence on Thomas as Frost is persuasive); Leighton is intrepidly associative, wayfaring from text to text. She appears to defend the "self-justifying mystique of literary writing" against the deconstruction of aesthetic pleasure into cultural capital, disguises for the operation of hegemonic power, and so on. While this is valuable (we need to read poems as poems, to respect the cognitions of form), it leaves much out. To eliminate content altogether seems misguided, and in fact reductive, of the work sound does.

For this reason—to pick one example, from a poet about whom I must confess to feeling possessive—I was disappointed by her reading of Elizabeth Bishop's "Twelfth Morning; or What You Will." In it, Leighton finds echoes of Frost, Eliot, Bishop's own "Sandpiper," and possible leaps to Woolf, and Robert Browning's *The Ring and the Book*, but not much of Brazil, where the poem is set. Content is treated summarily—the poem "describes the banal ordinariness of a backstreet scene in a seaside town"— and Leighton lingers on the third and fourth stanzas (I quote the first five):

> Like a first coat of whitewash when it's wet,
> the thin gray mist lets everything show through:
> the black boy Balthazár, a fence, a horse,
>   a foundered house,
>
> —cement and rafters sticking from a dune.
> (The Company passes off these white but shopworn
> dunes as lawns.) "Shipwreck," we say; perhaps
>   this is a housewreck.
>
> The sea's off somewhere, doing nothing. Listen.
> An expelled breath. And faint, faint, faint
> (or are you hearing things), the sandpipers'
>   heart-broken cries.
>
> The fence, three-strand, barbed-wire, all pure rust,
> three dotted lines, comes forward hopefully
> across the lots; thinks better of it; turns
>   a sort of corner . . .
>
> Don't ask the big white horse, Are you supposed
> to be inside the fence or out? He's still
> asleep. Even awake, he probably
>   remains in doubt.

"Hearing things" is also Leighton's title, a phrase that finely apprehends the experience of reading; the feeling of a poem as a "thing" which itself hears, as well as things and people in the world, other texts it may echo; then the idea of the critic accused of "hearing things" that aren't really there, of fantasizing ghosts in the machines that poems have been said to be.

Leighton worries less about this than I do. In fact, I'm glad she doesn't, and that she wrote this continually nuanced book. But the danger lies in not really listening to the poem, the person, right in front of you. Of not seeing the forest for the trees. Leighton zooms in, for instance, on Bishop's ellipsis, the three dots, glides into talk of the three-strand fence, its dotted lines, and then finds triads, like "faint, faint, faint," in the poet's other poems. Though it's wonderful to listen in on a deep reader of verse, thinking her way forward or (a favorite word of Bishop's) sidewise, much of this seems to me unconnected to sound except in a figurative way, and it leaves most of the poem undiscussed.

Concentrating on sound, there's the three-stress sequence, or molossus, rearriving throughout: "thin gray mist," "black boy Balthazár," "all pure rust," "big white horse." It's typical of Bishop to turn detailing of a place—see the slant rhyme too, on "horse" and "house" and the internal rhyme of "doubt" and "out"—into cultural exploration. The threes could be Trinitarian, given the dating of the poem to the Feast of Epiphany, and the ending, where the

> four-gallon can
> approaching on the head of Balthazár
> keeps flashing that the world's a pearl, *and I,*
>   I am
>
> its highlight!. . .
>   . . .
> "Today's my Anniversary," he sings,
>   "the Day of Kings."

It's a poem that wants to be religious, and whose ending echoes one of Bishop's favorites, Gerard Manley Hopkins: "I am all at once what Christ is, / since he was what I am, and / This Jack, joke, poor potsherd, / patch, matchwood, immortal diamond, / Is immortal diamond." Balthazar's "I am" emerges out of Hopkins's ingenious rhyme, but his act of lyrical transubstantiation isn't possible for Bishop. This has to do with unbelief, but also that she's writing about Brazil from the perspective of an outsider. Hence the talk of boundaries, the unease with which description approaches symbol, and then retreats; the desire to ennoble, sans sentimentality; and, indeed, the effort to understand race through a painterly or aestheticizing treatment of color ("Florida," "Cootchie," "In the Waiting Room," "Memories of Uncle Neddy," and her *Time-Life* book *Brazil* also do this).

Listening carefully to a poem, and its sounds, may take us back toward the world: "the agonies, the strife," said Keats, "of human hearts." Leighton prefers the involutions of the act of listening itself and is more religious than Bishop: one chapter begins anecdotally with her trekking in the rain to Lindisfarne, and she moves beyond tangible sounds to consider the "inner ear" that may "hear beyond hearing, or even hear innerly an absent sound that shapes itself as a presence." She claims "it is not 'news' that matters in poetry, good news or bad, but the sound of riding to bring it": "Poetry is predominantly something heard, and what we want from a poem is not ultimately a message, a story, a graspable or paraphrasable content of some kind, but rather an invitation to listen, and to listen again. It is the curious self-sufficiency of the act of listening which seems to say something about the arts of sound." Leighton's focus isn't on actually sounded verse, in the sense of performance. She explains that this leaves out much Black writing, for one. A scholar must be free to examine what interests them, without including minorities tokenistically. Yet—given her emphasis on a community of writers tuned in, primarily, to each other—one can't help but notice that, with the exception of a brief, sensitive reading of Toni Morrison's *Beloved*, all those Leighton examines are white and canonical (I suppose even W. S. Graham, the working-class Scot turned Cornish isolato, is published by Faber). To reaffirm the exquisiteness of their verse, its tapestry of echoes and self-echoes, might then appear a defense of privilege for privilege's sake: a closed world.

"Art for art's sake" is the phrase on the tip of my tongue, for, as in *On Form*, Leighton spiritualizes the legacies of aestheticism. Her lingering over the phrase and concept "je ne sais quoi" had me—and I've always thought of myself as a bit of an aesthete—craving some Pierre Bourdieu, or an equivalent citation, just to make the point that rich people (it's true) deploy standards of gentility to keep the less rich at bay, to deny others serious consideration; that social mystifications may parade as art talk. And I began to doubt Leighton on Tennyson. Examining "The Lover's Tale," she writes brilliantly of how "incremental repetition, which presses words into slightly altered variations of themselves, thus turns them into events, into dramatic actors rather than motionless disclosers of the story." But her riffing on Penelope Fitzgerald's suggestion that in Tennyson we hear "the sound of the language talking to itself" is too unbridled:

> The ear, as so often in Tennyson, tells its own love tale, one which may be at cross-purposes with the plot, but runs its sweetly melodious course, not only within the poem but also from poem to poem, as if telling of sadness and strangeness beyond any mere local interest. . . . Indeed, the sound of the language talking to itself, across line breaks, paragraph breaks, even breaks between poems, becomes what we also start to want to hear. What may sound like laziness, like the "sad sweet oversweet Alfred" pursuing his verbal fetishes, becomes a noise-haunting which in fact accounts for something always going on elsewhere—even if nothing more than a "lovetale" for the sounds of words, or for the memory of those other voices: Shakespeare's, Milton's, Wordsworth's, Shelley's, telling their own tales in the buzzing hold of a poetic tradition.

"Sad sweet oversweet Alfred" is Stevie Smith's narrator Pompey in her *Novel on Yellow Paper*, and Leighton also softens and reverses Woolf's critique of Tennyson's sonorousness, aligned with the robotic masculinity of Mr. Ramsay in *To the Lighthouse*. But these writers had a point to make about Victorian verse: in acknowledging Tennyson's continuing allure, they wished to draw attention to a sentimentality that, crystallized and preserved within so many gem-perfect lyrics, in fact gave voice disguisedly to a twisted bullishness, a vast emotional displacement connected to a jingoistic solipsism and the pluriform repressions of that era.

Tennyson has been thought of as two poets: the tediously patriarchal bore ("Alfred Lawn Tennyson," Joyce called him), and a measurelessly sensitive sufferer wishing to lose himself in dreamscapes of sound. But these roles are connected, as in the narrative of his monodrama *Maud* (whose lovelorn narrator finds his purpose, at last, in going to war), and Leighton's validation of failed communicativeness and self-enclosure brought to mind John Addington Symonds's account of Tennyson's meeting with William Ewart Gladstone, with whom he argued over the rebellion of plantation workers in Jamaica:

Tennyson did not argue. He kept asserting various prejudices and convictions. "We are too tender to savages; we are more tender to a black than to ourselves." "Niggers are tigers; niggers are tigers," in obbligato, sotto voce, to Gladstone's declamation. "But the Englishman is a cruel man—he is a strong man," put in Gladstone. My father illustrated this by stories of the Indian Mutiny. "That's not like Oriental cruelty," said Tennyson.

"Obbligato" is key, for, recalling Leighton's characterization of verse as music, it shows that Tennyson is uninterested in conversation. He takes refuge in the sound of his own voice, with a defensiveness passing into hatred of what's foreign, and therefore felt to be potentially intrusive, if it isn't firmly excluded on the outset from one's sympathies.

Although John Stuart Mill doesn't appear in Leighton's index, her stance is of the nineteenth century and extends his contention "that eloquence is *heard*; poetry is *over*heard. Eloquence supposes an audience; the peculiarity of poetry appears to us to lie in the poet's utter unconsciousness of a listener." In Symonds's ugly tableaux, Gladstone, the politician, is an exemplar of eloquence, which is (in Mill's words) "feeling pouring itself forth to other minds, courting their sympathy, or endeavouring to influence their belief, or move them to passion or to action"; Tennyson's withdrawal into a bigoted refrain provides a caricature of poetry, which is (says Mill) "feeling confessing itself to itself, in moments of solitude." He's there in the room but not really listening to anyone else—these surly outbursts are really a form of self-talk.

I don't mean by this to suggest that Leighton is wrong to examine poetry formally, insisting on qualities elusive of cruder critiques. It's more that I wonder what it would mean for us to maintain the aesthetic dimension while also considering poetry as a type of communication. Not browbeatingly linear or rhetorically manipulative or socially chameleonic (it's not about fitting in or flattering), but an attempt nevertheless at getting something across, at the same time respecting the challenges and opportunities both, that exist within a shifting language. This isn't a new idea (one precursor would be William Empson), but it's worth recovering and renewing in our atomized times in which everyone, it would seem, gets to have their say, though it's unclear who's actually listening to anyone else. A poetics of communication might now seem a must: what Leighton offers instead is a finely modulated self-consciousness that may amount to gussied-up self-regard.

This approach undersells, for one, the verse of W. S. Graham, for he is one of those who—I quote Søren Kierkegaard—"has an individual conception of what communication is . . . perhaps the distinctive characteristic, the reality of his historical importance is concentrated in precisely that":

> Meanwhile surely there must be something to say,
> Maybe not suitable but at least happy
> In a sense here between us two whoever
> We are. Anyhow here we are and never
> Before have we two faced each other who face
> Each other now across this abstract scene
> Stretching between us. This is a public place
> Achieved against subjective odds and then
> Mainly an obstacle to what I mean.
> —FROM "THE CONSTRUCTED SPACE"

Leighton says this poem "raises expectations of matter and purpose which are soon quashed"; she grants that its "space" contains "human presences, between which there is a kind of communication, transaction, or exchange," but her phrasing reveals a reluctance to take seriously these verse possibilities, and she reverses toward the aestheticist position: "Finally, the poetic space is constructed, like a formal box or design of language, in order that 'somehow something,' whatever it is (perhaps just another je ne sais quoi or sense of beauty?) might ride the 'habits of language to you and me' and make it stranger than we think." I don't buy that "finally," or the "perhaps"-initiated dismissiveness of the parenthesis, and "it" is hollowed out by the end of the sentence.

In fact, "The Constructed Space," Graham's masterpiece (one of them)—first published in *Poetry* in 1958—argues an aesthetic of communication, conceding as it goes impediments essential to that process, not overthrowers of it. Whenever people meet, it is in a (socially, politically, technologically) "constructed space": this phrase also, as Leighton explains, applies to the poem itself envisioned as an encounter between writer and reader. Why are the rhymes touching? Because they outline a river of talk desirous of an audience, which wonders out loud if there's "something to say," throws its hands up in resignation—"anyhow here we are"—and yet, with each coincidence of sound, suggests an impending confidence (in both senses), ghosting the desired connection of speaker and auditor that Graham can't assume. This poem isn't a formal box: it's siphonophoric (see-through and cloudy in volatile portions, fluidly shape-seeking) in how it connives an aphoristic sensibility, capable of lifting an empowering précis—"This is a public place / Achieved against subjective odds"—out of the nervous noise of onstreaming speech.

When those insights surface, the temptation to frame them on the wall is undone, always, by another thought, a courageously concessionary rather than acquiescently deflating coda: "and then / Mainly an obstacle to what I mean." Graham likes the word *obstacle*—"Have I not been trying to use the obstacle / Of language well?"—whose sticky sound has a mimetic stopping power or slowing power. This caution relates, however, not only to the crosscurrents and undercurrents of language that may either stymie or enable but also to the emotional risks involved in reaching toward another person:

> It is like that, remember. It is like that
> Very often at the beginning till we are met
> By some intention risen up out of nothing.
> And even then we know what we are saying
> Only when it is said and fixed and dead.
> Or maybe, surely, of course we never know
> What we have said, what lonely meanings are read
> Into the space we make. And yet I say
> This silence here for in it I might hear you.

The second stanza can't assume a reader, or listener, in agreement with what came before. It aims to persuade, but with qualifications—"it is like that / Very often at the beginning"—and only out of the effort to get its meaning across is the slant rhyme, "met," produced; under the pressure, that is, not only to speak but also to be heard and (however dilutedly) understood. "Met" then turns out, over the line break, to concern not an interpersonal but an intrapersonal meeting, with an "intention" arising from within; although we could also see those intentions as coming from outside ourselves (that division, of inside/outside, is breaking down), encoded within the language we inherit.

Graham suggests that a sort of mutual unknowing, a shared negative capability, a determination to be susceptible and a willingness to be surprised, is essential; the danger is always that one will be misunderstood, either in the moment or after it. We all become literary critics concerning our experiences of insecurity, cussedly sifting what we or others have said for reassurance that we won't be unseated by "what lonely meanings are read" into our untethered remarks. The poem includes these worries, but the stanza ends sturdily, where a verb is licensed to transcend its meaning in ordinary speech: "And yet I say / This silence here for in it I might hear you." You can't say a silence, strictly speaking: but your words can open a space for others to be heard.

I can see why a deconstructionist reader (Leighton compares Graham to Derrida) might discern a continual undoing of meaning. Graham has a sequence called "What is the language using us for?" that repeats the question, and in his "Private Poem to Norman MacLeod" we're told that "communication is always / On the edge of the ridiculous" (still, the word itself is present; he cares for what it represents). "The Beast in the Space," which we might read as a companion or counterpoem to "The Constructed Space," begins

> Shut up. Shut up. There's nobody here.
> If you think you hear somebody knocking
> On the other side of the words, pay
> No attention.

Leighton's central fecund reading is of de la Mare's "The Listeners," a poem where a knocked-at door yields no response; she moves into Robert Frost's intriguing remark, that the best way to catch what he calls the sound of sense, is to hear voices arguing behind a closed door that cuts off the words but not their acoustic contour. She convincingly aligns Graham's poems with his letters to friends (several of the poems call themselves "Letters"), but it's important to recognize that for every moment of real, not pretended, doubt in his verse as to whether communication is feasible—given the opacities of language and psychology both—there is time for a message struggling through, which may not be a pure transmission of what was intended yet still amounts to something: "See. / This night moves and this language / Moves over slightly / To meet another's need / Or make another's need"; "These words this one night / Feed us and will not / Leave us without our natures / Inheriting new fires." Language both creates and assuages desire, in a telephone game that may thwart a face-to-face meeting (Graham returns to this idea) but nevertheless postulates a real interaction.

Within "The Constructed Space," the assertiveness of "say," renovated in the previous stanza, can't be maintained, and the poem's speaker is pressed to rephrase:

> I say this silence, or, better, construct this space
> So that somehow something may move across
> The caught habits of language to you and me.
> From where we are it is not us we see
> And times are hastening yet, disguise is mortal.
> The times continually disclose our home.
> Here in the present tense disguise is mortal.
> The trying times are hastening. Yet here I am
> More truly now this abstract act become.

Ralph Pite explains that "disguise is mortal" in "two contradictory senses": "It is temporary and it belongs to the human condition. Disguise will pass at last, and yet its passing is a trial to us because we are wedded to it. Graham places against this paradox the 'abstract act' that provides an escape from both the thrill and the fear of losing your disguise and being exposed to another person." The poem—Pite discusses visual art too—is such an abstraction, but it's also a speech act from which these angsts can't be extirpated; its power, in fact, depends on that proximity. It's so marvelously discomforting, intimate-seeming, specific in being nonspecific: what it says about times, trying times, hastening times, and how they "continually disclose our home" has a power to touch readers in sundry situations. The recognition of a limited but real agency, and a partial yet true perspective, is given in language steered by a purpose, yet wavery and plural.

The convoluted final sentence continues the work of nuanced affirmation: Graham queries his own assertiveness without descending, pronto (Wallace Stevens, a philosopher-poet Leighton admires, can be like this), into mock-heroic bathos. So the poem doesn't click shut like Leighton's formal box: it's a touch ragged, unguarded, it knows it may sound frustratingly abstruse, pointlessly gnarled. The slant rhyming of "home," "am," and "become" approaches closure while remaining suspicious of it; what's ventured, with the verb *become*, echoes a comparatively translucent, if not transparent, love poem of Graham's, the seventh of "Seven Letters":

> A sweet clearness became.
> The Clyde sleeved in its firth
> Reached and dazzled me.
> I moved and caught the sweet
> Courtesy of your mouth.
> My breath to your breath.
> And as you lay fondly
> In the crushed smell of the moor
> The courageous and just sun
> Opened its door.

Does the first line say all that needs to be said? Maybe not, because the poem goes on. The sounds—the slant and full rhymes, the assonances, the glissade of "caught" into "courtesy," then "crushed" and "courageous"—point to a content within immediacy, a depth to touch, and a process of intellection, beyond and within feeling, to do with two people, not one.

Elizabeth Bishop, Robert Penn Warren, Cleanth Brooks, Communication, and Other People

I'd like to consider, as well as the form and texture of Elizabeth Bishop's poems, aspects of our political predicament. I refer to the risks and the rewards of communicating across distances—geographic, political, and to do, of course, with the jaded necessary triad of race, class, and gender. Bishop is aware that oceans of uncertainty—or bad, restrictive certainties—may separate two people speaking even in the same room. This is why she writes to Randall Jarrell, in a letter of December 26, 1955, that communication "is an undependable but sometimes marvelous thing."

We can politicize this. I'll begin with Robert Penn Warren's *All the King's Men* and the scene where Lucy, wife to the future governor, Willie Stark, wishes to cheer him up after an election loss. The persisting dichotomy of male/provider and female/homemaker makes this an archetypal situation: ambition carries a man outside of the domestic space it is supposedly a woman's task to turn into a soothing, curative realm. Lucy's trying to dismiss his rivals—"They'd be crooks, wouldn't they?"—but Willie doesn't appear to be listening:

> She kept watching his face, which seemed to be pulling back from her and from me and the room, as though he weren't really hearing her voice but were listening to another voice, a signal maybe, outside the house, in the dark beyond the screen of the open window.
>
> "Wouldn't they?" she asked him, pulling him back into the room, into the circle of soft light from the lamp on the table, where the big Bible and the plush-bound album lay. The bowl of the lamp was china and had a spray of violets painted on it.

Warren's verse suffers, as Calvin Bedient observes, from his tendency to "oversing." He loads every rift with ore, turning the verse more purple than purple—empurpled, engorged. Masturbatory. A touch embarrassing. But his prose, in his best-known novel, can be sure and brisk. Here it's Willie Stark who morbidly frigs his imagination, not the author. He, says Jack Burden, the narrator, fails to respond; sinks "back into whatever he was brooding over"; his "face seemed to be pulling off again into the distance which was not distance but which was, shall I say, simply himself."

The distance which was simply himself. I don't think that's just a prose riff (though Warren is given to them; he's incurably stylish): this sentence has something to say. Brexit, Donald Trump, identity politics, hate speech, and safe spaces: we're all worried about people unable, or unwilling, to speak with one another—a form of Internet-enabled twenty-first-century tribalism which diminishes the possibility of there ever occurring (can you imagine it, really, of yourself?) a conversation that might change minds. Yet Elizabeth Bishop's is a poetics of communication, rather than self-expression, in touch with the contention of Warren and Cleanth Brooks, in *Understanding Poetry*, that it, "like all discourse, is a communication—the saying of something by one person to another person." Some poets (Brooks himself, off on a rampage) work themselves up to the point of forgetting this. Bishop, never.

Consider the close of "The Moose," which famously took twenty years to write and was published in *Geography III* in 1976. As a meandering bus journey in Nova Scotia reaches its conclusion, Bishop dares to assert an experience of unifying joy. A moose wanders into the road, forcing the bus to stop, and it has a beauty seeming to exist in the eye of every beholder, although Bishop acknowledges multiple responses:

> Towering, antlerless,
> high as a church,
> homely as a house
> (or, safe as houses).
> A man's voice assures us
> "Perfectly harmless. . . ."
>
> Some of the passengers
> exclaim in whispers,
> childishly, softly,

"Sure are big creatures."
"It's awful plain."
"Look! It's a she!"

Taking her time,
she looks the bus over,
grand, otherworldly.
Why, why do we feel
(we all feel) this sweet
sensation of joy?

I'm struck by the mansplaining at the end of the first stanza—the patronizing voice that, in an incident I'll go on to discuss, Bishop had also to confront in person. Also by how Bishop rediscovers the cliché, "safe as houses"—idioms presume common ground—and moves toward a shared value judgment: the phrase "we all feel" affirms an undivided community expanding beyond the bus to include the reader too. Yet this emphasis on union combines with a stoic downplaying of what's actually possible. The desired connection occurs in parenthesis, and we end on a flatter note, as the bus moves on and the "dim / smell of moose" is overwritten by an "acrid / smell of gasoline." For while Bishop cherishes this distinctively Nova Scotian moment (strangers brought together in a closed space) I think she's also wary of it. Parochial groupthink isn't far off: communal stupor. What she wishes to get into poetry is the estrangement essential to communication, which is a touch across distance. If speaker and listener begin in the same place, with the same idea or opinion or sentence, then what happens between them isn't, according to this perspective, communication. It is instead a species of team-confirming amiability; a spree of reassuring in-signals; that confirmation of the language of one's coterie which also builds big, unbeautiful walls around its city limits. The spirit of the age—I mean, the way we've started to talk following the referendum on the EU and Trump's election—refers to this phenomenon as the "echo-chamber," or the "filter bubble," a more Internet-specific term coined by Eli Pariser to explain how algorithms prevent us from seeing online any content that disagrees with us.

Seeking a poetic equivalent, I think of Thomas Gray's "Elegy in a Country Churchyard," which one of Bishop's favourite literary critics, William Empson, claimed was complacent, because though it would have us pity wasted lives, "the reader is put into a mood in which one would not try to alter" the situation: "by comparing the social arrangement to Nature," Gray "makes it seem inevitable, which it was not, and gives it a dignity which was undeserved." For Empson, "good writing is not done unless there are serious forces at work; and it is not permanent unless it works for readers with opinions different from the author's." This is what makes literature, in the phrase of Ezra Pound, news that stays news—and not, to return to the parlance of our times, fake news. John Guillory explains that Gray's poem achieves an effect of universal truth by, in short, becoming a storehouse of commonplaces.

In "The Moose," the experiencers in the bus of the creature's arrival don't equate to the passive and uncritical audience implied by Gray's verse voice. The event is providential rather than reliable and leaves the passengers unhypnotized: individuals who, rather than sitting silent, actively whisper. I take the metaphor of hypnotism from *Understanding Poetry*, where Brooks and Warren deconstruct a commonplace of literary criticism pertaining to "the hypnotic power of verse":

> People think of hypnosis as a condition of sluggishness or sleep artificially induced. But the fundamental characteristic of the hypnoidal state is not—it must be remembered—sluggishness or dullness but the vastly increased concentration of attention and suggestibility. The person who is in such a condition hangs upon every word of the hypnotist and attends to and accepts even the slightest suggestion. In a similar fashion, by the regularity of the meter, the reader of poetry may be put into a state of greater susceptibility to the suggestions of ideas, attitudes, feelings, and images contained in the poem.

Consider the poetry of Swinburne, whose oceanic rhythms take priority over meaning. In contrast, Penelope Laurans writes of Bishop that "the reader is never allowed to forget himself and to be transported by the momentum of the verse. Instead, the metric roughness keeps him detached, his attention concentrated on the complexity of the event the poet is describing." This isn't only a technical point, for if we consider rhythm as essential to the communicative apparatus of a poem, it means that Bishop refuses to take for granted the reader's sympathy with its speaker. She isn't a hypnotist, and I wonder if one reason she's suspicious of her tendency toward an iambic beat—she frets she's just an "umpty-um" poet—is because it resembles the metrical equivalent of a mesmerist's swinging watch.

In Warren's *All the King's Men*, Stark fails, initially, to get elected because he can't communicate with voters. His ideal vision of what a politician should be has him build his speeches out of dry facts and bloodless statistics. Then he develops a style of preacherlike spontaneity whose gusto is, one feels, both sincere (he has convinced himself too) and pragmatic. In short, he becomes a hypnotist, and one of the anxieties of Warren's novel, I would say, besides whether or not a politician must become pragmatic, that is, corrupt, relates to whether or not a politician must also become a hypnotist. *All the King's Men* considers themes of silence and slow time, the momentum of history, solipsistic reverie, and the excitements of imagining oneself into the lives of others. It's a political novel in its plot, characterization, and its true-to-life detail. But it's also political when it is most poetic. Take the paragraph where Warren describes Stark on the verge of giving a supposedly impromptu speech—revealing how the politician, the hypnotist, touches us in the very place we are most alone:

> You saw the eyes bulge suddenly like that, as though something had happened inside him, and there was that glitter. You knew something had happened inside him, and thought: *It's coming.* It was always that way. There was the bulge and the glitter, and there was the cold grip way down in the stomach as though somebody had laid hold of something in there, in the dark which is you, with a cold hand in a cold rubber glove. It was like the second when you come home late at night and see the yellow envelope of the telegram sticking out from under your door and you lean and pick it up, but don't open it yet, not for a second. While you stand there in the hall, with the envelope in your hand, you feel there's an eye on you, a great big eye looking straight at you from miles and dark and through walls and houses and through your coat and vest and hide and sees you huddled up way inside, in the dark which is you, inside yourself, like a clammy, sad little foetus you carry around inside yourself.

The telegram we might see as the message to be conveyed, from politician to voter. But the drama trumps the message. The drama is the message. Warren's prose uses repetition, rhyme, and the syntax is eventually pulverized. The politician is commanded, we remember, "by the distance which is himself," the voter by "the dark which is you." Something has happened inside the politician, and now it's going to happen to other people—those unsure of themselves until they're gripped by his conviction. (I'm reminded of Emily Dickinson's poem beginning "He fumbles at your soul"—about a preacher or God or a rapist or music or how the wind bashes the trees: really, about all these things.) This is prose true to shocking political events: to how intensities are broadcast, or evoked, and how fear evolves into commitment. "It's the economy, stupid": well, yes. But it's also something else.

Let's compare the experience Warren records, and tries to communicate in onrushing prose, with the prosaic verse of "Over 2,000 Illustrations and a Complete Concordance." The speaker of this poem, maybe Bishop herself, finds in Morocco

> what frightened me most of all:
> a holy grave, not looking particularly holy,
> one of a group under a keyhole-arched stone baldaquin
> open to every wind from the pink desert.
> An open, gritty, marble trough, carved solid
> with exhortation, yellowed
> as scattered cattle-teeth;
> half-filled with dust, not even the dust
> of the poor prophet paynim who once lay there.
> In a smart burnoose Khadour looked on amused.

The traveler whose idioms and diction match Bishop's, and whom we might therefore consider American, white, well-off, has an experience one might characterize as terror; and this is a poem that has previously evoked "the squatting Arab, / or group of Arabs, plotting, probably, / against our Christian Empire." (The cognitive hop from "squatting" to "plotting" catches and ironizes a racist thought on the move.) Something is happening inside her—but the Arab, Khadour, who acts as her guide, is unaffected. The assonance linking "burnoose," "Khadour," and "amused" lends him an integrity of identity; the line is perfect blank verse, with an extra syllable at the start; "amused" rhymes (blink and you'll miss it) with the "dust" of two lines previous. We feel the contrast between their perspectives, but the expected hierarchy is reversed—both sound and meter hone the effect.

This poem ends with a yearning to feast one's eyes on a Nativity scene—to have "looked and looked one's infant sight away." As if the narrative of Christianity might still terminate the bewildering relativism—and cleanse the ominous absolutes—of other faiths, including Islam. Cleanth Brooks argued a poem is a "pattern of resolved stresses." I believe that Bishop's stresses, in the literal sense, are unresolved: her verse rhythm interpolates, and extrapolates, moments of indecision. "Over 2,000 Illustrations" is a poem about the impossibility of organic form. Its river of unconnected detail and its alternation of verse rhythm with the sound of discursive prose argues the incommensurability of world cultures. If people disagree more than they agree, then, Bishop suggests, poetry may be what happens when communication—that would be prose—breaks down. But, of course, other, awfuller things also occur when communication breaks down. In this sense, poetry comes into being, always, on the brink of a political crisis.

We have the "holy grave, not looking particularly holy," and Khadour, who "looked on amused." Although Bishop's verse of this kind may seem to relax into prose, her word choices matter. "Look" is also an important word in the unprepossessingly titled "Poem," in which she admires a tiny, crude painting of Nova Scotia by a distant relative:

> I never knew him. We both knew the place,
> apparently, this literal small backwater,
> looked at it long enough to memorize it,
> our years apart. How strange. And it's still loved,
> or its memory is (it must have changed a lot).
> Our visions coincided—"visions" is
> too serious a word—our looks, two looks.

"Look" isn't, perhaps, an unserious word, but a limited one. Our acts of gazing, is what Bishop means, or our perspectives; she's interested in what can be shared between two people—Bishop and Khadour, Bishop and her great-uncle—as well as what can't be. "Coincided" is a tricky polysyllable. I think of her wry, subversively ironic description of herself as a "minor female Wordsworth," itself an echo of Auden's self-portrait as a "minor Atlantic Goethe," because Bishop, like Wordsworth, makes a four-syllable word poetically plausible by welding it smoothly into blank verse. Using the same verb, Carole Doreski writes that, "faced with the intriguing strangeness of Key West, Brazil, and even black America," Bishop "could not make her available language and socialization entirely coincide with the immediate resources of the culture." I'd say Bishop's prosaic verse is properly wary of such unearned coincidences. It acknowledges distinctions presumptuous to deny, yet incorrect—and here we find a challenge to present-day identity politics—to consider ungetroundable.

It's because Bishop believes in conversation, that is, in, given luck and effort, the possibility of understanding another, and having one's mind changed—that she and her poems grow vulnerable. During her first stay in Paris, in 1935, she got into an argument. Harriet Tompkins Thomas gives us the details:

> For her beauty really was one of the eternal verities, the most important thing in life. Beauty meant a great deal to her. John was taking the part of the *advocatus diaboli*, arguing that beauty was in the eye of the beholder and that one's ideas of value conditioned what one thought and how one defined beauty. Bishop was trying to argue with him and he was getting the better of the argument because he was a practiced debater. Bishop got very upset, threw off her coat and hat—I don't know why she had her coat and hat on—and went into the kitchen. I found her there ten minutes later drinking a large glass of gin and weeping profusely. She said, "Well, you know, people shouldn't discuss things like that."

Elizabeth Bishop, the victim of more mansplaining—one wishes she hadn't been reduced to tears and gin. She wasn't pleased when Anne Stevenson applied Wittgenstein to her works, and I wonder what she'd make of my bending this anecdote toward the writing of another man, the ordinary-language philosopher Stanley Cavell. (In my monograph on her, I carry this quotation toward an extended reading of her masterpiece "Santarém," but with a great poet there are many paths through the work, and it's a pleasure to return to a crossroads and take the road previously untraveled.) Cavell remarks "the feature of the aesthetic claim, as suggested by Kant's description, as a kind of compulsion to share a pleasure, hence as tinged with an anxiety that the claim stands to be rebuked. It is a condition of, or threat to, that relation to things called aesthetic, that something I know and cannot make intelligible stands to be lost to me." If I say to you, of a Bishop poem, *isn't this beautiful?*, I've no way to coerce your agreement. If, in the end, we disagree, it'll get awkward. Maybe we'll part with a joke, to quash the tension. I'll have revealed myself to you, through trying to share what I care about (disapproval, dislike, is more immediately, if limitedly, impressive, as reviewers of poetry well know). Disagreeing with my opinion, it may seem that you disagree with me as a person. Why, at family dinners, is it said one shouldn't speak of politics or religion? ("People shouldn't discuss things like that.") One answer might be: because we always *do* discuss these things at family dinners. There are arguments whose intensity, on one side or both, is really there not to convince, but for each party to confirm, partly to themselves, where exactly they stand. But actual conversation, like falling in love or writing, or reading, a poem, requires an experience that may change, rather than confirm, who you are. This, to borrow the language of "Over 2,000 Illustrations," could be what frightens us most of all.

It isn't that we don't crave conversion experiences, breakthroughs—but usually in terms of a furthering of our current stance, a boon gained, an amplification of one's existing idea of oneself. What I'm talking about— what I hear Bishop talking about—is more disturbing and utter. It's a question of being changed at the cellular level, of being urged by astonishment to reconsider, dizzyingly, exactly who you are. (What would it mean to seek such changefulness, and not through self-loathing or self-doubt: to be content, yet unaverse to transformation?) I take the language of cells from Robert Frost, who, writes Tim Kendall, "thought about walls at the cellular and the bodily level" and protested: "Look! First I want to be a person. And I want you to be a person, and then we can be as interpersonal as you please. We can pull each other's noses—do all sorts of things. But, first of all, you have got to have the personality. First of all, you have got to have the nations and then they can be as international as they please with one another." Frost, like many today, fears a global monoculture, erasing of the lifestyles, and speech sounds, he loves, and somehow (I'm trying to follow his convolutions) the death knell of rational individualism as know it. Consider Brexit, and the idiom of "taking back control" uppermost in voters' minds, as they sought an alternative to what was perceived as the tentacular horror of the European Union—a malevolent kraken of red tape, swallowing and annihilating in its maw a core Englishness, which, however, no one can define. Bishop, on the other hand, suggests, if not an "escape from personality," in T. S. Eliot's phrase, then a willingness to soften one's borders. She has the courage to underline, and not downplay, those moments when it's possible for us to stop being ourselves—and become, perhaps, someone better.

She gives a curious answer to Elizabeth Spires, in the *Paris Review*:

> INTERVIEWER: In your letter to me, you sounded rather wary of interviewers. Do you feel you've been misrepresented in interviews? For example, that your refusal to appear in all-women poetry anthologies has been misunderstood as a kind of disapproval of the feminist movement.
>
> BISHOP: I've always considered myself a strong feminist. Recently I was interviewed by a reporter from the *Chicago Tribune*. After I talked to the girl for a few minutes, I realized that she wanted to play me off as an "old fashioned" against Erica Jong, and Adrienne [Rich], whom I like, and other violently feminist people. Which isn't true at all. I finally asked her if she'd ever read any of my poems. Well, it seemed she'd read one poem. I didn't see how she could interview me if she didn't know anything about me at all, and I told her so. She was nice enough to print a separate piece in the *Chicago Tribune* apart from the longer article on the others. I had said that I didn't believe in propaganda in poetry. That it rarely worked. What she had me saying was "Miss Bishop does not believe that poetry should convey the poet's personal philosophy." Which made me sound like a complete dumbbell! Where she got that, I don't know. This is why one gets nervous about interviews.

Bishop won't appear in "all-women poetry anthologies" because she refuses to be placed in a box. She's talking about coteries, and the binary rivalries necessary to literary histories and (some) journalists. And she's also talking about talking.

The shift from "I" to "one"—"this is why one gets nervous about interviews"—is defensive. "Nervous" takes me to a lovely metaphor from a neglected poem (one of my favorites; I never got to discuss it in my book on her), "Quai d'Orléans." It's a poem I admire for its failure to cohere; for its ending, which seems to me unduly enigmatic, forming as it does an imagined speech act within a poem removed from such unfettered communication, between friend and injured friend, as no longer seems possible:

Each barge on the river easily tows
   a mighty wake,
a giant oak-leaf of gray lights
   on duller gray;
and behind it real leaves are floating by,
   down to the sea.
Mercury-veins on the giant leaves,
   the ripples, make
for the sides of the quai, to extinguish themselves
   against the walls
as softly as falling-stars come to their ends
   at a point in the sky.
And throngs of small leaves, real leaves, trailing them,
   go drifting by
to disappear as modestly, down the sea's
   dissolving halls.
We stand as still as stones to watch
   the leaves and ripples
while light and nervous water hold
   their interview.
"If what we see could forget us half as easily,"
   I want to tell you,
"as it does itself—but for life we'll not be rid
   of the leaves' fossils."

This is from Bishop's first book, *North and South*, published in 1946. It's a poem, as I'll discuss, with a trauma behind it, but also a work whose drift—magnificently if inconsistently managed—concerns the relationship between imagination and reality and, more specifically, subjectivity's debt to the world outside ourselves. The way, that is, that ideas may be given to us, or inflicted upon us rather like events.

Not a great deal has been written on this poem, and the best sustained reading may still be Bonnie Costello's. She suggests that Bishop borrows her Parisian setting from Proust, but to outline a view of memory different from his: no chance epiphanies, but the mind as a "helpless receptacle of memory traces"; speaking of the poem's rhymes, she uses the fine phrase "aesthetic logic," applicable to the delicate sonic patterning with which the poem commences. As often in Bishop, an act of attention develops incrementally, never taking itself for granted, and by means of stepping-stones of sound. "Each," for example, passes on its sound—its moment of confidence—to "easily." If the barge wakes correspond to the lasting memory, in one's life, of a painful event, then the word "easily" raises the question of what, in the poet's mind, isn't easy but hard to process or move beyond.

"Wake" then moves together with "gray," an adjective that repeats like a brushstroke: this is painterly verse, announcing its precision, although Bishop's turning of the verb "alights" into "lights," which briefly reads as a noun, does make for a moment's ambiguity, because that "giant oak-leaf of gray lights" seems to hang together as a unitary impression. We then return to the long *e* sound in "real leaves," and "sea," with the feeling of a tension relaxed, although Bishop will return to this Wordsworthian phrase with another repetition later on: touching the idea nervously, as one tries a bad tooth with one's tongue, over and over. Or—revisiting the idea of the painterly poem—one could find in it a sympathetic feeling for what it might be like for an artist, to depict the scene on canvas, but hesitantly, following an injury; as if to paint the "Quai d'Orléans" meant learning how to paint all over again.

I allude to an event the poem tries to process—not to depict it gruesomely, as a confessional poem would, but to, I think, work through in the manner of dreamwork. Bishop visited France as a student in the thirties and was involved in a car accident in 1937. Her friend Louise Crane was driving, and they were forced off the road—Margaret Miller's right arm was severed. It was a cruel injury, because Miller was a painter, who'd now have to learn to work left-handed. Bishop's poem is dedicated to Miller—Bishop's dedications to her poems are important—and it describes the view from the apartment where they stayed after leaving the hospital. Dismemberment is intimated by the "fossils," and the walls against which the ripples extinguish themselves "as softly as falling-stars come to an end / at a point in the sky"; that mathematically exact "point" suggests a harsher severance than the surrounding imagery is willing to evoke. The broken look of those short lines, compared with the long, also does this, and I think that the way the lines come through fairly forcibly, before being softened by enjambment, initiates its own quiet drama.

To explain what I mean by this—if we look at the next section of the poem:

Mercury-veins on the giant leaves,
    the ripples, make
for the sides of the quai, to extinguish themselves
    against the walls
as softly as falling-stars come to their ends
    at a point in the sky.

The line division on "make" suggests the argument we see often in Bishop's poetry, that the poet isn't conferring a design on her surroundings, but that nature—in this case, an urban space, with water in it—is already shaping itself into art, really "making" something of itself. It also initiates a series of lines ending firmly, possessing a clear sonic outline for the micro-instant prior to their being regathered gently into the movement of a single sentence. The ripples "extinguish themselves"—"against the walls"; "falling-stars come to their ends"—"at a point in the sky." In both cases, the detail arriving with the next line tempers the initial blow. A violence is recognized and softened.

Bishop's water patterns may draw on the experience of skin-grafting Miller underwent, as described in a letter to Marianne Moore: "they take specks, a little larger than a pinhead, from the thigh, and transplant them and after a while they begin to grow and spread together." Bishop writes, hopefully, that her friend is beginning to draw with her left hand: "the lines were perfectly clear and firm. So we are not worrying so much about whether what resides in the right hand is in the left too, or not." That process of dermatological accumulation, and the cheeringly distinct pencil lines, are present within the poem. We wish on falling stars, and I wonder if it's too fanciful to hear "wish" in the sound of "extinguish"—the speaker hesitates to give wholly her yearning for her depressed friend's recuperation and a new closeness between them.

I mentioned the confusions of the poem's ending, and, knowing about the car accident, it is possible to resolve the uncertainty of the verse into a sort of apology to Miller, for Bishop's own role in the accident. But I wonder—we've a new biography of Bishop, from Tom Travisano, and a new cache of her letters to her psychoanalyst, which has renewed the biographical approach to her work—if it's really the role of the critic to, with information from the poet's life, explain away torsions in the verse. David Kalstone, for instance, writes that the poem "is colored by all the losses the accident entailed and recalled, though none of them is specifically its subject: her friend's mutilation; her own childhood losses; the loss of self-control and surge of vulnerability." This packages things too neatly. The poem ends:

> We stand as still as stones to watch
>   the leaves and ripples
> while light and nervous water hold
>   their interview.
> "If what we see could forget us half as easily,"
>   I want to tell you,
> "as it does itself—but for life we'll not be rid
>   of the leaves' fossils."

The river imagery prefigures the late poem "Santarém"; "Quai d'Orléans," too, balances the poet's desire to submerge human awkwardnesses within a description of flowing water ("our knowledge," to quote the famous lines from "At the Fishhouses," is "historical, flowing and flown") against an impediment that won't allow the substitution. Frank Bidart thought Bishop was in love with Miller, though she knew her feelings could never be reciprocated by a heterosexual woman.

So we can keep redescribing the gnomic material at the poem's end in terms of the biography overdetermining it or go on—with the, to me, more interesting idea—that we have here an example of Bishop writing at her best and then falling away from that achievement. The description is marvellously sensitive: the speech act fails, both in itself and as an ending to the poem. Unsure of the poem's structure, Bishop tries to bring it full circle, with an obviously coordinating element: the word "easily," encountered already at the start. But the poem ends with those "fossils," acknowledging a resistance to its attempt at closure—"fossils" rhymes only very mildly with "ripples" several lines earlier.

What I find here is a movement away from a common language toward a privacy that refuses to be shared: in this way, a poem that seems horribly personal can also be read as a political poem. Bishop begins by rejuvenating a cliché, about standing "as still as a stone," and ends with a sentence hard to understand. To repurpose an idiom in verse is to situate herself, and Miller, safely within an interpretative community, in which all speak the same language. And it's out of this trope that she develops the wonderful metaphor—"light and nervous water hold / their interview"—where a conversation between two people (Bishop and Miller) is displaced onto the environment. I say Bishop and Miller, but the interviews pressed on the women after the event by the patronizing French police may also be relevant:

> The driver who had forced them off the road returned and drove Miller, accompanied by Crane, to a doctor in the nearest town, five miles away. Bishop waited at the car, where she was pestered by questions from passersby, among them a priest who said the accident had occurred because there had not been a man driving. When she arrived in town, Bishop found the medical techniques antiquated and the police's insistence on interviews ghoulish.

Bishop's metaphor of the light and water holding their "interview" reimagines the painfully pointless interactions surrounding the event. We then move toward language at the opposite extreme to a cliché: a verbal pileup whose gist we ascertain but cannot be transparently parsed. Even the statement the speaker will not bring herself to utter protects itself against understanding.

We have here an isolated speaker—Bishop, feeling separated from her friend by an unshareable trauma—and also a reworking of her notebooks, where she describes the other separation, of Miller's arm from her body, surrealistically:

> The arm lay outstretched in the soft brown grass at the side of the road and spoke quietly to itself. At first all it could think of was the possibility of being quickly reunited to its body, without any more time elapsing than was absolutely necessary.
> "Oh, my poor body! Oh my poor body! I cannot bear to give you up. Quick! Quick!"
> Then it fell silent while a series of ideas that had never occurred to it before swept rapidly over it.

"Alongside this passage," observes Alice Quinn, "running vertically up the notebook page, Bishop adds, 'So this is what it means to be really 'alone in the world!'" The experience of isolation, of being left behind, that Bishop ascribes to the severed arm, may draw on her own experience of waiting by the ruined car while her friends went to the hospital. There is in this case no "interview," such as light and water tenuously achieve within "Quai d'Orléans," or comparable to the literal "interview," with the *Paris Review*, where Bishop sought to describe her failure, elsewhere, to describe herself adequately to other people, to be recognized by them as the sort of the person and poet she considered herself to be.

I wonder if the poem, and the notebook passage, have something to say to us about pain and appropriation. Let's imagine a conversation between Miller and Bishop, where (in the place of the compromised speech act in the poem) she were to say to her friend: "I understand how you must be feeling." (In England, there exists the milder phrase, "I can imagine," perhaps due a renaissance, although its evolution toward "I can't imagine" tells us something about our changing culture.) Miller might then respond, refusing the gesture: "You can't understand! You've still got your arm!" It is this refusal or rejection, I'd suggest, that the end of "Quai d'Orléans" reverses away from into what is for Bishop an unusual opacity.

The question of the shareability of experience is a part of all our lives, though it has a special political value today, connected with the impulse to identify with particular groups and particular experiences. Marilyn Lombardi writes, of the notebook passage, that "Bishop clearly identifies with the lonely arm—the analytic arm of the artist detached from the woman and from the sensual memories that a woman's form retains." Certainly, to recover the gender of the body enriches the notebook passage, suggesting a parallel between the body and its severed arm (longing to return to it) and a mother and her child. And the marginalia, about being completely alone, also suggests such an identification with the arm. But this would be self-pitying, wouldn't it? And Bishop, unlike her version of Robinson Crusoe, in "Crusoe in England," tries to refuse self-pity at every turn. She tries, as Travisano wrote marvelously in his previous study of her work, to take self-pity and turn it, from line to line of different poems, into something else. I'm not sure that, reintroducing biography into the poems to explain them (and turning Bishop into the sort of confessional poet she, if said poet wasn't named Robert Lowell, loathed), we're in the right.

The poet abroad is aware of projecting her emotions onto the Parisian urban landscape, but suggests she only recognizes her own feelings by looking closely at the place that is—though she won't say it outright—in some way to blame. Lombardi thinks the arm "analytic" because it gives up on the reconnection it initially desires, stops talking, and instead begins to think. But it remains passive, with the experience of thinking described as an onslaught: "Then it fell silent while a series of ideas that had never occurred to it before swept rapidly over it." The repeating word "it" jars—the arm isn't a person, a woman, but an object—and the "series of ideas" sweeps rapidly over the arm like a sequence of feelings, rather than thoughts. The verb "occurred" is important: "that had never occurred to it before." Ideas occur to us, but so do events; if we replace "occurred" with "happened," this becomes clearer. Perhaps an idea can happen to us, with the force—almost—of a car accident; just as we can be alienated from those close to us by the events in our lives, we can also be separated from them by the thoughts, opinions, ideas speaking themselves through us.

In Ralph Waldo Emerson's famous essay, which Bishop would certainly have read, he describes "The Poet" thus:

> By virtue of this science the poet is the Namer, or Language-maker, naming things sometimes after their appearance, sometimes after their essence, and giving to every one its own name and not another's, thereby rejoicing the intellect, which delights in detachment or boundary. The poets made all the words, and therefore language is the archives of history, and, if we must say it, a sort of tomb of the muses. For, though the origin of most of our words is forgotten, each word was at first a stroke of genius. . . . Language is fossil poetry. As the limestone of the continent consists of infinite masses of the shells of animalcules, so language is made up of images, or tropes, which now, in their secondary use, have long ceased to remind us of their poetic origin. But the poet names the thing because he sees it, or comes one step nearer to it than any other. This expression, or naming, is not art, but a second nature, grown out of the first, as a leaf out of a tree. What we call nature, is a certain self-regulated motion, or change; and nature does all things by her own hands, and does not leave another to baptise her, but baptises herself; and this through the metamorphosis again.

"Quai d'Orléans" is many things. It's one of Bishop's marvelous feats of description (of Paris); it is a verbal event, enriched and estranged by diverse feelings; and I wonder if it is, also, an intricate reading, in verse, of this passage from Emerson, using as a springboard his aphorism, "Language is fossil poetry." This could be the source of Bishop's "fossils," and the feeling, in the poem, that we are both part of, and separate from, processes of nature resembling fate. I've examined the water in the poem as expressive of "motion, or change," as the "archive" of a more than personal history, and as a querying of other forms of horrendously anatomical "detachment or boundary." We might call Emerson's passage one source for Bishop's poem, as the car accident and Miller's injury is another source. But Bishop's poem, like Emerson's poem, if you like, in prose, on the subject of nature, also questions what is meant by a source, or, as he has it, an "origin." Her verse is not symptomatic and refuses to be simply and healingly elucidated in terms of an event prior to its creation.

Phobic of collision, "light and nervous water hold / their interview"—they make contact, as that ruptured arm and body can't. A delicate image: the light and water appear like two people who can hardly hold each other's gaze. Neither dominates the other. "Nervous" brings empathy, the physical registering of pain, into the poem, as well as an anxiety about (social) disconnection. "Quai d'Orléans" circles around a trauma that can't be articulated explicitly because Bishop doesn't want to take ownership of her friend's pain. What can be shared by two people or even by different parts of the same person? "So we are not worrying so much about whether what resides in the right hand is in the left too, or not": she finds a language for the divisions between ourselves and others and also between ourselves and ourselves. The quest for definition that must be ever renewed—it's like writing on water—and out of which opinions, and political stances, evolve.

Ted Hughes, Keith Sagar, and the Poetics of Letter Prose

Ted Hughes's correspondence, like his verse—and the criticism he said it physically injured him to write—has a desperate, lunging quality. In his poems, he tries to codify this movement as a decisive violence: his "Thrushes" famously "with a start, a bounce, a stab / Overtake the instant and drag out some writhing thing." But this is (I'm using one of his favourite words in a way Hughes wouldn't like, as a personal, noncosmic term) a *myth*: a story he liked to tell about himself, his poetry, and the world it refers to. Really, that lunge is self-exposing. As if Whitman's "barbaric yawp" weren't affirmation but an uncontainable cry for help.

It's about communication—a gauche lurch toward another person whose rejection Hughes can't bear but feels the need to confront or even provoke. As he lamented in 1989, "audience—one's idea of audience—is the great problem": a concern repeating throughout his correspondence, a genre of writing necessarily prioritizing interpersonal dilemmas. There's a touching instance in Christopher Reid's Faber selection, where Hughes writes to Philip Larkin, dying of cancer of the esophagus, recommending the faith healer Ted Cornish. He knows Larkin will think this nonsense—just as he must have foreseen, before unleashing on the world his bizarre book on *Shakespeare and the Goddess of Complete Being*, something of the reception it would receive. Still, he sends the letter. "Please don't write back," he tells Larkin, "or mention this again—no point. But the impulse to tell you all this has been recurring more and more strongly. I just wanted you to become aware somehow or other that this fellow exists." It is a generous message, but not without, I feel, a particle in it of hurt selfhood. "This fellow" isn't just Ted C but Ted H too.

On the back of this new selection of letters stands a windswept man with a bleak, blurred tree behind him and a dog on a leash by his side. He has his hands in his pockets, a grimace on his face, and the loose hair about his forehead and above his ear looks like smoke. You might think on first glance it's Ted Hughes, but it's not. It's Keith Sagar, Hughes's most devoted critic and the editor of this volume as well as author of half its letters. Sagar, himself a poet, prints his own correspondence in a smaller font. He also reveals on the first page that Faber rejected his proposal for this book in 2009, commencing a series of revelations about his struggles with the world of academic publishing. A footnote on page 4 informs us that Cambridge University Press rejected his proposal for a third edition of *The Art of Ted Hughes*; Christopher Reid, we're told, rejected an early draft of *The Laughter of Foxes*, another study of Hughes, as "disconcertingly ventriloquial." Of *Literature and the Crime Against Nature*: "rejections from publishers mounted up in the early 1990s. When the number reached seventy-two, I gave up.... It remained unpublished until 2005."

There's an Alan Partridgesque quality to Sagar's footnotes (Seamus Perry, reviewing this same book for the *LRB*, mentioned Charles Pooter): "I was not even short-listed for the Warwick chair; a relief, since I had really no desire to leave house, area or job"; "In fact the insurance paid for a much better trailer-tent, which Melissa and I are still using." But I do sympathize with Sagar's rejections—in fact, I wrote this essay at a stage in my career when I identified with him intensely—since academics tend not to mention their failures of this kind, or do so only in an affectless, self-deprecating way. (I must also mention one more letter Sagar sent—to me, responding to this review nobly and with gratitude. He died in 2013.)

Sagar won't have any of that distance between his life and writing. His sense of Hughes's absolute importance to a spiritually and ecologically benighted world means that the critic's becomes a sacred duty. In the face of seventy-plus rejections, he sticks to his guns: more sure, perhaps, the more resistance he has to face. In this Sagar comes to resemble Hughes himself, and indeed one of the functions of their correspondence—and its weirdly evolving power dynamic—was the mutual confirmation of both parties in their sense of themselves as outsiders. Here is Hughes in December 1993, lamenting his status, or lack thereof, in the United States:

> The general opposition to me personally in the U.S. (Feminism in College & University English Faculty Committees—& in Libraries & Bookshops) has really made me, quite spontaneously, begin to delete the U.S. from all my reckonings. The males who might support don't

seem to raise their voices. Maybe what I write is simply of no interest to them. The damage has been done. That's my impression. I can't go lecturing/reading, to raise my stakes—because I meet crazies. So.

Spontaneous is a key word for Hughes, as it was for his hero D. H. Lawrence (Sagar wrote books on him too), and also for the Cambridge don F. R. Leavis, whose influence on Hughes—obscured by Hughes's myth of himself as a rebel at university—is now better understood. But here Hughes doesn't seem to understand what spontaneous means (this typifies writers obsessed with that word and concept: it flits restlessly through their sentences and can't be pinned down). To act spontaneously means of one's own accord without external compulsion. Hughes's letter denies his dependence on, his need to connect with, other people: the individuals that make up the poet's audience.

Hughes's neglect in the U.S. is the result of many things, including his destructive relationship with Sylvia Plath. Although Sagar and Hughes were at Cambridge at the same time, they didn't meet then, and their correspondence begins in 1969, six years after Plath's suicide. Also, Sagar didn't learn till years later that Hughes must have received his first letter "on the day before the death of his partner Assia and their daughter Shura." We encounter in this book an embattled and obliquely grieving Hughes. It's clear he suffered terribly, also that his experiences confirmed in him foolish beliefs. (What a parenthesis that is, summarizing the opposing ranks in a single waspish blurt—a single gender!) His sentences suggest a done deal, as if he has washed his hands of the matter. But also a reactive hypersensitivity, because he clearly hasn't.

Hughes deserves a better reputation in the U.S.—and worldwide— because, for all his personal and aesthetic faults (I don't mean to say these are one and the same thing, only that, as he didn't treat people, especially women, well, he also wrote a number of duff melodramatic poems) he remains a great, diction-inaugurating poet (the work of Seamus Heaney, who *is* a favorite in the States, simply isn't possible without Hughes) whose susceptibility is part, even if he denies it, of his power, a way we can relate to him. Poetic reputations are forged through critical discussion, about which both Hughes and Sagar had mixed feelings. Of Faber's aforementioned rejection of *The Laughter of Foxes*, Sagar retorts that "Ted had better things to do than spend his time putting words into my mouth.... I am content to disconcert those readers who are hoping for sterile theory and judgemental confrontation." What disconcerts me is such for-us-or-against-usness. As Hughes writes on March 9, 1984:

> You & I read an author by his best—or even by what we feel of his own inner idea of what he's after. But most readers are much more pragmatic. We read with idealistic good-will. Most readers read with actual ill-will. As Pascal says, at bottom most people hate everybody else. You & I, simple honest Northerners, (as distinct from bilious, rancourous [sic], envious, crooked ones) still think we should love one another, & operate on an instinctive expectation of good-will & affection, an assumption that in our foibles we'll always be given the benefit of the doubt—as we give others. Well, it's not so, is it.

The lovely warm sentence about Northerners (I am one) shows Hughes refusing to take himself seriously (I like this side of him very much). His letters remind me of a passage on Shakespeare where he remarks that dramatist's magnanimity, his giving of everything in himself with a maximum of emotional outlay and verbal inventiveness, regardless of the commission or occasion, or indeed the ability of his audience to understand him. Hughes writes this way, and it can seem either a helpless onrush of self-exposures or a moral choice he has made. Yet this passage also reveals the limitations of his polarizing imagination determined to divide readers up into those of "good-will" and "ill-will," another disappointingly black-and-white formulation. In his introduction, Sagar writes of Hughes continually seeking "good readers—readers who could be trusted to approach his work, or any work, in the right spirit"; he quotes Hughes asking for *Crow* to be read with "creative as well as sympathetic imagination, not just critical attention," and for readers of his essay on "Shakespeare and Occult Neoplatonism" to approach it "with the cooperative, imaginative attitude of a co-author."

I'm reminded of psychics who, when they're exposed as frauds by James Randi or another debunker, claim it isn't their fault but the result of negative energy in the room. Hughes is at war with that hard, unavoidable moment when, having moved toward someone else, the poet, like the letter writer, simply must accept the risk of being found boring or hostile. Rejecting the ideal of disinterested aesthetic judgment, he longs for a more organic community in which communication could rely (as in the poems of Mir Taqi Mir) on a repertoire of shared attitudes. You could say, and Hughes comes close to saying it, that in such a situation communication as such would disappear, because we'd already think and feel the same things. Sagar quotes from Hughes's essay, "Myths, Metres, Rhythms," his remark that when "the shared group understanding of all members is complete then a mere touching of the tokens of their mythology is enough for complete communication." Importing this into modern society, however, brings us to what the Romantic essayist William Hazlitt identifies as the "commonplace," which "operates mechanically, and opens an instantaneous and infallible communication between the hearer and speaker. A set of cant-phrases, arranged in sounding sentences, and pronounced 'with good emphasis and discretion,' keep the gross and irritable humours of an audience in constant fermentation; and levy no tax on the understanding." Hughes tells Sagar that "traditions—like Auden's—aren't changed by argument, only by death of skulls and brains. Argument changes the children, I suppose, who eavesdrop." So critical discussion becomes pointless. In a queasy letter of September 1, 1990, he defends the "tragic equation" he finds throughout Shakespeare's work and about which Sagar—among many others remains skeptical. The important thing, insists Hughes, is that Hamlet

> rejects his mother, does not murder her, & yet she dies, gulping poison (as Ophelia gulped water). As a tabloid journalist would see quite clearly—Hamlet murdered both of them. His Tarquinian madness was the direct cause of their deaths.
> In the same way, the tragic equation's requirement imposes the pattern on Goneril, Regan & Cordelia. On the mythic plane, which that tabloid journalist would recognise, Lear in his madness against them killed all three. Somehow. Exactly how does not matter—to the equation.

What disturbs isn't only the alignment of mythic understanding with tabloid sensationalism, but also the disavowal of what "matters" to Sagar. With that trademark dash—Hughes told Reid he wished he could write entire chapters as "one sentence—phrases linked by dashes"—he turns away from the reader, closing down discussion. The tragic equation sounds suddenly like Richard Dawkins's selfish gene, a self-reproducing entity of unstoppable fervor: becoming its prophet, Hughes makes himself invincible, because everything everyone else cares about seems but a limited glimpse of the underlying reality that he alone has the cognitive wherewithal to process.

Sagar's problems with *Shakespeare and the Goddess of Complete Being*, as well as the laureate poems, reveal a different understanding of the critical act. He believes a good critic should be on sympathetic terms with his author, but that this doesn't preclude disagreement. Reading these letters, we see him moving sometimes closer to Hughes, sometimes further away, as if trying to work out the correct distance between poet and critic. Traveling in Italy in 1978, he writes a short story called "The Beast" and then returns to find "uncanny resemblances" between it and Hughes's "The Head," just published. Juxtaposing their psychological coincidence with the geographical distance between them, Sagar remarks to Hughes, of "The Head": "Who beamed a preview of it across Europe?" Hughes responds by not only complimenting but also analyzing Sagar's writing, positively but appropriatively: "The beast is, I imagine, among other things, your original being in all its undeveloped aspects." Meanwhile, Sagar appends a footnote saying that he "had not interpreted it at all. . . . Had I done so, my interpretation would have borne no resemblance to Ted's, which is not to say that I rejected his." It's a curious role reversal: putting aside verse and coming together as storywriters allows Hughes to act the critic for once, and Sagar the creative artist. The footnote reinstates, as we watch, the distance between them this exchange of letters seems, back in 1978, briefly to have collapsed.

Hughes's rejection of academic prose is well known. In a letter of July 16, 1979, he writes of going at Cambridge, "through some kind of crise. The problems attached themselves to the writing of the weekly essay." Again, the problem is with critical distance. He can't write on those he doesn't side with: "I remember writing fluently about Blake," he says, and that night was writing "an essay about Samuel Johnson (a personality I greatly liked)," when

> I dreamed I was still sitting at my essay, in my usual agonising frame of mind, trying to get one word to follow another. The door opened & a creature came in, with a fox's head, & a long skinny fox's body. . . . He came across, & set his hand on the page & said "Stop this. You are destroying us."
>
> . . .
>
> I connected the fox's command to my own ideas about Eng. Lit., & the effect of the Cambridge blend of pseudo-critical terminology &

social rancour on creative spirit, & from that moment abandoned my efforts to adapt myself.

Rereading this letter—previously cited by Sagar in *The Laughter of Foxes* and included in Reid's selection—I wonder if Hughes actually suffered from an excess of critical sensibility, not a lack thereof. Literary criticism is, after all, not only about the "Leavis-style dismantling of texts" he repudiated but also the drawing of such imaginative "connections" as he does here. Hughes interpreted his dream, rather as one might interpret a novel or poem, to suit his needs: "I connected the fox's command to my own ideas." Postulating the fox as a spirit-messenger meant picturing the kind of encounter with an alternative intellect that, in other contexts, he was prone to shirk. (Hughes's repeated misspellings of people's names in his correspondence—an infuriating tic—also demonstrates a wilful solipsism passing itself off as a helplessness of rapid composition.)

In an important letter of April 11, 1981, Hughes connects the aggressive style of his verse with his intellectual proclivities:

> Odd feeling re-reading such things as Brother's Dream etc—I see what it is about much of my writing that repels people—again & again I seem to be starting some sort of fight for life that admits only rough & ready counters of language—a sort of makeshift language . . .
>
> The ugliness in all that, for me & I suppose for others, is that it is a fight—and not a talk, or a marriage, or an agape, or a sweet friendship, or a debate.

Few could so acutely describe their own style. Hughes loves, in his letters, to interpret his own poems, and it seems to me the meanings he comes up with weren't necessarily there in the first place—this may instead be happening as he writes the letter without his realizing. Because, like his dream, the poems were his to begin with, there is no critical distance to cross. It's a way of writing literary criticism without intersubjective risk; of talking about oneself, but as a mainspring of mystery of whose motivations one can't be sure.

The letter continues, intriguingly, by comparing his critical prose, which "somehow expresses very little of what I want to say," with his father's letters:

there was something about them so vehement, so much in over-drive, that I often couldn't read them. (He was mostly a very silent man.) Is it possible to inherit a brain-rhythm? Very curious—in a biological way, to see it in myself so clearly, really as plain as a colour in a calf. The rest of me observes it with some dismay.

When I see it in such things as my exegesis of Orghast—in Anthony Smith's book—I feel slightly horrified—I see what barren wastes of intellectualism—in the worst sense—lie in wait if I let that monster fly off with me. What a fury of ingenuities! The real relieving thing comes from elsewhere if it comes at all.

As Hughes writes in "Thistles," "sons appear, / Stiff with weapons, fighting back over the same ground." What this letter misses out, or steps around, is the trauma of his father's experiences in World War I. "The fight for life" Hughes identifies in his own style may, suggests Tim Kendall, represent a displacement of "wartime brutality from its specific historical contexts." Hughes says he couldn't read his father's letters because, as with his own poems, they possessed an intensity not geared toward, in fact at odds with, communication—sound and fury signifying nothing. (Given Hughes's immersion in Shakespeare, the assonantal phrase "fury of ingenuities" seems to remember that passage from *Macbeth*.) He writes here a bit like a critic, and indeed pseudoscience is a way of continuing to opinionate discursively while purporting to address deeper than literary facts.

Orghast, a play he wrote with Peter Brook, featured an artificial language of the same name designed for physical, visceral communication; so the second paragraph gives a glimpse of Hughes's fears. "The real relieving thing" appears to be free, sensuous, unencumbered perception; he fears his critical prose expresses only a private neurosis. This explains the frenzy in which he claims, in *Shakespeare and the Goddess of Complete Being*, that the most canonical writer of all could, by expressing *his* own dilemmas, also give voice to an English culture torn between Catholicism and Protestantism: the idea of the individual creative consciousness as a microcosm of the national imagination is absolutely central for Hughes, and reemerges in the notes to his laureate poems. In that book on Shakespeare, the unachieved meeting with the reader is supplanted by a "fury" of esoteric linkages that never quite seem to satisfy the need for a real, lasting connection. When Hughes discusses it with Sagar, his correspondence takes on the "over-drive" quality he lamented in his father's. It sounds, that is, like the book itself, begun as a series of letters to the director Donya Feuer; Hughes's study, like his correspondence, manifests a kind of fevered improvisation whose extempore quality is both a way of excusing its incoherence and of insisting on its access to primal truths.

Given its reduced scope, it's unsurprising that Sagar's collection of letters doesn't contain as many singing passages as Reid's, although there remain instances of Hughes's life-givingly undisciplined prose style (I'm trying to describe it—his salmon fishing draws me also to the adjective *upriver*: there's an always upriver—striving, that is, oppositional if not confrontational—gusto to his sentences). On March 31, 1976, he thanks Sagar for his book on *The Love of Tropical Fish* and composes a paean to the Australian outback, unavailable in the Faber selection of his letters:

> Thank you for the book—a lovely generous gift. The Australian book is spectacular, some of the best impressions of the place I've seen. My 5 days, or 6, in that country was one of the best jaunts I've ever had. I saw very little of the land. Just the primaeval scrub of Ti trees between the bijou bungalows on the promontory south of Melbourne. Then on my last day I visited a farm—an 18c Manor farm—70 miles or so outside Adelaide. I got a taste of it there. The whole place hit me very hard & deep. The most peculiar thing is the light—a glare even when there's cloud. It casts a weird disastrous starkness over everything—like a primitive painting. A dream brilliance & strangeness. Everything stands or moves in some eerie significance—rather sinister & very beautiful. I couldn't get over it. And I couldn't quite locate exactly what created the impression—except the light. The second great wonderful surprise is the birds. Every bird behaves at least as queerly as our cuckoos. And they have a class of cries utterly different & unique—imagine the calls of lizards & prehistoric freaks. Cries completely unmodified by the revisions & bird-masterpieces of the last 50 million years. And behaviour to go with the cries.

Like D.H. Lawrence, Hughes is a white Englishman traveling the world in search of "primitive" landscapes releasing him from the moribund preoccupations of his own heritage. It's important to realize that these writers often practice, like Gauguin in Tahiti, a sort of aesthetic colonialism: they find in foreign places the values they themselves have put there. One doesn't, or shouldn't, go to Lawrence or Hughes to discover what these places are really like, although their more factual descriptions of flora and fauna can be some of their best writing (as Gāmini Salgādo observes, it's "characteristic of Lawrence"—and, I'd add, Hughes too—"that even his most portentous writing is veined with a fine literalism of fact—little ants are liable to run through even his most gigantic metaphors.")

Here are many instances of Hughes's dash, identified by Reid as "part of his characteristic sentence music." (Sagar, unlike Reid, puts a space either side of each em dash that highlights them further.) The first sentence sets up the device as it thanks his friend for the gift of his book. What follows is the sensitive poet-correspondent's "gift," in return, of his own "impressions," a transaction one often finds in literary correspondences; in, for instance, the letters shared between Elizabeth Bishop and Marianne Moore. Each clause excitedly appended with a dash to the end of its sentence is another spoken exclamation, an exhilarated pointing-out reaching toward the reader. Which means Sagar, because this letter couldn't have been written to anybody except him. This is true of all correspondence, but the evolution of Hughes's style out of that grateful first sentence confirms it and makes all this rather tender. Another gift Sagar has given him seems to have been the energy to write this way, recapturing and perhaps even reexperiencing bygone events. (Reid's selection includes another letter, written the same day to Richard Murphy and reusing the same imagery; I suspect Sagar's letter was Hughes's true inspiration.) The language is playful—"one of the best jaunts I've ever had"—as Hughes enjoys his alliteration, bundling those "Ti trees" with the "bijou bungalows." Then, characteristically, there's the quest for the absolute: "I got a taste of it there." "Taste" echoes "Adelaide," so we hear him discovering the word, before "it" gets dropped into the main word in the next sentence, with a sense of impact: "The whole place *hit* me very hard & deep."

Hughes clarifies: it's "the light" he's concerned with (a transient perception, rather than a discovered Australian essence), and which the dashed-off clauses explicate, time and again, trying to reproduce the experience for Sagar or to evince, like one type of excited, participatory criticism, a vividness cognate with the work under analysis. The assonance linking through *casts-disastrous-starkness* tries to communicate through embodiment a quality unavailable to straightforward reportage. This makes Hughes's letter a kind of primitive painting. It doesn't follow the literary equivalent of the rules of perspective. It isn't a poem or prose designed for a wider audience. But it still has a sense of itself as something shaped and of "eerie significance." Hughes's prose has an improvised quality preventing its rush of sibilance from sounding too staged or purple. The *o* connecting "over" and "locate" lets us hear, in the first of two thrown-off "and" sentences, the sound of him thinking: "And I couldn't quite *locate* exactly what created the impression—except the light." This is convincingly humble: he isn't Hughesplaining Australia to us. When he returns to the "light," repeating himself, there's a necessary roughness—he hasn't finalized the perception. But it's also a kind of rhyme.

"Every bird behaves at least as queerly as our cuckoos." Australia's strangeness reminds him of home. "Queerly" reaches back to "eerie" and alliterates or assonates with many words to follow. Birdsong is traditionally linked with poetry, and Hughes is thinking about the relationship between spontaneous utterance and literary composition when he contrasts these ancient bird cries with "the *revisions & bird-masterpieces* of the last 50 million years." This description of natural selection in literary terms reveals his fusion, again, of multiple discursive registers. He identifies with, I suspect, the single-mindedness of those birds who have refused to change or haven't had to. Rather like the poet deleting "the U.S. from all my reckonings," or refusing to "adapt" himself to the milieu of Cambridge English, they fly their own course.

That such letter prose is marvellously pitched at its reader reminds us that Hughes's relationship to his audience wasn't always agonized. His most anthologized poems are so for a reason. They make immediate sense and possess an attractive vitality just this side of rawness. Yet as his career progressed he was driven, for reasons we can understand and some we can't, to write an uglier, more menacing, abrasively ornery, style: a paradoxical fusion of exhibitionism and concealment. His final collection, *Birthday Letters*, isn't only an attempt to set the record straight about Sylvia Plath but the culmination of this drive, related to his griefs and grievances but also to other more abiding vectors within his personality.

Sagar includes a letter of 1974 from Olwyn Hughes, commenting on the first typescript of *The Art of Ted Hughes* in her capacity as her brother's agent. So it's the poet's sister trying to pass on, formally, the poet's opinions to his friend who has also written a monograph about him; the tone is wonky to say the least, as the distance between Hughes and Sagar is renegotiated by a third party. She discusses "Dawn's Rose," which Hughes apparently composed "deliberately as an imagistic poem in the style which—in all the rest of CROW—he was trying to get past. DAWN'S ROSE is in contemporary 'poetic language'—our present version. He intended to write a few, because he thought if he didn't, he would lose touch with some readers altogether. It's dismaying to see it repeatedly chosen as the best piece in the book. Though he likes it too." As Reid said in his editorial refusal of *The Laughter of Foxes*, such writing is "disconcertingly ventriloquial"—we hear Hughes speaking through his sister, particularly in that last turn. It makes me wonder if mainstream success arrived too quickly for his dissenting temperament and if much of the travail recorded in his letters relates to his consequent need to reposition himself.

Hughes's debut, *The Hawk in the Rain*, was published simultaneously on both sides of the Atlantic as early as 1957, after it won the New York Poetry Center First Publication Award judged by Stephen Spender, W. H. Auden, and Marianne Moore. With Sylvia Plath sending off his poems for him to magazines, he bestrode the hills, carrying himself like one of those prehistoric birds, unbesmirched by the realities of literary career-making—unselfconsciously (or so he liked to believe) himself. He then found (it's a common fantasy) that having imposed his terms on the world, it had accepted him anyway. He seems to have reacted to his ascendancy with eventual suspicion—perhaps he didn't want to meet his readership so soon, so smoothly. The encounter had to be rougher than that; something of, as he puts it, a "fight," such as would augment his sense of himself. We are left with poems and prose and letters disfigured and transfigured by this suspicion of his own charisma, of the eloquence immediately attractive to such distinguished judges and eventually to a broader public few modern poets reach. As he wrote to Daniel Weissbort in 1969, "I've been trying to write verse in completely the wrong way for some years. I've been excluding the real thing. I institutionalised the mode of one or two successes in 1962—and got stuck on the board of management." Despite Hughes's love of the primitive and spontaneous, his work is shaped by a fundamental unease, as well as a corrosive fascination, with what came, or seemed to, *naturally* to him. In one sense he is the archetype of the cis-het Major (that is, self-mythologizing) White Male Poet, as bemused by his privileges as by the doors beginning to close in his face.

Rae Armantrout's Lonely Dream

"It is easier to think," wrote Keats to John Taylor, "what Poetry should be than to write it—and this leads me on to another axiom. That if Poetry comes not as naturally as the Leaves to a tree it had better not come at all." Bouncing ludically onward, Keats is, in his correspondence, at once the Romantic genius parading his licensed idiosyncrasies and the "camelion Poet" with no identity at all. This famous letter presents us with the drama of consciousness. Reading it, one agrees with Rae Armantrout in her interview with *Prac Crit*: "objections could be raised to a human consciousness being a unified thing. The present is something that the mind does. They say the subjective present is about three seconds long." In comparison, Keats's hotly provisional axiom has turned to marble, his moment of excited phrase making will last forever. And it hasn't palled, at least with me, for though we've learned cautiousness as to what appears to come "naturally" (especially while reading Armantrout; she makes you contemplate even the back of your hand with bedazzled skepticism), Keats never says that leaves arrive all at once or without a fight.

Nothing is natural in the work of Rae Armantrout. Our words, gestures, and relationships are conventional, scripted, deformed—or outright produced—by, as she has it, "the interventions of capitalism into consciousness." On the subject of "nature," I notice plenty of leaves, and leaf shadows, and leaf reflections (in both senses of the word) in her poems—but her plants are urban, compromised, possibly parodying of Keats:

> Evenly hovering attention:
> pocked concrete.

> Long tangles of gray-
> green eucalyptus leaves
>
> twizzle,
> throwing sharp shadows.
>
> If I could just signal
> so variously.
> — FROM "TWIZZLE"

Armantrout's short lines, and short stanzas, inhabit that "subjective present" she mentions. Her style observes, engages with, and would redeem our attention deficits. Championing the experimental verse of Lyn Hejinian and Lorine Niedecker, she insists that "clarity need not be equivalent to readability. How readable is the world? There is another kind of clarity that doesn't have to do with control but with attention, one in which the sensorium of the world can enter as it presents itself." And so she asks that we look closer and try harder, but also suggests that willpower may itself be an illusion.

What's salvageable? Armantrout seizes the overweening falseness of our culture as a creative opportunity. We're so denatured that the poetry appears, paradoxically, to come, as Keats says, naturally. So encoded are her environs by modes of power, so thoroughly embosked by media jargon just yearning to be critically ravished—so multiplex, all in all, with capitalism's oozy-woozy contiguities—that the poet discerns everywhere a bad and mighty significance:

> The other day I drove past a typical strip mall and noticed the names *Comics City*, *Video House*, and *Taco King* side by side. Since that configuration seemed indicative of "what is wrong" with American society (the commodities are real, the polis is virtual), I considered writing it down for later use in a poem. I decided against it though—on the grounds that it was "too ironic." The problem with merely noting shop names is that it leaves the viewer (me) unimplicated and in a generally superior "I know better, but they're ignorant" position. Used that way, irony seems snotty.

Though it can become smug, this is a position one has sometimes to take. When "Canary" begins "Some folks got tortured/ by folks," we may rush, with the poet, to condemn U.S. military policy, noticing the homespun idiom Obama and others weave emolliently into their rhetoric; "Thing" compares a cat licking herself to (Armantrout's scare quotes) "balanced reporting"; and what about the parody of business speak, evilly near military speak, in "Prayers": "All we ask/is that our thinking//sustain momentum,/identify targets?" These poems identify their own targets, they skewer, and I'm grateful for every moment of it. This is guerrilla condescension, a way of making our world livable and pressing back against the immense money power that comes at us every which way and vulgarizes whatever it touches. (I'm especially tickled by "Haunts": "On how many bookstore shelves,/ lovely, fanged teenagers,/ red-eyed, smeared with blood.") And though Armantrout writes of sex, pornography, and gender with serious intent, there's space for innuendo, a phallus-withering giggle: "When certainty is high, / we grunt or yelp— // the agreed-upon signal. // One of us does."

Yet Armantrout usually places both reader and writer within a compromised situation, rather than safely outside. "In Front" refuses to leave its viewer, or speaker, unimplicated:

> Tree in new leaf
>
> in front of
> a brick building
>
> with narrow
> white-wood balconies
>
> slung under panes
> of glass
>
> in which a tree
>
> is being
> dissected
>
> before an audience
> of one,

> none,
> hundreds.
>
> •
>
> New twigs
> do the splits
>
> as I once did

For other poets, a "tree in new leaf" remains, innocently, a trope for new life. But Armantrout describes her way alternatively into that "brick building" and its reflections, replacing the green thing itself with its mediated and multiple echo—it's "dissected" like a corpse before an audience, though is anyone watching? The panes of glass resemble television screens, the cluster-eye of a fly. "Dissected" turns vision into analysis, perception into commentary—so it's perfect for Armantrout, who takes from William Carlos Williams his mechanical caressiveness, a stagey and often wondrous ponderousness of focus, and also bends observation toward social critique. A characteristic section break has the poem continue, slightly—with a conclusion, or a second thought? It's that turn to the personal typical of our times (and maybe the self-interest of everyone, everywhere); whenever you think Armantrout's setting up a steady lyrical voice in her poems, she's probably just poking fun at this tendency. She frames the exclamations of a personality jockeying for position—"Look at me!"; "Don't look!"; "Each poem says, / 'I'm desperate' // then, 'Everything / must go!;' " "I want to go back!"—I would identify this voice with the neediness of the child within, if that wasn't precisely the kind of warmed-over media cliché her verse lines up and delights to knock down like dominoes. She remarks upon our inability to really see anything except in relation to ourselves—we rethink what it would mean for a poem, or a personality, to come as naturally as the leaves to a tree.

In her lovely, pellucid essay on Lorine Niedecker, Armantrout observes how in that poet's *North Central* "humans are implicitly compared with trees. A tree is said to "put forth" leaves as a person is said to put forth effort. But a tree is consistent, untiring.... The little joke is that such behavior, if maintained, would cause humans to die of exposure." She also sees Bob Grenier parodying Romantic verse when he writes an "ecstatic address to bountiful nature in the form of a tree." But it is in her interview with Tom Beckett that we really see what Keats might bring to Armantrout's own thoroughly unantiquated poetics. "What are your hopes," Beckett asks, in 1999—before 9/11, the invasion of Iraq, the financial crisis, Facebook, Twitter, the iPhone, the Arab Spring, the Occupy movement, coronavirus, Black Lives Matter, and a spate of both ironic and pretentious superhero movies—"for the future of poetry?"

> Trying to answer this question makes me feel a bit like a politician. "Building a bridge to . . ." etc. My poetry isn't built on hope. I don't know what it is built on, but it isn't hope. I guess I could say this: Right now the audience for serious poetry (of any kind) is small. It seems as if what most people expect from poetry is a kind of ego-tonic. They want to identify with the speaker of the poem as one might identify with an action figure. (That may show just how powerless people are feeling.) I don't think this was always what people wanted from poetry. "Ode on a Grecian Urn," for instance, doesn't make you feel particularly empowered. You don't say to yourself, "I'm just like that. I appreciate antiquities!" So here's my wish—I wish people would stop looking to poetry for confirmation of what they already feel (or wish they felt) and that they would instead rediscover "negative capability." Or, to put it another way, I wish that, in art and politics, people would seek a power other than that of voyeuristic identification.

In "Two, Three," Armantrout asks a related question:

> Is it the beginning or end
> of real love
> when we pity a person
>
> because, in him,
> we see ourselves?

Poetry doesn't confirm what we already feel about ourselves and other people; it challenges those preconceptions. So we might see Armantrout as inspiringly out of step with the orthodoxies urged upon women poets, those of color, and other minorities who are pressured to find an empoweringly consistent "voice" and smoothly depict, rather than analyze or be inventive in relation to, their everyday lives. The prescribed task is to offer an "action figure" to identify with—photographs of ourselves in mighty poses, rather than poems—instead of contesting, as literature must, our prevalent, culturally sculpted guesstimates as to what a person actually is and could be. Armantrout's having none of it: "Various voices speak in my poems. I code-shift. I am many things: a white person, a working-class person with roots in the South, a woman, an academic of sorts, a '60s person who still likes rock and roll, someone who was raised on the Bible, a skeptic, etc. My voices manifest their own social unrest." Armantrout is insistent on her "various voices," which prevent her writing simply and straightforwardly "as a woman." But where women have been simplified into sexual objects and commercial provocations, she wishes to recover the possibility of "social unrest." "Easily" scrutinizes a strip club ad, with sympathy for the women "posed" in it to titillate the male gaze—and also as a question can be "posed":

> The models
> in the Gentlemen's Club ad
> are posed
> with pink mouths slack,
> eyes narrowed
> to slits.
>
> Show me stunned resentment—
>
> the way
> the world absorbs
> an insult
> it won't easily
> forget

Every calculated word choice, every line break, adds a nuance, a point where meaning condenses. (Armantrout's memoir, *True*, mentions the teaching of Denise Levertov: "Most of the suggestions I remember her making about my poems involved line breaks. She caused me to think more seriously about the possibilities involved in breaking lines.") The poem's anger is compelling, as Armantrout counters what has been done to these women and what they've been made to stand for: what a grisly technological word "model" is, when you really look at it! The "Gentlemen's Club" isn't exactly the Athenaeum, but a strip club—still, the euphemistic pretentiousness of its moniker captures a continuity relating to these male spaces, while even "club" has its tinge of caveman violence. The "pink mouths" and "eyes narrowed /to slits" are vaginal, while the eye-narrowing also gives us the hijacking of sexual signals (working on the viewer unconsciously) by the strategies of advertising—which is thus able to bypass those rational decision-making processes so insisted upon by academic economists. "Forget," hanging there in white space, with no period, sounds like an instruction: "forget." We see ads like these every day, and then we "forget" about them, taking their cynicism as a given, as immutable as the physical laws making apples fall from trees and our bodies age. But don't these messages actually stick in the mind and shape our attitudes? Really, we're all insulted by them—I don't mean "offended," in the conventional sense; I mean, there is inside the ad an idea of us as small, stupid, and malleable.

All of Armantrout could be read this minutely. This poem highlights a continuing interest in sexuality and gender; another new one, "Assembly," seems to me to rescramble, in a characteristic mixing of science language with relationship language, the fish-woman imagery of Sylvia Plath's "Mirror." This fusion, or colliding, of registers has become more and more important to Armantrout. "I try to somehow ground abstract physics in human psychology," she says; "I do so feeling that the two are somehow incompatible and that they will clash in tragicomic ways." In the first section of "End Times" (a religious phrase we're prompted to query) the expansion of the universe becomes a game of hide-and-seek (freighted, of course, with longing and shame):

> Galaxies run from us. "Don't look!"
> Was this the meaning
> of the warning in the Garden?
> When a dreamer sees she's dreaming,
> it causes figments to disperse.

Writing to Benjamin Bailey, Keats compares the "Imagination" to "Adam's dream—he awoke and found it truth. I am the more zealous in this affair, because I have never yet been able to perceive how any thing can be known for truth by consequitive reasoning—and yet it must be."

Armantrout is as skeptical of what we take for "reason"—the trains of thought following their supply lines to the centers of commerce—but less assertive as to the power of the imagination. Her dreamer in the garden of Eden (a woman, is it Eve?) falters in the middle of a lucid dream—it all comes apart. (A "figment" is a fictional "fragment," but I also wonder if Adam and Eve's shamed wearing of fig leaves over their genitals applies here.)

The poem's second section blends with science the vocabularies of art appreciation and computer programming:

> Black bars and dots
> of low cloud,
>
> almost a signature,
> reflected on a sunset marsh.
>
> Luxuriant and spurious code
>
> as art,
> as if we were meant to think,
>
> "Beautiful!"—
> so we do
>
> and a ripple
> travels in one spot.
>
> When something reaches
> the speed of light
>
> it will appear to freeze,
>
> growing gradually
> less meaningful.

I read this and I do think "Beautiful!" for Armantrout does, sometimes, choose to write that sort of poem. The description works as description and also as "code"—those "black bars and dots" are like Morse—and the notional "signature" alludes to natural theology, the view of nature as an artwork created by God with secret meanings and a confirmation of his existence within. The line break on "think" is (I think) especially "meaningful." Were human beings—it's admirable how Armantrout brings together such an all-pervading corrosiveness as to social arrangements and the postulation, nevertheless, of a collective experience—truly "meant to think?" We've evolved to consider ourselves more reasoning and reasonable than we in fact are; all our philosophizing comes down to, from a biological-anthropological perspective, a survival strategy. The recognition of the beautiful is, Kantianly speaking, what lifts us above all that—beauty has no utility—but perhaps even here we're only finding patterns and making sense and trying to feel more secure about our environment.

The paradox of the ripple traveling in one spot may describe not water but an emotion, and the subsequent talk of the speed of light is conscious of the point at which scientific description becomes "meaningful", or stops being so, as metaphor. New age pablum seizes irresponsibly on the figural residue of science—the media, and media scientists, often have a vexed relationship with this (rather salable) aspect—think of Richard Dawkins, for instance, and the "selfish gene." Just as the speed of light can never be reached, so language (within a poem or outside it) may approach vacuity but never truly get there, for words are constantly effusing significance, however uncorralled. "The Creation," a poem from Armantrout's earlier selected, *Veil*, states pretend-biblically, mock-scientifically that "in the beginning / there was measurement":

> Let us
> move fast
> enough, in a small
> enough space, and
> our travels
> will take first
> shape, then substance.

This is physics-flavored but also concerns ambition, identity, and the meaning, or meaninglessness, of life. (See also "Once": "The opposite / of nothingness // is direction"). How provincial must we become, or remain, to be coherent to others and ourselves?

A poet's *Selected Poems* is a chance to shape into integrity their scattered outpourings. So for Armantrout to call her second *Partly* is roguish. Her title foregrounds doubt and announces (to borrow from her conversation with Hejinian) a political poetics of uneasy "parts":

> Devices and strategies arose, I suspect, because they correspond with conflicts in the modern and postmodern world. They reflect an uneasy relation between part and whole. How does the individual relate to his or her society? Representational democracy doesn't seem to represent us. How do individual neurons add up to a single consciousness (to revert to the problem of knowledge)? Many poets continue to pose the unsolved part/whole problem on the page.

"Pass": "Single cells // become like-minded, // forming a consensus // or quorum." This metaphor grows courageously experiential in *Versed*, published three years after the diagnosis—of a rare form of adrenal cortical cancer—Armantrout received in 2006. She says her poem "Own" was begun in the ICU: "Woman in a room near mine moans, 'I'm dying. I want/ to be fine! It's my body!/ Don't let me! Don't touch me!'" Reading that "the part is sick / of representing the whole," we may think about a categorized person (a woman, a cancer survivor) refusing to position her experience as representative or otherwise exemplary; also, of the parts of one's body, its cells, turning on each other in revolt. The personal becomes political in the most terrible way.

"Later" philosophizes about disease, and personhood, with a lived inventiveness reminiscent of Donne in his *Devotions Upon Emergent Occasions*, evoking his own body as given over to civil war. It's a poem about how parts add up, or don't add up, to wholes. Here are the first and second parts:

1

To be beautiful
and powerful enough
for someone
to want to break me
             up

into syndicated ripples.

>   Later I'll try
>   to rise from these dead.
>
>
>   2
>
>   How much would this body
>   have had to be otherwise in order
>   not to be mine,
>
>   for this world
>   not to exist?
>
>   When would that difference
>   have had to begin?

A cancer sufferer might shift from conceiving of her own body as convulsed by internecine war to feeling that a separate demon wished to destroy her—and then ask, *Why me?* "Later," you might say, about something you don't want to sort out now, or the word might continue a story following a major incident. But can a person with cancer—Armantrout's, happily, went into remission—rely on "later?" She will not rise from the dead, but "these dead"; she has been, to go back to "In Front," split, divided, into many possible selves. Section 2 is gauchely gluey on the subject of identity, precise to the point of pedantry—no poet could write "have had" without wincing, but Armantrout does it twice. The experience of alienation from one's own body, the agony of its tissues being no longer "in order," turning other: academically inert diction insists, perversely, provocatively (with a constructed aloofness) that this is a philosophical question.

Armantrout has written about wishing to describe her experience from outside, but also, feelingly, from within:

> When we think about other people's subjective experience, we ask ourselves what it's like to be them. What is it like then to be told that you have adrenal cortical cancer, a disease so rare you have never heard of it and from which you will probably die? What is it like to discover this when you have been feeling no pain, feeling, especially well even?

That is the situation I faced in June of 2006. In the months following my diagnosis, I tried to describe the experience, to say what it was like, in poetry which was later published in a book called *Versed* (sometimes confused with the anesthetic Versed).

To say what the cancer "was like": does this mean, snaring the essence of it, or, contrarily (and with no lapse of authority/sincerity/authenticity) using it as the basis for simile, metaphor, comparisons of the person with the state or with another person? The poem isn't exactly an allegory; it creatively rejigs what actually occurred in trying to get down on the page what it was "like." Cancer provides an imaginative route into the question of selfhood and how we are constituted in relation to our sometimes abrasive interactions with other people:

> They drive me
> out to sea.
> Secretly, I am still
> ____, the mysterious.
> I speak in splashes.
> Later
> I have the lonely dream
> — FROM "LATER"

In the run-up to diagnosis, Armantrout "began to have rather ominous dreams." One involved "being towed out to sea in a little boat and left there. Do I believe in precognition? Not really. But I think it's possible that your body may sometimes know more than your conscious mind does." The six-syllable couplet beginning this section has the pronoun "me," which throngs the poem—*me, me, me,* it cries—run harshly up against "they." The speaker is driven out to sea—ostracized, exiled (because infected)? Or does the poem describe only a kindly excursion, a patient taken for a recuperative drive by her caretakers? We know also that a person is composed of psychophysiological "drives," so "they" could refer to her cells, a disease acting from within.

Yet the social, or antisocial, language of the poem is surely crucial. "They drive me/out"; this hurting phrase has a psychoanalytic primacy and situates the speaker among other people. "Mysterious" insists on a special identity that can't be touched or tarnished because it's secret and protected from however others might act. Does "I speak in splashes" describe her capacity for a heightened elemental language—like that of poetry—or is the alliteration self-defeating, does it suggest that she only emits noise, can't say very much at all, can't communicate? The "lonely dream" posits a realm of subjective privacy into which the speaker may retreat or where she could be trapped—also a possession or an aspiration ("I have the lonely dream") adding glamour to her remoteness. "Later" concerns suffering, the self, other people, and a threat that appears, like inspiration, to arrive both from within and outside. It's about victimhood and uniqueness—overlapping concepts feverishly central to our culture but treated here in such a firmly diagnostic way. We're left wondering if the speaker of the poem will, like Adam, wake from her dream and find it truth.

Dreaming the World
Vinod Kumar Shukla's Extraordinary Sentences

What do you do—as a critic—when you encounter a writer so gladdeningly cajoling, so sweetly weird that you're convinced anyone who read him deeply and carefully would be delighted, but who also, stylistically, can be studiously bizarre in a way that you worry will scare off the very readers who might love him?

Born in Rajnandgaon in 1937 and now resident in Raipur—locations that inspire his work—Vinod Kumar Shukla is the author in Hindi of novels, poetry collections, and also short stories. Though he lives outside of the limelight, he has won practically every major prize available to a Hindi writer, including a Sahitya Akademi award (from India's national academy of letters), the Atta Galatta–Bangalore Literature Festival Book Prize, and, just this year—he's now eighty-four years old—the inaugural Mathrubhumi Book of the Year award for *Blue Is Like Blue* (2019), a collection of stories translated into English by Arvind Krishna Mehrotra and Sara Rai. Published in 1979, his fiction debut, *Naukar Ki Kameez*, or *The Servant's Shirt*, was turned into a 1999 film by Mani Kaul; this novel and three more have been translated into English by Satti Khanna.

Alongside his writing career, until his retirement Shukla taught agricultural techniques to farmers: we find in his work an intimate understanding of rural and small-town landscapes and communities. One must look closely, however, to spot his emancipatory politics, for he writes playfully and unprogrammatically. The Indian journalist Paromita Chakrabarti describes Shukla as shaped by India's history but also by its rich literary legacies. His mother, whose father was killed in the violence around Partition, read to the family the "works of Rabindranath Tagore and Bankim Chandra Chattopadhyay, Sarat Chandra Chattopadhyay, and other

Bengali greats ... poetry was a common love"; Shukla was influenced in particular by the Marxist poet Gajanan Madhav Muktibodh, whom he met. Shukla writes about painful experiences, and often specifically of the Indian poor, but without sentimentality or melodrama, and while his characters always have money on their minds, they never say it in so many words. Comedy and wonder are there for the asking:

> The first time that Muktibodh read me his poems it was late by the time I reached home. One of them had been a long poem about the sky. It had seemed as though a kite, tied to the string of time, were flying above the world and had been given plenty of line. Muktibodh handed me the spool after he'd finished reading. The poem had ended but it had not yet finished; it still hasn't.
> —FROM "OLD VERANDA"

"Old Veranda" and all the other short stories I quote appear in *Blue Is Like Blue*, translated by Mehrotra and Rai. Muktibodh's poem "still hasn't" finished: Shukla's phrasing leaps surprisingly from the past into the present, reminding us that the writer's basic unit of meaning and wonder is the sentence. Each of his makes you stop and think, or tumble flat on your face. Here's another example, also featuring a veranda, from his 1996 novel *Once It Flowers*: "His wife awaited him on the verandah. She continued to gaze expectantly even after he had reached her". Shukla defamiliarizes whatever he touches, making the world plastic and askance. You put the book down, turn it over, glance at the back cover and then out the window, with a shiver. Something has changed, but you can't put your finger on it. His words haven't "finished" with you.

It could be the best thing is simply to step aside, pointing you to "College," a story characteristic in so many ways. The emphasis, for instance, on darkness, distance, situations where the clear grows unclear, and who knows what's what—"In the dark, the neem tree did not look like a real neem tree. . . . It looked like some other tree dressed up as a neem"—and, following on from this metaphor, acting and role-playing. Also, the people-watching narrator—"walking in the bazaar was what I liked best. . . . Watching other shoppers was more fun than being a shopper oneself"—who, like Walter Benjamin's flaneur, heeds what others miss, smelling out a deeper reality beneath everyday surfaces: "In the history class my attention would invariably be drawn to the floor. I would tap it with my foot and it would sound hollow. I was convinced that there was an underground chamber there."

My title is from Jorge Luis Borges, who isn't a magical realist, just as Shukla isn't, not quite. They are philosopher-magicians, special-effects wizards in literature. Why act, think, create this way? Because, says Borges, we "have dreamt the world. We have dreamt it as firm, mysterious, visible, ubiquitous in space and durable in time; but in its architecture we have allowed tenuous and eternal crevices of unreason which tell us it is false." Shukla is Indian, writes in Hindi, but he isn't your standard postcolonial writer. Arvind Krishna Mehrotra and Sara Rai make that (combatively) clear in their translators' introduction to *Blue Is Like Blue*:

> Shukla must be among the few writers alive whose work has appeared in journals where world literature is published or discussed—*Granta, Metamorphoses, Modern Poetry in Translation, Some Kind of Beautiful Signal, The Baffler, n+1*—but who has heard neither of these journals nor of world literature. In contrast to his unawareness of the term and his indifference to the subjects that keep the assembly line of global fiction moving (historical trauma, acts of terrorism, personal turmoil) is the attention he lavishes on the fleeting observations, thoughts, memories and gestures that for most of us, regardless of where we live, constitute our lives.

As this suggests, Shukla is tough to pin down. His supernaturalism suggests magical realism. (People turn into birds or become invisible; falling down infinite holes, they learn to fire real bullets out of imaginary guns by shouting *bang*.) But in that mode, writes Maggie Ann Bowers, "it is assumed that something extraordinary *really* has happened." Shukla's slyer. He gives strange events in the conditional tense, so it's unclear if—within the overall narrative—they've really occurred.

Approaching his stories and novels through his poems, where the sentence effects I mention are allowed free rein, it becomes clear that his real subject is the porous membrane dividing perception from imagination. Here's a poem that quick-wittedly investigates objects, animals, buildings, and people, without activating the standard literary process of illumination through comparison. It's a refusal, I think, of the cultural "production line" mentioned by Rai and Mehrotra. Living beings are not, the poet suggests, things for transactions:

> That man put on a new woollen coat and went away like a thought.
> In rubber flip-flops I struggled behind.
> The time was six in the morning, the time of hand-me-downs, and
>   it was freezing cold.
> Six in the morning was like six in the morning.
> There was a man standing under a tree.
> In the mist it looked like he was standing inside his own blurred
>   shape.
> The blurred tree looked exactly like a tree.
> To its right was a blurred horse of inferior stock,
> Looking like a horse of inferior stock.

Concerning images that echo in other works, what relationship is there between the neem tree in "College" and, in this untitled poem, the blurred tree which "looked exactly like a tree?"

These tics, or tricks, suggest a type of ineluctable facticity—such as we'd expect from reportage of Indian poverty—before refocusing on language itself, which glitters like dust in the light between us and what we're trying to examine. Shukla isn't surreally escapist, but sensitive to overtones realists skip. "That man" has a "new woollen coat"; the speaker struggles in rubber flip-flops, requiring hand-me-downs; it's implied that to his "master" he's a beast of burden and, like the horse, "of inferior stock." The poem could refer to a caste system in which people suffer roles they can't escape, and the strength to redefine oneself ("I wasn't that horse") is often unfeasible; or—I'm grateful to Vikrant Dadawala for this thought—Shukla might be concerned with the kind of servility that many low-income jobs seem to require, even from Brahmins, in South Asia. Poetry—considered as a network of images—connects here with frameworks of exploitation. You get from Shukla an excessiveness announcing itself, paradoxically, through tautology—"Six in the morning was like six in the morning"—as if to extract from nullity a vim that surmounts, without denying or sentimentally transcending, the constrictions his work records.

I'm aware, reading Shukla in translation, that part of the eeriness I respond to in his short-circuited tropes may relate to their appearing in English. The novels and stories and poems are, like his sentences, two-sided, for in them English and Hindi, like the magnetized halves of a simile or metaphor, meet suggestively. The translated work is neither one thing nor the other, belonging neither here nor there—though it may aspire to a universality undone each time we encounter in the work a strangeness that shifts the reader from eye-skimming fluency to scrutiny of individual sentences and paragraphs.

I was caught off guard, for instance, by the opening of the twelfth chapter of *Once It Flowers* (or, in the original, *Khilega Toh Dekhenge*):

> A rural railway station was about to arrive. Or else the scene of a rural railway station was arriving seated on the train. The previous train had already brought most of the image of the railway station with it. When a passenger disembarked, it was like an image of the passenger disembarking. When a passenger got on, it was like an image of the passenger getting on. The rain shower was like an image of the rain shower. The sun emerging was like an image of the sun. The images kept changing, but there was one image that seemed to have disembarked for good—the image of a rural railway station. It may not have bought a ticket for its journey. Otherwise, wouldn't the image of the station have walked off like the other passengers?
>
> This was the same station as before. Musua station.

This paragraph seems to untether from the narrative, becoming a laboratory space in which Shukla's experiment with the independent sentence is repeated over and over. No sooner is a detail enrolled than it's scrutinized and compared to the image of itself.

The novel is about—though it unstintingly expands to ponder a community—the family of Guruji the schoolteacher, who after their roof is blown off by a storm move into "an empty police substation left over from British times." Shukla explains in an interview with Khanna, appended to this translation: "New architects must have been hired after Independence, but many police stations built by the British are still in use. For instance, the Central Jail in Raipur was built by the British." This foreign-homely place, both anomalous and intimate, imposed and chosen, provides for Guruji, his wife, and their children, Munna and Munni, a starting point for adventures of the mind.

To read the previous paragraphs is to go on such an adventure, and, as I've said, I was wrongfooted. "A rural railway station was about to arrive" sounds—a solecistic shimmer!—like pidgin (or translationese), for *trains* arrive, not stations. But Khanna's version respects, carrying the syntax into English, where it chirrs unexpectedly, one way of putting things in Hindi: "station aa rahaa hai." This translinguistic peccadillo pinpoints a real-world strangeness. A railway station changes how people see themselves and act (sexual harassment becomes a problem; we learn that "for many women, train travel becomes one more source of distress"). Once provincial lives are touched by places formerly distant, communities could be decimated by flight to larger townships. Guruji's son asks him if more people are getting on the train than getting off. The dance of separation and fusion is played out by the paragraph itself: it reads briefly as a prose poem with its own integrity, before slotting back into the plot.

I say *prose poem*—seeking a vocabulary for how Shukla's fiction turns, at times, away from plot toward the often ouroborotic microplots of individual sentences—but we might use the language of film. The self-contained epiphanies of modernist prose resemble movie set pieces that take your breath away and are remembered long after you've forgotten the rest—or that are highlighted in publicity materials, trailers, prior to release. Taking this route, Shukla's railway station echoes the great moment in Satyajit Ray's *Pather Panchali* (1955) when Durga and Apu race to a railway through a field of kaash (pampas grass), a cinematic inscape with its own dizzying momentum.

But my fascination remains with those sentences where the filmic intrudes, alternatively, as a perpetual self-consciousness. Every object is really a prop on a film set, every utterance might be altered or edited out or rerecorded for superior fidelity. In the aforementioned interview, Shukla also raves about the "talkies" he saw growing up in Rajnandgaon, which introduced a heroic, or mock-heroic, feeling into ordinary life: a reimagining of the everyday in terms of actors playing roles. His sentences grasp at reality (indicating their target's escape, like water running through your fingers) by means of a circumambient daydream—the mental slipperiness that, when you think about it, coats with oblivion all we experience and will soon forget or misremember. Guruji and his family watch a film with playback singing (songs not actually performed by those onscreen); his wife speaks in the darkness, and he says: "That's not you speaking. Somebody else is performing playback for you." It's that neem tree again from "College."

Films and books redeem the evanescence of our lives by making moments conscious of themselves, placing them within a frame. But that doubled awareness also threatens to steal from the passing instant its spontaneous flavor. Depicting Indian small-town life, there's often an elegiac perfume to Shukla's unforeseen sentences as they relay swift-moving experiences: "Children picked up flint stones from the hills and played with them, striking them to watch sparks fly. The sparks were beautiful—too many and too rapidly vanishing to keep count. Their flaming and dying were the being and passing of instants." This cinematic passage from *Once It Flowers* zooms in on the leaping glow of the sparks. (Shukla uses this metaphor in *Moonrise from the Green Grass Roof*—published in Hindi in 2011 and translated by Khanna in 2017—where six-year-old Bolu "arrives suddenly as if transported by a zoom lens," and his friend Bhaira looks at his father without understanding: "the zoom lens would not focus on his father; he looked hazy.") The final sentence, equating one thing with another—going beyond simile—is philosophically assertive: the children, though they wouldn't speak in such terms, do what they do out of a feeling for the texture of time. I think again of a sentence from *Moonrise*, about stars in the sky: "They were the questions children wanted to ask, but had never asked out loud."

Why do children play? To take between finger and thumb, and test tactilely, the fabric of reality (as we do, reading novels, and especially when pulled up short by puzzling, agential sentences, each becoming, like a koan, an event in itself). Do we live in a world of realities or of images? There's Plato's allegory of the cave, but also, closer to home (or Shukla's) the insights of Advaita, the Hindu philosophy asserting that the self is at one with a reality whose plurality of appearances is an illusion.

Shukla's prose explores our wavering focus on our surroundings: how the mind sizzles for a minute with excitations, then is flattened and neutralized by boredom, bouncing from one mood to another. In the short story "Man in the Blue Shirt," another Indian flaneur—"I had time on my hands"—is people-watching, picks one in particular, and then becomes (mildly) obsessed with who the man is and where he's going. It's a story about crowds—"The crowd was like a crowd"—and how they can be alienating, yet how (outside bigger metropoles) strangers act like intimates. It's funny, and resembles, like *Moonrise from the Green Grass Roof*, a story for children or a folktale or a joke, as strangers try differently to explain the man in the blue shirt. This is where Shukla's poetics of prose meets his handling of narrative. On the one hand, his circular sentences match, microcosmically, stories with no clear beginning, middle, and end; when you get one such sentence after another, they also coalesce into a picture of Indian small-town life that, unlike traditional realism, can suggest thought behaviors shaped by hardship, happenstance, and the collision of long-standing traditions with new, unevenly allocated, technologies.

In the Bajrang Snack Shop, for instance, in *Moonrise from the Grass Green Roof*, "The tables were rickety. If you set down a teacup the table trembled the way hot tea in a cup trembles when you blow on it. By the time the legs of the table stabilized, the tea would have cooled enough to sip." The first sentence sets the scene, before Shukla's trademark effect. It's as if Andrew Marvell, through a portal in the gardens of Appleton House, stepped out of seventeenth-century England into a twentieth-century Indian backwater—the perception is as exquisitely self-enclosed as a couplet he might graffiti on the snack shop wall. But how to get back to Indian lives? By suggesting how people accommodate themselves to circumstances, learning to, if you like, rhyme with their environment, just as the trembling of the table consorts with the trembling of the tea. In this way, Shukla suggests without mawkishness the tiny satisfactions clung to by people without privilege, hidden in the wrinkles and folds of the nondescript: what the Oulipo writer Georges Perec identified as the "infraordinary" or—as opposed to the exotic—the realm of the "endotic." There follow remarkable sentences about light—"The dim light that entered the room seemed to apologize for being the little that was left over from the brightness outside"; "the shaft of light" entering the room after sunrise "seemed to be a clothesline to hang darkness on, after the darkness had been beaten clean"—but he's really talking about technology: "a weak light bulb," the "neon tube in the verandah"; "transient electricity, ready to be on its way out soon." In *Once It Flowers*, it's said the "police never made rounds" of what they list as an "underilluminated" village: "underilluminated meant unimportant."

Likewise, a sentence can be a window on a personality: "Bolu . . . had a way of merging into the background that made him hard to detect." The prose stylist is determined to avoid autopilot and see everything afresh: in some, this can become showing off and a means to attain a position of superiority through irony. Yet Shukla's style radiates energies also discoverable in the lives and loves of his characters: "It needed practice to see things in familiar and unfamiliar ways. The practice for seeing a wife as more than wife required to love her more often. People kept looking for cozy little worlds to settle in." I don't think Shukla is wholly at odds with that coziness: his man in the blue shirt is irruptive, singular, but has a way of bringing people together. It's a question less of orthodoxy smashed than (returning to Perec) of the strange and disconcerting inhering in the material holding communities together. Rather like Wallace Stevens's man with the blue guitar, Shukla's man in a blue shirt is less an individual than a principle of the imagination. Time and space shimmer and warp around him, and the narrator scurries to keep up:

> The man in a blue shirt left in a hurry.
> "Your shirt isn't really white," the old man said to me as we started walking. I tried to remember if I'd ever worn a blue shirt. In my mind I went over all the things at home that were blue. The sky isn't particularly blue. Blue is like blue. A group of boys strolled past wearing clothes that were of five different colors. We came across an ochre-colored house in Gudakhu Line. The old men wore dirty white shirts.

Color provided Wittgenstein with the epitome of private experience: we've each a peculiar, even unique idea of what *blue* is; nevertheless, our language games situate idiosyncrasies within a collective framework (you understand when I ask you to hand me the blue book, not the red). Though Shukla stresses perceptual thaw, he does this in sentences that, touching base with pellucid sense units, place their ruptures in a shared lifeworld.

If, at one moment, as we've seen, he seems unsure what a tree blurred by mist really is, at others, he talks matter-of-factly, restoring the horizon he'll later sponge away. This process of retrieval followed by dispersion crystallizes in a single paragraph from *Moonrise from the Green Grass Roof*:

> People who have sight share the visible world. A person with eyesight sees a particular tree much the way another person with eyesight sees that tree. That disc which is known by one sighted person to be the moon is known to be the moon by another sighted person as well. Knowing the moon by seeing it is one way. Knowing the world by not seeing it is another. One must draw close to something to be able to touch it. The blind live closest to creation, so close they can run their hands over it.

The moon reappears throughout the narrative to heal each child's experience of disconnection: "it was the same moon, and it shone more radiantly as all the friends came together." Children only gradually grow assured of the stable world assumed by realist fiction (it's why they like to hear the same stories over and over again). But does this process ever end? Even as adults, we gain then lose this confidence; we think we know what's going on, then realize our certainties were false and that what Keats called "negative capability," or the capacity of "being in uncertainties, Mysteries, doubts, without any irritable reaching after fact and reason," is essential. Then we go back to feeling fixed and grounded: Shukla's sentences give each stage of what could be a cyclical process. Novelists may philosophize, but they aren't philosophers operating under the obligation to a final truth. To butt one's head against the brick wall of mental fatigue—being certain, only, of the tautology "blue is like blue"—might seem like failure. But Shukla's prose has to it a singing sweetness, a return upon itself suggestive of plenitude rather than depletion. His style doesn't corrode but promotes curiosity: the narrator looks around, becomes more interested in familiar buildings and unfamiliar people.

Shukla's characters typically enter our field of attention visually, through becoming, that is, visible. Guruji sees his wife arrive in the dark—"A woman who looked like his wife was running towards them, holding a lantern. The patches of what was visible and what was not visible jumped strangely together." From a narrative point of view, the first, cinematic sentence is more important than the second, whose provocation is unique to literary prose; one feels, however, that for Shukla it's the other way around. He doesn't describe faces or bodies especially, but stresses clothes, because they define others in terms of their responsibilities, grievances, fortunes, while allowing for role-playing.

In one paragraph in *Moonrise from the Green Grass Roof*, that visual or, as I've said, cinematic sensibility is deconstructed into—the word actually appears—"sentences": what's heard takes priority over what's seen. It's a touching scene about a minor incident: a mother loses sight of her child briefly, then finds her again; it's also an inquiry, I suspect, into the limits of literary representation. Whose lives, and which experiences within those lives, can fiction accommodate? Shukla foregrounds anxieties rarely explored in fiction (or film); "The Burden" concerns a man who worries he's forgotten to lock his door, returns to check, and cycles on with an ephemeral lightness of heart now considerably immortalized: "He smiled and shook his head, then continued to go along at the same speed. If someone had then seen him smiling they would have been surprised." Discomforts pass, and we laugh about them in retrospect. At the time, however, they can be all-consuming:

> Her daughter had vanished. Koona's mother thought she heard Koona say: "These yellow flowers are fragrant" just before she disappeared.
>
> At first, Koona's mother thought she had heard the entire sentence before Koona disappeared. Afterwards she thought Koona was visible as far as "These yellow flowers . . ." The rest she heard only after Koona vanished. Or it may have been that she heard Koona's entire sentence after Koona was no longer visible. She panicked. Where could Koona be?

Shukla's hyperscrutiny of objects, people, and relational threads aligns with everyday panics. There's nothing rarefied about his preoccupations. A mother loses sight of her child: suddenly, she analyzes her environment like a detective; she goes over remembered sentences like a literary critic; she tells and retells the story of how she got here, like a novelist.

Moonrise from the Green Grass Roof has children as its main characters, dressed vibrantly, and in noting this Shukla's prose approaches in its conscious naivete the amazement with which children encounter the world. Each has their quirk, which Shukla develops with gusto. Bolu, for instance, can only talk while walking, so Koona exclaims, "Please don't say anything, Bolu. If you speak, you'll move away from me." Talking is a way of moving both toward and away from people, and Chhotu, an impressionist of his friends' voices, finds that he can only speak in a persona, not as himself:

> Chhotu's shorts were a dark navy, easily mistaken for black. His shirt was iridescent, one color in the sun, another in the shade—indefinite like his voice. The indefiniteness might extend over time to his appearance as well. His appearance might change as he grew older. At first he would appear to be Chhotu. Then he would appear to be like Chhotu. Then he would become quite different. He would come to meet his friends and say, "I'm Chhotu." His friends would recognize him because he spoke in Koona's voice. What if he used a voice unfamiliar to his friends?

This is an example of Shukla writing in the conditional tense, suggesting (with cinema again in the background) scenes that—it gets nebulous— may or may not have happened, or are about to, or are of dubious canonicity, like deleted scenes restored in the editor's cut. Are these the novelist-narrator's fantasies, or Chhotu's, or those of other characters who care about him?

The future can be frightening. Is the person Chhotu may become the same person he is now, if personhood is (as it would seem to be, in qasbah communities) fundamentally relational? ("Friends" repeats provokingly, appearing three times in three successive sentences, stressing Chhotu's agitation.) The sadness is in the transition: becoming other to the memory of himself, he first changes enough to be (enlisting the structure of simile) "like Chhotu": the sort of person, like the man with the blue shirt, who reminds people of other people. Because his role was to speak in other people's voices—he was never self-identical—only through impersonation can he confirm his identity. Children aren't themselves for long, but always becoming someone new (as, no matter how clever a sentence is, we read it primarily to reach the next): if we map this onto a province being integrated into a national culture, then the future of these children becomes doubly precarious. They may drift away, and even if they don't, their hometown may in their lifetime change beyond recognition.

I mentioned in *Once It Flowers* women molested on trains—Shukla's is a feminist intervention, concerning a country where, given practices ranging from "Eve teasing" to outright rape, women aren't safe in public spaces. This generates another imagined "scene" in which a traveler is abducted. She escapes her kidnappers and returns home, but the situation resembles Chhotu's:

> She will hear the familiar chirping of birds, but the birds will not be those she knew in her village. She will see familiar trees, but they will not be trees she knew in her village. The morning air will be different from the night air. She will notice a tribal person from whom she will seek directions to her village. She will hear the footfall of her pursuers and run into the afternoon. Many days will go by in this way, many years. The girl will grow middle-aged and become safe for that reason.
>
> The scene can include the middle-aged woman meeting a man. The man should be familiar to her, someone from her own village, someone who has aged like her father. Will he recognize his daughter in this middle-aged woman? She will recognize him. The scene may well show Guruji as the father. Guruji will address the middle-aged woman: "Munni, my child!" The man doesn't have to be Guruji.

To repeat the future tense in successive sentences introduces into the prose the noise of composition. Shukla doesn't only supplant—dazzling the reader—the story we're reading with another, occurring at a different level of fictional reality: he also reminds us that any story is only made of words coming together according to the grammatical and literary rules that we're used to.

But to recognize this isn't—as experimentalists of other stripes have argued—to deny fiction's link to reality, nor its ability to probe and process experiences of the heart. When the escaped woman is identified as Munni, with Guruji for a father, the devices of fiction are laid bare and with them the limitations of the reader's empathy. It's the main characters we feel for and whose destinies concern us, so for this woman to actually be Munni, grown up, amplifies the crisis. Shukla inserts a representative event (the abused and kidnapped woman) without, by strictly assigning it to one of his protagonists, reducing her character to a cliché without interiority. The woman needn't be Munni, and her father needn't be Guruji; it forces consideration of those on the margins of stories, and of miseries elusive of representation: so many women have suffered this way. There's arid wit to the sentence about the woman aging and therefore becoming safe from molestation by men; and, as with Chhotu, the idea that if we're different people at different times in our lives this is because people alter in how they see and treat us.

We see in Shukla's art how the movement of prose toward the curvatures of verse can further the fiction writer's work, discovering (with each sentence) a new angle on individuals and their ligatures. He doesn't appear to believe that verse and prose are different (that's why his images float unconcernedly out of poems and into stories and novels and back again). You've the feeling he wrote his work out of the same wonderment it conjures in the reader. "I don't know while I am writing," he says in his interview with Khanna,

> when something real transpires in my fiction and when dream takes over. I believe in the truth of the imagination. I believe that I am capable of exercising my imagination. I can imagine how sweet happiness is, and I derive happiness from what I have just imagined. I want to save my capacity to dream in the world of stark reality. I feel assured if someone says to me "It'll be alright" when I am in pain. There isn't much happiness in stark reality. We use the happiness of imagination

to extend the happiness possible in life. We want happiness to stay fresh a long time, but it is pain that persists like a splinter lodged deep under the skin. It is difficult to extract that splinter. "It'll be alright" is a fantasy. The fantasy gives us courage to fight with painful reality. Everything doesn't become all right, but it is still possible to hope.

What a deliciously contrarian approach to writing of poverty and structural injustice. India is a thoroughly unequal country, and the prejudice-fomenting Hindu nationalism of its prime minister, Narendra Modi, has reduced the rights of minorities and endangered their lives. Discovering Shukla in this context, one may find that a bit of Indian sweetness and light isn't escapist but what's required to go on hoping and believing that things can get better.

Shukla—aligning with other Hindi writers who, from the 1950s onward, sponsor the imagination over a narrow realism—finds ingeniousness in the lives of the dispossessed. He dares to write of "happiness." There remains the feeling that literary fiction and poetry must be gloomy. Yet Shukla, writing of Indian people, doesn't reduce them to their circumstances: "The sky could be seen as sorrow or happiness. The sky of happiness would not be pale red or dark blue. The sky of sorrow would not be yellow or black. One needed to know judo or karate to see the sky of happiness. This skill was useful for self-defense as well. There was happiness in moving from the glare of the sun into shade. There was happiness in the touch of air." Shukla holds back—in *Once It Flowers*, quoted here, but also throughout his work—from saying outright that it's in our power to choose to see the world as either a happy or an unhappy place. Guruji and his neighbors, terrified of fires, carry around buckets of water just in case. Except it's hard to do, so they tote empty buckets—doubling as containers for groceries—thinking they'll fill them up later; but even this is a fantasy, for "drinking water had become scarce in villages. Water to put out fires was a distant dream." Shukla doesn't paper over poverty, but he also won't dismiss as delusion people's ways of coping. He certifies an experiential sweetness that, felt along his rhythms, can't be denied. In what he says about sun, shade, and air, he tries for a definition of happiness available to everyone.

Srinivas Rayaprol and Gāmini Salgādo

This is an essay on two writers long invisible: authors out of print whose works have been tough, if not impossible, to acquire. With Srinivas Rayaprol, I'm pleased to have helped set this right, editing a new *Selected* with Graziano Krätli; Gāmini Salgādo's literary criticism, however, and his memoir of growing up in Sri Lanka, *The True Paradise*, remain elusive.

It's a pity for any book to disappear. But there are some it becomes the critic's duty to reintroduce to popular awareness. What makes them special? Well, there are any number of reasons why we keep reading a writer—where I say "read," one might add "publish," "review," and "teach"—and yet the truest goal must be an experience of literary complexity. A style of thinking contingent upon their uniquely disposed forms. Postcolonial literature is insufficiently considered as art. In fact, there are those for whom aesthetics seem fatuous, beside the point, or, worse, one of the disguises worn by hegemonic power. But I don't agree. And, in fact, I think it's about time that authors from underrepresented, and misrepresented, communities were taken seriously as *writers*—not witnesses unto atrocity or speaking wounds.

Srinivas Rayaprol's verse, and prose, has to it a peculiarly hightailing swiftness that—resembling Louis MacNeice, whom he met—makes discoveries as it goes:

> For me it was the step yesterday
> That makes me see
> That the release I've always sought
> The knot I've wished to unknot

> Is nothing more
> Than the crab's dignity in the sand
> —"CRABS IN THE SEINE"

"For me" qualifies what is to follow: we bounce from the past into the present and back again; "the awful daring" of, in T. S. Eliot's phrase, "a moment's surrender" coexists with fatalistic processes. Rayaprol devises with his syntax and lineation a "knot"—one of, as Graziano Krätli writes, his key images— which, unlike the Gordian one, can't simply be cut asunder. You can't paraphrase, that is, these cussedly tortuous lines, that are also a movement of thought, or the opposite—a stalling action that remains totally compelling.

The problem is this. Rayaprol writes strong poems and weak ones, and, worse, even the intertextures of his best poems can fray. Graziano and I worked with, to produce our edition, texts mobbed by misprints and skew-whiff English, not all of which can be blamed on Rayaprol's editors. The poems evince, when they become unidiomatic or phrasally clenched, an Indian English distinctively his. He writes of an emotional disorder his language to some extent reproduces, but with felicities that imply deliberation. The power of "Sometimes," for instance, seems to depend on an inability to verbally pin down the poem's referent, an inability we could relate to the poor fit between Rayaprol's complex sensibility and the English language as he inherits it:

> Sometimes it is the tragedy of words and meanings
> Sometimes of ambitions and fulfilments
> Sometimes it is the nameless fear at the base of your skull
>
> Sometimes it is the private pain of love
> Living under the surface like an unhealed wound.
> Sometimes it is the distortion of your face
> In a cracked mirror.
> The unrecorded thoughts, the unregistered feeling.

His language here is clear and powerful, combining ungrammatical anaphora with, arriving in the second stanza, more conclusive syntax. The negative prefixes in "unhealed," "unrecorded," and "unregistered" coolly analyze failures the verse doesn't manifest. But this isn't always the case with Rayaprol, and it prompts the big question: are the poems consciously (not haplessly) wonky? I think so, though I also prize in them a voice that isn't wholly and perpetually self-secure, expressing without undue defensiveness a hybrid intelligence informed, and deformed, by both Indian living and U.S. writing.

During and after his stint in the States, Rayaprol was nourished by his friendship with William Carlos Williams ("when in the winter of 1950 I found myself in New York on a winter vacation, I wrote to Dr. Williams that I would like to meet him . . . though he had mis-spelt my name, his welcome was warm and genuine"). He writes of Williams that "his poetic line has been organically welded to American speech like muscle to bone." This organic relation, even simultaneity, between speaking in English and writing in English wasn't possible for Rayaprol; yet he learned from Williams to forgo crypsis, detail sincerely, and to be explorative rather than confirmatory in his lineation:

> Each night the flesh moves
> its heavy weight on the air
> and at morning the distant
>
> wall of a broken barn breaks
> through the nightlong snow.

From night, to morning, and then back to "nightlong"—the mixed time signatures do so much, but I was stuck to explain the force upon me of "Here It Is Spring Again" until I read "Yesterday": a poem about U.S. race relations, spoken from the perspective of an African American woman amid bus passengers "with blank eyes / and unlovely faces" who won't sit next to her (only a blind man does). "Unlovely" took me back to Alfred Lord Tennyson and the best-known section of his elegy for Arthur Hallam, "In Memoriam A.H.H.":

> Dark house, by which once more I stand
> Here in the long unlovely street . . .
>
> He is not here; but far away
> The noise of life begins again,

And ghastly thro' the drizzling rain
On the bald street breaks the blank day.

Rayaprol engages unconventionally with the developments of Anglo-American modernism, but his reading goes back still further: words and sounds ("bald street breaks"; "broken barn breaks") migrate—I can think of no better word, for doctors also use it to describe the transference of pain from one limb to another—out of Tennyson's verse and into his. When the image recurs in "Pastorale"—"the first broken wall of a barn / broke the rhythm that monotony / sometimes has on the moving eye"—we see that his inquiry into perception is also, as in Williams, a self-consciousness of poetic style.

These borrowings need to be distinguished from the sentimental copy-and-pasting by Indian poets writing in English, of the banalities of Victorian and Edwardian verse. Rajeev Patke tells us that nineteenth-century poetry was "diligently imitative"; what you get from the colonized's first attempts at artistic originality is "mimicry, incongruity, and ineptness." In his memoir *The True Paradise*, the Sri Lankan writer and critic Gāmini Salgādo tells of being defended, absurdly, in court, for playing truant. At first glance, his lawyer appears to speak the kind of malformed, wordy, and in Arvind Mehrotra's phrase, "babu" English evolving grotesquely out of what the Raj left behind. But this scatter plot of fevered citations from Palgrave's *Treasury* is in fact quite brilliantly constructed, as de Silva (hired with a couple of rupees the boy was meant to spend on biryani at a cricket match) preens in court as marvelously as Oscar Wilde:

"Your Honour, we have here a truly piteous case of oppression and harassment. Consider this young lad setting off at break of day with shining morning face, eager to arrive at his alma mater and there imbibe the invigorating waters of learning from the Pyrennean springs."

The magistrate looked imploringly at Mr de Silva but he was too far gone for imploring looks.

"Education, Your Honour, is the inalienable right of every citizen of this resplendent isle. It is the cornerstone of our democratic system, the stepping stone on which each and every one of us rises from our dead self to fresh fields and pastures new."

It's funny, but there's a point to it, because English was, and perhaps remains, an aspirational matter to Indians and Sri Lankans, a "stepping stone" to power: magnificently authoritative, it seems to promise, if conquered and internalized, an eloquence putting one forever beyond harm. The colonial dreams of taking the master's language and, with it, his magic. I'd like to believe the event really occurred as Salgādo pictures it, but there is a stylistic debt to a book, and a scene, mentioned in his lecture on "Shakespeare and Myself": the bit of *Huckleberry Finn* where the supposed duke of Bridgwater staples together Shakespeare quotations from multiple soliloquies into one spectacular farrago. Salgādo quotes this speech in his lecture before identifying it and asking "who does not feel a warm glow of recognition steal over him as the familiar phrases in such a passage as this fall softly on the delighted ear?" He's sincere, but in a lecture focusing his own otherness, "who does not feel . . . ?" is more than a rhetorical question; in both Twain's novel, with its U.S. vernacular, and his own, where Shakespearean English meets Ceylonese diction, a point is made about colonial power and literary canonicity.

Salgādo was one of England's first nonwhite full professors of English—joining Exeter University in 1977 after studying at Nottingham. He wrote on both Renaissance literature and D. H. Lawrence, a strong influence on his memoir. Constructed posthumously of gathered fragments by Salgādo's widow, Fenella Copplestone, it was published by Carcanet in 1993, including as an appendix that inaugural lecture on "Shakespeare and Myself." Because it's unlikely you'll be able to acquire it—I've tried to no avail to interest publishers in reprinting it—I quote large sections here. The lecture contains several assertions, stances, positionings, that speak forcefully now, to what literary criticism might and should be:

> Personal involvement with literature is not an accident or an inadequacy to be apologized for, but an essential and integral element. . . . The point is so obvious and so simple that some of you might wonder who had ever denied it. But such is the prestige of scientific method in our day that more than one effort has been made to . . . propose as an ideal for the study of literature that independence from the nature and aspirations of the knower which is characteristic of scientific knowledge. Disregarding all our human experience, some people write about literature as if the only criteria for meaning, value and

truth are those deriving from quantification, measurement and the most brutally reductivist notions of utility.

The first and most obvious difficulty is that the language of Shakespeare is not my own. We all know, of course, that Shakespeare is universal, not only for all times but for all places. But if we allow this universality too early and too easily it becomes all too often a matter of playing ritual obeisance to a conventional monument. The universality then becomes the stock recognition of a collection of Wayside Pulpit platitudes or the baleful glitter of Gems from Shakespeare; and this can only lead us, if we are honest, either to indifference or to sympathy with Shavian iconoclasm. Like any universality worth talking about, Shakespeare's is a matter of particularities, the particularities of language.

Among the many passages and corridors of history, few can be more cunning and contrived than that which led to the establishment of Shakespeare's tongue as a second language in a little island thousands of miles from England, where Englishmen had scarcely set foot in Shakespeare's lifetime. Of that ambiguous legacy I am one of the beneficiaries.

The phrase "the heresy of paraphrase" gained a wide currency some years ago and was used to indicate that great poetry communicates on its own terms and cannot be put into others. . . . But apart from making clear, for what it is worth, the plain sense of a passage, the real virtue of paraphrase is that it makes us realize, in particular detail, its own inadequacy. I remember wondering what Macbeth meant by "If it were done when 'tis done, then 'twere well / It were done quickly." Then, when I had lurched into some such paraphrase as "If whatever action is necessary would be really concluded, then the more speedily it is done, the better," I began to ponder the pathetic discrepancy between the extractable "sense" and the felt power of the original line. In doing so, I realized among other things, that the gong-like tolling of "done," the nervous flurry of "tis" and "twere" and the breathless, panic-vibrant movement of the whole line as a whole were the very shape of the meaning and that what I had extracted was only what could be extracted. But the effort of paraphrase had made this clear to me with a force I might not otherwise have felt.

The language through which I encountered Shakespeare showed . . . two faces. It was the language of school, of getting on in the world, of the alien in our midst and later, more emotively and less specifically, the language of imperialism. I could well understand, within that framework of feeling, the reaction of a French audience in 1823 to a performance of Shakespeare by the first English Shakespearean company to visit France: "Down with Shakespeare! He's Wellington's lieutenant!" But English was also the language of an inner life associated with domestic and familial relationships, though not a language we ever used at home. And this paradoxical combination applied not only to the language but to the world which it rendered real. Many things about the Shakespearean world were and remained for a long time utterly unfamiliar to me. The most obviously unfamiliar were the trees and flowers and, intimately linked with them, the deep feeling for the rhythms of life associated with the pageant of the seasons.

. . .

I am not, of course, talking about dictionary definitions which could be come by easily enough, but the sort of understanding and response that is felt in the blood and felt along the heart. Nor do I imply anything remotely analogous to the view of Aldous Huxley who, in a single sentence of his essay "Wordsworth in the Tropics," contrived to misunderstand both Wordsworth and the tropics. "Nature under a vertical sun and nourished by the equatorial rains," he wrote, "is not at all like that chaste mild deity who presides over the *Gemütlichkeit*, the prettiness, the cozy sublimities of the Lake District." No one who can thus characterize Wordsworth could be expected to see that "the pantheistic worship of Nature" which is felt to be unexportable to the tropics is precisely what distinguishes such a poem as "The Cloud Messenger" by the great fifth-century Sanskrit poet, Kalidasa.

My mother was taught at Jaffna Ladies College Wordsworth's "I wandered lonely as a cloud," though she'd no idea what a daffodil was—a Sri Lankan version of the absurdity described by Edward Kamau Brathwaite, where he explains how into the Caribbean educational system arrived "the imported alien experience of the snowfall". Children in Sri Lanka didn't know daffodils; those in the Caribbean had never seen snow; the actual experiences, the unique knowledge field, of colonized people got overwritten. Yet when Salgādo considers the flora and fauna he as a Sri Lankan couldn't recognize in Shakespeare, he begins to construct, delicately, counterintuitively, an argument for the tactical, minoritized imagination. He's *not* saying it was a good thing that Empire left its stamp on educational practices in the Global South, but he is saying that this could be understood not only as a grievance, related to subjugation, but also— seeing disenfranchised people as not just victims of history but creative reinterpreters of it—as a mental opportunity. In this way, his poetics of resistance opposes Empire without chucking the baby (Shakespeare!) out with the bathwater:

> I do not draw from this difficulty the conclusion that some may expect me to draw, namely that this aspect of Shakespeare was either indifferent or, worse still, irrelevant to my understanding and appreciation. This would be a notion of relevance so barbarously short-sighted that one would gladly believe that no one could take it seriously—if only there were not such overwhelming evidence to the contrary. Far from this being the case, the effort to conceive and imagine that which in real life was simply not there was one of the most stimulating and enriching aspects of the study of Shakespeare and English literature. The lily that grew in the mind may not have been a recognizable botanical specimen but it was truly a plant or flower of light. And I would want to argue that, trivial as it is, this instance is a type of what literary understanding is, the imaginative effort to recognize the remote as present, to understand the other, be it time, person, place or thing.

Salgādo's recovery of subjective knowledge anticipates the personal, or postcritical, turn in literary studies, especially as practiced by people of color who can't take a position of objective (read: white-coded) authority for granted, but feel they must outline *where they're coming from*. He argues for clear writing in academic criticism and close reads without shame, because, in a sophisticated point, he sees the "particularities" of literature as the only route back to what some consider the exploded concept of "universality."

What was previously spoken of as the "universal" was merely a disguise for the perspective of a global elite: but Salgādo's return to that term haunts me. It seems to speak of the most important things, as I've felt afraid to.

Salgādo commences a view of literature that, though it doesn't assume that everyone's had the same experiences, holds the same views, or reads from the same position, nevertheless forsakes the alternative logic of subcultural identification (i.e., Sri Lankan readers, only wanting to read Sri Lankan writers on the subject of Sri Lanka) for a heuristics of the imagination. This isn't the sort of imagination that worships Shakespeare as a type of all-conquering marble hero, which would be just another type of disguised identification (the passage on the "baleful glitter of Gems from Shakespeare" takes us back to Twain and de Silva's speech in court, both of which introduce surprise, humor, and alterity into the reciting of Shakespeare, to get us beyond "stock recognition.") It is rather such imagining as, risking alienation and injury, encounters literature with a willingness toward the unfamiliar and a susceptibility to wholesale transformation.

Salgādo also defends the practice of memorizing poetry, or learning it off by heart, the idiom he prefers, for "if we remember what we love, we can also learn to love by the effort of remembering. . . . In our educational activity we have lost any sense of the connection between memory and love." *The True Paradise* is also about the "effort of remembering," as that effort combines with, for the émigré, a more involuntary Proustian recall of one's childhood in another country. It records a middle-class boy's Buddhist-Sinhala upbringing prior to Independence and the civil war. (That violence exists in the book as a futurity casting its shadow on a remembered past: playing as a boy with "a wooden sword with the blade painted silver," Salgādo "used to beat down the tall reeds by the river with it, King Gāmini driving the Tamils back across the sea to India.") Here is a homegrown response to Leonard Woolf's *The Village in the Jungle,* shaped by an imagination conversant with diverse literatures. The title is from Proust himself. "Les vrais paradis son les paradis qu'on a perdus"; or, in sadly unalliterative English: *the true paradises are those we've lost.*

Considering Sri Lanka, Salgādo writes lyrically, yearningly, but is cognizant of his distance from a homeland reshaped not only by the civil war and its aftermath but also an unevenly globalizing modernity. He confronts the imperfections of memory both at the level of the sentence and that of the narrative (Fenella Copplestone put it together of fragments after his death), whose arcs make his memoir a work of art, not straight autobiography. Describing the local Buddhist temple, Salgādo hints uneasily, in his description of the priest's bald head, at that faith's collusion with state violence (after the civil war, Hindu sites were erased and replaced with new, bright-white *stupas*): "The chief priest's head, completely shaved and oiled, twinkled like a polished copper ball in the yellow morning sunlight, and the tendrils of hair on his ears glimmered like fine wire. His chin often had a whitish stubble, but no matter how close you looked, his head presented only a burnished metallic surface." I'm reminded of the gaze-obscuring aviator sunglasses worn by Boss Godfrey in *Cool Hand Luke*. Such is the hard unyielding surface of power; a purity ethic always on the verge of intolerance. "I hated him with the boundless hatred of childhood": the priest's a sadist who flicks his student's ears and tears out his hair.

It's notable that when the boy does have a genuine religious experience in the temple, it's impure and confused. Buddhism meets Hinduism, in a prose style inspired by D. H. Lawrence:

> Inside, the walls from left to right were lined with blue-painted statues of the Hindu gods, their fantastically complicated golden head-dresses and the whites of their bulbous eyes gleaming eerily out of the incense-laden darkness.
>
> Buddhism has no god of its own so through the centuries we have borrowed a few from Hinduism, because it is difficult for men to live without doing homage to the gods, even if they don't believe in them. At the foot of each figure was a little ledge on which were laid offerings of candles, joss-sticks and sometimes even flowers, though most of the flower offerings were laid before the gigantic sleeping Buddha which took up the entire back wall and reached, at the shoulders, right up to the ceiling. The altar before the statue seemed almost as big as the statue itself, but often it was difficult to find room for your handful of flowers on it, so thickly was it piled with shallow reed baskets or cones of flowers among which the candles and joss-sticks flickered like fire-flies. The even, ochre-coloured stone folds of the sleeping Buddha's robe fell away towards the enormous feet like ribbed sea-sand. I could not cover the nail of the big toe with both my palms. The vermilion lips seemed strangely out of place in the gentle, candle-coloured face.

The orchestration of this passage reveals Salgādo's control of sound, syntax, and tone. The *o* sound prominent in the sentence about the Buddha's robe is picked up by "big toe," as the astonishment of the child-observer is reinserted thrillingly and livingly into what might become a static description; the long *a* sound of that gigantic "nail" generates in the final sentence a rhyme linking "place" and "face." Salgādo learned his refrains from Lawrence, whose poem "Reading a Letter," for example, features both "earth-coloured life" and "chalk-coloured tulips." Applying this to a Buddhist temple, he draws on what he identifies, in his study of Lawrence, as that author's displaced religiosity, his sentences with "the hallucinatory and incantatory quality we associate with ritual." Both Salgādo and the Indian novelist-critic Amit Chaudhuri find in Lawrence, so easy to pillory as a racist, sexist antique, an aesthetics of difference.

Lawrence's white unease at foreign cultures—an unease bordering on fetishism of the "noble savage," and what he imagines as instinctual, pre-civilized freedoms—is turned towards a different sort of intracommunal discomfort, pertaining to how in Sri Lanka the Buddhist-Sinhala majority has failed to do justice by the Hindu-Tamil minority. The "bulbous eyes" of the Hindu gods threaten; they're assimilated not only within the temple architecture but also the prose itself, which, however, comments intelligently on this process. In her afterword, Copplestone notes that on Salgādo's last trip to Sri Lanka "he experienced the horror of hearing at first hand how his brother had had to protect Tamil neighbours from the murderous mob which had burned and looted his home area."

Salgādo's estranged perception (it is the author himself who'll soon be, culturally and geographically, "out of place"; he knows, too, he's discussing Ceylonese sculpture in stylized English prose) is nuanced by the shift from the Buddha's "ochre-coloured" robe to his "gentle, candle-coloured" visage. This adjective takes a changed inflection if we remember its precursor— the soft jostle of "gentle" against "candle" also contributes to its judged exquisiteness. In the chapter "A Journey to School," Salgādo is arrested for squeezing onto a crammed train and, asked by the authorities for his name, provides that of James Joyce's Stephen Dedalus. A portrait of the artist as a young man: this chapter moves from lyrical excitement to humiliation to eventual triumph in a way strongly reminiscent of Joyce's novel, with a hint as to this early on, when Salgādo reads the "rust-pocked enamelled station advertisements," including one for "STEPHEN'S INK with the big blue splotch like congealed blood except the wrong colour (though for a long time I had believed that 'blue-blooded aristocracy' was a literal description of English aristocrats)." Color, blood, nation: the Irish writer lends Salgādo something crucial in his attempt at a Sri Lankan literary style: an exactitude of perception borrowed from modernism is used, in particular, to evoke the intonations of Ceylonese English, revealing how class and community is expressed through linguistic registers.

The town crier deploys a "kind of pompous pseudo-classical Sinhalese, rather like that used by monks in their sermons," delivered—skipping ahead a few pages—"in a uniform sing-song drone which was inescapably soporific"; the white registrar-general who arrives to certify the marriage of Salgādo's parents speaks not "the English read in Father's beloved books but a dry airless tongue, a language clipped, filed and orderly, a bald impersonal necessary language." And on that train journey to school "a trousered and solar-topeed gentleman in the corner seat" takes the boy's bag but is disappointed by the copy of *Portrait* it contains: "'Once upon a time and a very good time it was there was a moocow coming down along the road met a nicens little boy named baby tuckoo . . . I say, I say, what is all this nonsense, man? You're sure you are not bringing your baby brother's Beacon Infant Reader by mistake, hah?'" This "Joyce James," the gentleman avers, must "be American—English authors know how to write better than that. Not even a single comma or full stop anywhere that I can see. After all their own bloody language no?" Salgādo shares with Stephen Dedalus his politically nervous relationship with English as well as a final move away from an aesthetic of suspicion and toward a cosmopolitan freedom claiming that language as one's own.

What is available to Salgādo, then, given the breadth of his reading, his transhistorical awareness of English style, and his academic authority, is a position of mastery that, though it ramifies within his unsullen lyrical prose, nevertheless remains a wellspring of surety. Those descriptions of Sri Lankan voices sound like close readings of literature: writing of Jacobean tragedy, for instance, Salgādo mentions "Marston's determination to make every line count, coupled with the nearest thing to a tin ear among any of the important dramatists of the time," which makes "his language sound turgid and bombastic." I wonder if these style-noticings express his own insider-outsider relation to the English language, a situation his niche in academia allowed him to safely intellectualize.

Rayaprol didn't have such luck, but it could be that never quite knowing the dress code is precisely what makes his English so alive and prepossessing. It's not just the glitches I've mentioned, and the nonavailability of his books up to this point, that prevent his accession: it's also that he's never so boring as to put the postcolonial position plainly (I doubt, in fact, that he could put anything plainly). As with Salgādo, we recognize the historical dimension of such writing through attention to style (in this case, Rayaprol's idiosyncratic and sometimes internally inconsistent, within a given poem, verse forms). Let's consider *white* as it appears from poem to poem, accruing depth as it goes, becoming what William Empson once described as a "complex word" (like *honest* in Shakespeare's *Othello* or *sense* in Wordsworth's *Prelude*). It's often applied to snow, which as we've seen, fascinates Rayaprol—as with the Caribbean children described by Brathwaite, he'd likely never seen it before coming to the U.S.—and which he often turns into an abstract "white" weight descending from the sky. He also writes frankly, sexually, of complexions. Sometimes, the incongruence of his brown skin with those environing him is displaced into nature: "How like white / is the white snow // Before tomorrow's sun / takes it all away // and leaves the streets / brown as before." But he can also be explicit:

> Fat old men with flat white faces
> That shine out of the pages of *Time*
> And speak to me
>
> Of the unspeakable pleasures possible
> Between our bodies.
> —"ALL KINDS OF LOVE"
>
> I speak not of the mystery that is woman
> Nor of the great white being that is God—
> I do not speak of love, or of people,
> For I have known neither father nor lover
> And none have I reached with what I cannot utter.
>
> But I speak of the lonely word
> That will not reach beyond my tongue
> Nor fulfill my frustrations.
> —"THIS POEM"

Sexuality can also be a matter of aspiration to reach a locus of power and fame—this is what *Time* magazine stands for—where all one's yearnings will convert, like caterpillars becoming butterflies, into a banquet of unanxious pleasures. "Many years ago, when I was about seventeen or eighteen, my one ambition was to be a great poet, but I did not know what it meant except to thrill at a line of Auden or a word of Wallace Stevens, and imagine the unimaginable—that one day I, too, would join the galaxy. Poets were lonely people, I had heard, and was I not the loneliest of the lonely?" As an Indian immigrant (and then an Indian back home) it was harder for Rayaprol than for others to "speak" of his homosexual feelings, but the slap-bang candor of the first poem and the braggadocio (the inversions, the syntax) of the second suggest that it was never easy for him to "speak," in his verse on any subject. There were always obstacles, and he couldn't make up his mind whether to glide above them in the passenger jet of a refined high style or to make his way on foot (again, like Williams), incorporating into his poetics the textures of the terrain.

Can a frustration be "fulfilled?" Perhaps: it's another of those moments where we see Rayaprol seeking the foothold of a received phrase, or the contour of a preexisting idiom, only to veer toward a perhaps unintended originality. He admired in the painter Jamini Roy that "at a certain stage of his life, he had the courage to discard everything he knew and had learned as an artist, and to plunge in the dark: a certain light within his head must have been his only direction." Rayaprol's prose suggests of his plunging verse that we're concerned here with a total experimentalism, a risking of the basic unit of coherence. A refusal to turn the project of self-understanding into self-assuagement:

> I have never been more
> than the occasion demanded
>
> have never been in an occasion
> which demanded more than me
>
> I have never had the mind's argument
> dislodged by the horses of the heart
>
> have never ridden horses
> which did not know their riders
> —"POEM FOR A BIRTHDAY"

Because the English words are strange to him, Rayaprol inhabits his first idea like Hamlet having nightmares within a nutshell. He tries out a phrase, turns it inside out, seeking a mathematical equivalency; projecting an ideal fit between a person and his environment (an immigrant's dream), he begins to realize that what is lost from such a zero-sum game is personality itself. We might think "riders" is another typo (should it be "rider?") but the point may be that you can never ride the same horse, just as you can never step in the same river, more than once: there are an infinite number of both horses and riders.

Returning to India and becoming a civil engineer, Rayaprol wasn't happy. It could be he needed to be on the move, to (like Philip Larkin visiting Ireland) at some level not belong. Certainly, his one masterpiece, "Poem" (his titles are revealing, the hurriedly applied labels of tryouts in test tubes, haphazardly shelved) seems a love letter to those who, rooted in the one place, grow identical with it, but also a sort of prayer—you can hear it as you read, a countermelody—to never be that person:

> In India
> Women
>
> Have a way
> Of growing old
>
> My mother
> For instance
>
> Sat on the floor
> A hundred years
>
> Stirring soup
> In a sauce-pan
>
> Sometimes staring
> At the bitter neem tree in the yard
>
> For a hundred years
> Within the kitchen walls.

The woman, "my mother," is exactly where, it would seem, she belongs; how does she feel about it? The transferred epithet "bitter," the trick done, once again, with time—so Rayaprol seems to present a visionary instant and also a grief-stricken duration—it's a poem to anthologize, and canonize, and there are many others here that deserve to be read the world over.

You Can't Close Your Eyes for a Sec
Arvind Krishna Mehrotra

They don't make just anybody a Penguin Modern Classic. "Born in Lahore in 1947"—I quote from the solid paragraph of author description, bristling impressively with the italicized titles and dates of his many books—"Arvind Krishna Mehrotra is the author of four previous collections of poetry" and "two of translation," notably *Songs of Kabir*; he has also edited the "ground-breaking" (the adjective is applied only to the first of these books, but could well describe all three) *Oxford India Anthology of Twelve Modern Poets*, which appeared in 1992, *An Illustrated History of Indian Literature in English*, arriving just over a decade later, and the *Collected Poems in English* of his close friend and poetic peer, Arun Kolatkar. Published in 2010, it was Mehrotra's Kolatkar that, published in the UK by Bloodaxe, changed my life by introducing me to Indian verse in English: I'd thought previously of postcolonial literature as something urged on me by cack-handed, if well-intentioned, white academics, seeing my brown face and leaping to mentor me; as a jargon-infested realm obligating one to consume, and then regurgitate, a thousand theory-mauled sentences before being permitted to begin to think about one day intending to eventually read a work of literature. But Mehrotra's Kolatkar was funny, savage, complex, no doubt in ways that answered to such analysis, but also immediately pleasure-giving—it revealed to me another path. I had been stuck in a dark wood and saw now through the trees a glimmer of light.

And then I'd always wanted to write essays more unbuttoned and diverse than academic prose allowed for and been disappointed to see that, with the exception of some extraordinary women (Susan Sontag, Barbara Everett), such books were inevitably written by white men about other white men. Mehrotra's collected essays, *Partial Recall*, arrived in 2011, the same year as his Kabir translations, and once again opened my eyes. If you haven't read those essays, you must; but not before reading his own poems, which I've now had the privilege of editing for New York Review of Books. As this list of publications makes all too clear, Mehrotra's importance to the world of Indian letters (which he also criticizes plentifully, for its amnesiac vanity) is indisputable—but the verse itself remains to be analyzed. What kind of poet is he?

Seeking a description, let's consider his introduction to the *Oxford India Anthology*, now in its sixteenth reprinting: "I have wanted to reveal through a particular choice of poets and poems the sharp-edged quality of Indian verse." These poems dissect, can wound, and don't match up with the boisterous (maximalist) salability of much Indian fiction in English. Salman Rushdie called his own process a *chutnification* of English; the Kashmiri American poet Agha Shahid Ali preferred *biryanization*. The concept of hybridity, linking these metaphors, has become definitive. But Mehrotra's sharp-edgedness, though it draws on multiple sources (*bhakti* poetry, Anglo-American formalism, surrealism, and the Beats) is different. The verse style he cherishes as an editor and practices as a poet isn't concerned, like Rushdie or his imitators, with stretching the English language to its bursting point.

What's Indian about this verse, that is, isn't evinced by blatancy, an over-the-topness that fizzes, seethes, and may finally cloy, nor by the profusion of exotic details that can turn writing about South Asia, and indeed the Global South more generally, into a sensationalistic parading of otherness. (When details do feature, they can be ironic: "If I told you the names of the mango / Varieties we had here," drily remarks the tenant narrator of "Number 16," "you'd think I was / Speaking from an imaginary textbook / On horticulture.") These poems resist overt displays of nationality and have a minimalist rather than maximalist distinctiveness. Acerbic, saddened, they arrive in clear spurts and outline a bullshit-free zone. Here's "January," from the 1982 collection *Distance in Statute Miles*:

> The gate wide open; chairs on the lawn;
> Circular verandahs; a narrow kitchen;
> High-ceilinged rooms; arches; alcoves; skylights.
> My house luminous; my day burnt to ash.

This small and perfectly formed poem depends on the versatility of the semicolon, which can both divide the items of a list and separate the terms of a binary opposition. As with all short poems, what's excluded or bracketed out performs a vital absence, and it's also notable how the sound of "rooms" is dropped into "luminous," troubling that otherwise smoothly lyrical adjective.

My essay's titled for the last line of "Looking Out," a newish poem that connects with semicolons water beads on willow branches, squirrels on the verandah, parrots in flight, and, finally,

> The spotted owlet in the mango tree,
> Looking in through the open window where I
> Sit at a jade table looking out, in a house
> Where nothing happens that so much happens
> You can't close your eyes for a sec.

The house serves as a metaphor for India—"O house by the mill we're trapped in," remarks Mehrotra in a poem dated June 26, 1975, the day Indira Gandhi declared the state of emergency—but "January" also recalls and reverses the phrasing of a recent interview in *Mint*, where he complains of Allahabadis that "everyone thinks that it's all happening here, when actually there's nothing happening here."

"Looking Out" describes not Mehrotra's gardenless flat in that city but his house in Dehradun. A riotousness-in-quietness, an unmetropolitan locus of more-than-personal, even spiritual meaning, is captured with a burst of pace and a whip-crack vernacular finish reminiscent of the American verse that has nurtured him. "We belong to the houses we live in," writes Mehrotra in "Hoopoe," and buildings feature strongly. He evokes their insides and outsides and his own emplacement with a delicate appraising eye, a sureness that never grows cosy. Both reposeful and alert, the poet keeps his finger on the pulse. I mention U.S. verse: Mehrotra is—pun intended—*at home* in verse enriched by multiple traditions. In "The Emperor Has No Clothes," a seminal essay (that adjective is desiccated, wince-worthy, but necessary in this case) published in the early 1980s, he complicates Rajagopal Parthasarathy's limited understanding of A. K. Ramanujan's work. Ramanujan wrote in, and studied works emerging out of, different languages; yet, for Parthasarathy, his own verse depends for its authenticity on a buried nativeness. "For the model to hold we have to agree"—it's a delight to watch Mehrotra's wickedly sparkling intelligence at work—"that Ramanujan arranges Tamil and Kannada in the lower strata,

English in the upper, and each time he chooses to write he descends, caged canary bird in hand, into the thickly-seamed coal pit of the mother tongue." This "inflexible, stratified order" must be replaced with an open-ended and nonhierarchical view of the "multilingual sensibility": Mehrotra links Ramanujan with writers like Vladimir Nabokov and Jorge Luis Borges.

We require, to appreciate this sort of poet-critic, an awareness of the overlap between poetic and critical style. As Amit Chaudhuri remarks in his introduction to the *Collected*, the "wonderfully scolding, imprecatory, cutting voice" (that sharp edge again!) that Mehrotra brings to bear on national book culture is also there in *Songs of Kabir*—his translations of that impish mystic are contumaciously eclectic, merging in active speech present and past—as well as his own verse. Hence the sting in the tail of both "January" and "Looking Out," where listed details emit, come the end, a blast of head-clearing insight. John Donne said a poem's power lies in its conclusion, which "is as the impression of the stamp, and that is it that makes it current." This coin metaphor is literalized in Mehrotra's short, snappy "For a Slave King 2"; unremembered for his reign (*Delhi*, 1211, reads the epigraph) of scarcely a year, this Ozymandias figure found time to strike a pose or, to be exact, "strike a copper coin, / Bearing on the obverse the legend, / 'The victorious Aram Shah, the Sultan.'"

Sharp closing twists also occur in Mehrotra's critical prose, as when he ends a paragraph with a note on "Aurobindo Ghose, who spent the last years of his life composing a worthless epic of 24,000 lines," or caps an amiable summary of Jayanta Mahapatra's "Hunger" by telling us the poem "is, however, spoiled a little towards the end when, in a careless moment, Mahapatra compares the girl's legs to worms." Nor is the device always destructive. Mehrotra's final endnote on his Kabir translations refers to the "shining nothingness" that "sums up, as well as anything can, Kabir's unclouded view of human life. It's a view he repeated in poem after poem, almost obsessively." After this, four-fifths of page 145 is blank. We're left to ponder Kabir's repetitions and whether they express a personal hang-up or a spiritual truth.

What fascinates in all these examples is the refusal of unified tone; an awareness of the poem as a grab bag of fancies, fillips, and velleities; the mixture of lingering sensitive focus and quarrelsome brush-off: Mehrotra prods, amuses, catches us off guard. Academics studying world literature could learn from his tonal variety, which resists at all junctures the cessation of cognition that is the perpetual allurement of a wafflingly untroubled and therefore dullard discursiveness. But listen too carefully, learn too much, imitate the poet too entirely, and you're done for; his is a terminal language, perpetually self-skeptical, whose words seek to vanish in an instant of illuminating surprise. Kabir's *ulatbamsi* or "upside-down poems," in which, Mehrotra has it, "language disrupts communication, forcing us to think in new ways"—"There's a fire / Raging in the ocean. . . . You're the cage, / I the parrot inside, / Watching death's cat / Meowing outside"— bear comparison with the surrealism of his 1976 debut, *Nine Enclosures*:

> Talking of animals I've seen cats
> Sulking beside the sea
> There lies at its bottom
> A submarine full of mice

This sequence appears in the *Collected Poems* with its title changed from "Eleven Cross-Sections" to "Songs of the Good Surrealist": "for me, who started writing in the 1960s, the discovery of surrealism helped resolve the awful contradiction between the world I wanted to write about, the world of dentists and chemist shops, and the language, English, I wanted to write in." The restored title reveals Mehrotra's surrealism as, however, always a form of irony or pastiche. Its bizarrerie morphs in eye-catching lines into something more like wisdom: "Mornings I fell from trees are poisoned wells."

Introducing the *Illustrated History of Indian Literature in English*, Mehrotra mentions intriguingly (the choice of adjective) the scholar William Jones's "universalist and surreal ideas of race." *Surreal* drops out when this piece is reprinted in *Partial Recall*, perhaps because the word has been imprecisely used. But in describing as surreal the theories of the man known as "Oriental Jones"—who came to India in the eighteenth century as a supreme court judge, learned Sanskrit to better administer, and discovered proto-Indo-European, the shared ancestor of several Eastern and Western languages—Mehrotra aligns that adjective with a wild mixing of races and cultures and the "notion of a common homeland for mankind, from which it had centuries ago migrated to different parts of the globe." What happens in his poetry is that, finally, the surprising juxtapositions are those resulting from colonial processes—the weirdness is already there in India; it doesn't have to be surrealistically and defamiliarizingly engineered by the poet. He finds a way of apparently jotting down, quite simply, the absurd facts while actually writing deceptively crafted poems.

My favorite of this kind is "On the Death of a Sunday Painter," which again I quote in full:

> He smoked a cherry-wood pipe, knew all about cannas,
> And deplored our lack of a genuine fast bowler.
> My uncle called his wife Soft Hands.
> Once in 1936 as he sat reading *Ulysses*
> In his Holland Hall drawing-room, a student walked in.
> Years later I read him an essay on D. H. Lawrence
> And the Imagists. He listened,
> Then spoke of Lord Clive, the travels of Charles Doughty,
> "My dear young fellow . . ."
> I followed the mourners on my bicycle
> And left early. His friends watched the cremation
> From the portico of a nearby house.

John Ashbery described Elizabeth Bishop as a "writer's writer's writer"; I'd call this the poet's poet's poem. It looks so easy and yet the sentence arrangement, the rhythm, the manipulation of the conflicting tissues and time signatures of anecdote is all so wonderfully precise. (There's a wistful new poem here, "The Sting in the Tail"—a phrase this essay borrows, for last lines—about reading Ashbery in Allahabad, "a glass of tepid / Fennel-flavoured sherbet by your side." He may influence Mehrotra's surreal poems, but this one ends with the concrete "thwack!" of a slapped mosquito; a rejoinder, I suspect, to the—it's Seamus Heaney—"centrally heated day-dream" of Ashbery's verse.)

Mehrotra's Sunday painter is Rabindra Nath Deb, a university colleague of the uncle who appears in the third line. Both taught English—that Deb also painted is typical of cultured Bengalis—and Mehrotra's uncle also appears in his discussion of his early surrealism: "How do you write about an uncle in a wheelchair in the language of skylarks and nightingales? It's as though I'd said to myself that since I cannot write about these things in English, let me do so in French, so to speak. The irony that the uncle in question was himself an Oxford-educated professor of English has struck me only now." Those Romantic "skylarks and nightingales" stand for a received understanding of what poetry is supposed to be—conventions exported to the colonies were, as I mentioned in the previous essay, imitated by nineteenth-century Indian poets. Objecting to such enmeshment, overcompliance, counterfeiting, Mehrotra writes "On the Death of a Sunday Painter" in a simultaneously lucid and disjointed English that cleaves to no expected pattern. The snippets are sturdy but the order to events is uncertain, and why they merit a mention—"Once . . . a student walked in"—isn't self-evident. *My dear young fellow*: Deb speaks a mannered Oxbridge English, and this antiquated soundbite is, poetically speaking, structural, for its ellipsis allows the jump-cut to the funeral and also suggests the vanishing of a stifled yet unique personality.

We move from a smoked pipe to the cremated man; from fast bowlers to "his wife Soft Hands"; from high modernism (uninterested in D. H. Lawrence, Deb mentions a book introduced by *T. E.* Lawrence) to the inauguration of the Raj, or an echo of it. For the mention of Colonel Robert Clive, and of Deb receiving visitors, resonates with Benjamin West's 1774 painting of Lord Clive receiving from the Moghul the grant of the Duanney. This work records the signing of the treaty of Allahabad marking the start of British rule: reproducing it in the *Illustrated History,* Mehrotra mentions the "touch of farce," for some "of the Englishmen appear to be talking in whispers to each other, as do some of the Indians. The reality was quite different: Clive actually received 'the Duanney' in his tent. . . . The emperor's throne, far from being a canopied, oriental affair, was in fact Clive's dining table surmounted by an armchair." Mehrotra's elegy may remember this painting. It recreates the scene, but with that Mehrotran spin. Knowing "all about cannas," Deb may have told Mehrotra, his student, the well-known story—a piece of untrivial trivia—about the hard black seeds from this plant, also called "Indian shot," being used as ammunition by British troops during the rebellion of 1857.

"Two Lakes," also from *Distance in Statute Miles,* reveals again the stylistic control with which Mehrotra attends to the colonial period and its legacies:

> The second lake lies
> At the foot of the hill and is clean
> To the point of invisibility. On one side
> Is the club where dead Englishmen
> Sit down on tigers and play bridge.

> Specks of dust drift through their moustached faces.
> In the billiard-room the table is still
> Intact, while the stained kitchen knife
> Has appeared in the region's
> Folklore.

The first line break, on the ambiguous word "lies," stresses truth's inevitable, as well as insidiously engineered, distortions (personal, colonial, industrial, poetic) and disappearances, as does the last, isolating as it does the rich word "Folklore." This word typically describes the untainted mythos of indigenous communities. Not so here: the "stained kitchen knife" is presumably blood-stained—sounds carom and constellate to focus on that adjective our scrutinizing attention—and although the English ghosts are presented as a cinematic special effect, Mehrotra's sometime surrealism is no joking matter. This is the phantom, contused, humdrumly malign, inorganic, geography of postcolonial India: patterns of existence collide and overwrite one another in verse that, feeling realism inadequate to this state of affairs, becomes artfully and tellingly dishevelled.

Poetic form is rarely discussed in the work of Indian poets. (I keep making this point in successive essays, in the hope it will catch on; I realize that, reading this book, you may tire of it.) Their poems drop out of sight; prior to this, they may only be examined as a species of avidly historical utterance it would be trivial to also appreciate as literary art. Poems become symptoms, windows on a damaged history. But the distinction's false. Mehrotra's verse shaping is a style of thinking about events; his cosmopolitan engagement with authors from many time periods and cultures isn't passive consumerism (in the dog-eat-dog world of postcolonial criticism, accusations of bad faith come thick and fast!) but ever inquisitive. Stylistic felicities pepper his poems. Take his translation of the Hindi poet Suryakant Tripathi, popularly known as Nirala:

> Those whose heart's thatch
> Hasn't caught fire, never find
> The treasures buried there.

"Inscription," from 1998's *The Transfiguring Places*, evokes the midnight arrival "unbidden, unsigned," of a line of "eight memorable / Syllables" Mehrotra didn't record and sadly forgot. Here, the flensing frankness of that first line, its four glowing monosyllables, becomes a treasure. There's the flow of "those" into "whose," the bookending alliteration of "those" and "thatch"; the refusal, even, of the crude possible rhyme of "thatch" and "catch"; and the sonic dalliance of "fire" with both "find" and the slant rhyme "there," which appears to confirm the epigram.

This concentration is one with Mehrotra's pointed authoritativeness—he writes economically, with a care for impact, and shifts from being a surreal to a historical to a philosophical poet in registering the limits of language and literary effectiveness. The adjective I want is *tidy*, if you could remove from that word the pejorative associations of smallness, harmlessness, pettiness; Mehrotra has invented a kind of unreconciled, not smug, neatness. There's too much verbiage in the world, he seems to say, so I'll add only what truly matters. *Nine Enclosures* may appear to speak on behalf of the Ganges with a Whitmanian expansiveness: "I go out into the world / I am the world / I am nations, cities, people / I am the pages of an unbound book." Yet "Songs of the Ganga" really meets his other work (it conjures Kabir too) in the river's concise skepticism about existing arrangements and assumptions—"I make two lines in the sand / And say they are unbreakable walls" (one thinks of Cyril Radcliffe's arbitrary division of India from Pakistan in 1947)—and its canny survivalism:

> From smoke I learn disappearance
> From the ocean unprejudice
>
> From birds
> How to find a rest house
> In the storm
>
> From the leopard
> How to cover the sun
> With spots

In a tale from Kipling's *Just So Stories*, the leopard gets its spots to better disguise itself for hunting. Inverting this, Mehrotra's river voice is playful, wary, self-constructed—even a little bit vulnerable: "In summer I tend watermelons / And in flood I stay / Near the postman's house." This is the poet—fact-attentive, sentence-conscious, image-curious, rhythm-considerate—who, in "Paradise Flycatcher," admires the "unvictimized, unnoticed" love life of birds, untroubled by the "boundary fence," with "no feathered / Father or brother / Beheading them in the street / In an honour killing"; and, in new poems reminiscent of his friend Arun Kolatkar, tenderly describes working-class people, including an ironing lady whose "clothes pile up, / Each fold a stanza break, / Till she's folded the last one, / Finishing the manuscript." Who, in "Dream-Figures in Sunlight," wakes "in the city where Kipling lived" and prays:

> A hundred, a thousand
>
> Years from now, may the sap-filled bough
> Still print its shadow on running water,
> And a dusty March wind blow its leaves
> Towards a page of Kipling, a home-grown page.

Thom Gunn's Shadows Hard as Board

In his introduction to his fine, vital, note-enriched edition of Thom Gunn's poems, Clive Wilmer argues for—a paradox to unpack—Gunn's style of unique impersonality: "People used to talk in the 1960s—perhaps they still do—about true poets 'finding their own voices.' Gunn appeared not to have a distinctive voice. Indeed, he appeared to have no wish to find one." Reading this, I pause. My pencil-end hovers, before marking the margin. Wilmer knows, surely, that blurbists (and not only they) have, alas, never stopped speaking thus. "I am not 'confessional' by nature," Gunn said; Sylvia Plath is "the last person I want to be!"; "Lowell . . . is obviously central to our period in many ways, even if sometimes I cannot help wishing he wasn't." Movement poets (the label came from the *Spectator* and never sufficed, for Gunn or the rest) revealed themselves more quietly, in verse larded with English speech fillers — or, as linguists have it, "hedges" — *perhaps*, and *I suppose*, and the rest. (Donald Davie, a transatlantic migrant like Gunn, criticized his own verse for its good manners.) Gunn's "Expression," which he began writing, Wilmer informs us, in May 1977, turns from the melodrama of "very poetic poetry" to an "early Italian altar piece" of the virgin and child:

> The sight quenches, like water
> after too much birthday cake.
> Solidly there, mother and child
> stare outward, two pairs of matching eyes
> void of expression.

The poem's last word repeats its title, scrutinizing a concept central to the modern lyric. Painting also plays this corrective role in a poem written almost two decades earlier, as Gunn's verse, in firm form, manages the miracle of seeming to emit perception unmolested by personality. The first stanza of "In Santa Maria del Popolo," from his third book, *My Sad Captains* (1961):

> Waiting for when the sun an hour or less
> Conveniently oblique makes visible
> The painting on one wall of this recess
> By Caravaggio, of the Roman School,
> I see how shadow in the painting brims
> With a real shadow, drowning all shapes out
> But a dim horse's haunch and various limbs,
> Until the very subject is in doubt.

An "I" appears and "conveniently" is witty. But the plaited rhythms and perception-enhancing meter really conjure the equivalent of a painting in verse. The speaker is present, but as a point of view in the literal and not the opinionating sense. Why should his feelings obtrude when the data can be given us untainted?

Gunn refused to position himself as a "gay poet"—though he wrote directly, and with compassionate acuity, about the sex lives of gay men (early on, he pretended a woman addressee in some of his poems). Of his poem "Carnal Knowledge," in his first collection, *Fighting Terms* (1954), he claimed: "anyone aware that I am homosexual is likely to misread the whole poem." Against Gunn's wishes, one could limn a psychobiographical trajectory in his *Selected Poems*: once he moved to San Francisco, shortly after the publication of *Fighting Terms*, he wrote more openly about being gay and accepted, with refinements, the idea of a free verse capable of true spontaneity. You could say the uptight Brit loosened up once he crossed the pond. But Gunn always accepted control and impulse as interlocking elements: he continued to write both freely and formally. He insisted on a verse tradition of greater antiquity than creative writing programs like to admit — he was a great admirer, for instance, of Ben Jonson, who reveals, in Gunn's words, that "artifice is not necessarily the antithesis of sincerity" — and liked to make remarks such as: "in his attraction to inherently awkward material, Ginsberg resembles Hardy" or, "I want to be an Elizabethan poet. I want to write with the same kind of anonymity that you get in the same way somebody like Ben Jonson did. At the same time I want to write in my own century." As a gay man, he was fortunate to live in the twentieth and not the seventeenth. But we shouldn't claim of his life and his desires simply a case of pre-Stonewall opacity replaced by post-Stonewall candor, or of individual self-liberation (that would be where the myth of "voice" comes in, and, as stated, he was no confessionalist). As Gunn wrote in "My Life Up to Now": "My life insists on continuities — between America and England, between free verse and metre, between vision and everyday consciousness."

Wilmer's selection is the ideal place to begin with Gunn — the major poems are here, and the facts of their provenance (over seventy pages of this book are given over to notes); sequences arrive happily entire. Wilmer is truly selective — he rightly takes just five poems from Gunn's first book. His second volume, *The Sense of Movement* (1957), made his reputation in England, and produced a couple of masterpieces. "On the Move," the first poem in the collection, is one:

> On motorcycles, up the road, they come:
> Small, black, as flies hanging in heat, the Boys,
> Until the distance throws them forth, their hum
> Bulges to thunder held by calf and thigh.
> In goggles, donned impersonality,
> In gleaming jackets trophied with the dust,
> They strap in doubt—by hiding it, robust—
> And almost hear a meaning in their noise.

Equally inspired by, or obsessed with, the films of Marlon Brando and the existentialism of Sartre and Camus, this is very much a young man's poem, but few young men can write like this. In his criticism Gunn speaks eloquently, and vividly, the language of metrical verse, and this poem uses variations in the pentameter available for centuries in the service of a contemporary astonishment. (The assonance, and the inverted first foot, outlining those "bulges!")

In "On the Move," the verse rhythm is already more susceptible, and uncertain, than it seems. The commas in the first two lines quoted are marvelously controlled—a delight for the savoring ear—but they also register that "doubt" eventually strapped in and hidden (where the fitting of rhyme to rhyme is the poet's own version of this process). Writing of Thomas Hardy, Gunn says his "poetry is almost always robust, never fretful or neurotic." Yet in this poem the hidden neurosis is acknowledged. And we shouldn't miss, in either the essay on Hardy or "On the Move," the genuinely mitigating (rather than habitual) word *almost*—as crucial here as when it appears twice at the close of Philip Larkin's "An Arundel Tomb," from which it tends to vanish whenever that poem is sentimentally quoted. The internal rhyme with "dust" and "robust" emphasizes the word: Gunn won't wholly idealize his kinetic toughs.

Comparing this with the verse of his following books, we see how Gunn gradually learned to combine his rhymes with soft-hard meter. "In Santa Maria del Popolo" is slicker, less insistent and more insinuating — the syntactical distensions have become second nature. In 1965 Gunn collaborated with his brother Ander on the photography collection *Positives* (only "The Old Woman" makes the cut here); two years later, *Touch* appeared, containing the sequence "Misanthropos" (solipsism diagrammed with a diamond-point chisel) and also the famous title poem. Here sexuality is held in abeyance, allowing a space for the metaphysical; the speaker melts toward, and into, his lover, and the experience requires of the poet a newly limber free verse:

> You are already
> asleep. I lower
> myself in next to
> you, my skin slightly
> numb with the restraint
> of habits, the patina of
> self, the black frost
> of outsideness, so that even
> unclothed it is
> a resilient chilly
> hardness, a superficially
> malleable, dead
> rubbery texture.

Present tense takes us directly into the scene. The conceptual language is tactfully makeshift. It captures that distance which can arrive between lovers at, it seems, any time—a sort of stubbornness coming of the fear of being either absorbed by the other or entirely cut off from them. The speaker has grown "cold" in both the literal and the emotional sense. His partner turns and holds him:

> do
> you know who
> I am or am I
> your mother or
> the nearest human being to
> hold on to in a
> dreamed pogrom.

The lineaments of identity are shed as Gunn seeks an experience, however elementary and insentient, that's universally shared. The infant's bond with the mother, global atrocities—this is the world in which we live, and where we find our happiness, or not at all.

> What I, now loosened,
> sink into is an old
> big place, it is
> there already, for
> you are already
> there.

The first line of the poem returns. Now there's no holding back:

> What is more, the place is
> not found but seeps
> from our touch in
> continuous creation, dark
> enclosing cocoon round
> ourselves alone, dark
> wide realm where we
> walk with everyone.

Wilmer explains that continuous creation "is one of the theories of the origin of the universe, sometimes called the 'steady-state theory,' in which the universe has no beginning and no end"; his gloss also relates the poem to Donne's "The Good-Morrow," and "The World," by Robert Creeley. Open form licenses the poet to seek, as we watch, for the correct word—and to find it. The separate shape of each lover is lost within the "cocoon" that both isolates them in a realm of two—which, for Donne, is grandiosely its own kingdom—and unites them, in tenderness, with "everyone." Soft *w* sounds, slipping from the repeated word "what," provide the momentum. You can't speak the lines without shaping your lips, as if for so many kisses.

There is a feeling, in Gunn, that sinuosities of syntax, given the scaffold of rhyme, and proved upon the pulse of meter, cannot fail in the quest for complexity; he has a habit of relentlessly finessing a perception until the rhymes begin to self-generate and the metaphysical contortions produced as a result are mannered, not cognitive. Rococo, not rational, though Gunn's no-nonsense aesthetic—he was hard on James Wright, for writing disconnectedly—packages these flourishes as a strict logic. This tendency survives into *Moly* (1971) and "For Signs," whose second stanza, and what follows, can't live up to the first:

> 1
>
> In front of me, the palings of a fence
> Throw shadows hard as board across the weeds;
> The cracked enamel of a chicken bowl
> Gleams like another moon; each clump of reeds
> Is split with darkness and yet bristles whole.
> The field survives, but with a difference.
>
> 2
>
> And sleep like moonlight drifts and clings to shape.
> My mind, which learns its freedom every day,
> Sinks into vacancy but cannot rest.
> While moonlight floods the pillow where it lay,
> It walks among the past, weeping, obsessed,
> Trying to master it and learn escape.

The last three lines are superfluous: they only fill out the form, with a bit of mind-body confusion. A "mind" can't lie on a pillow or walk "among the past, weeping"; nor can the perfectionist's cleaving to ten syllables excuse the compressed clumsiness of "learn escape."

The first stanza gives us, as Gunn writes of a poem-opening of Fulke Greville's, the spectacle of "the observing intelligence ... making careful distinctions." Gunn scopes out the area (he did two years of national service) and goes on from there. "Hardness was a quality," he writes, "sought after by the avant-garde poet during the period marked approximately by the years 1910 to 1925. It was considered a corrective to what appeared the softness of the poetry in the years preceding. It took the form of an emphasis on clarity, explicitness, and sharpness of language and image, accompanied by an equal emphasis on objectivity or the appearance of it." "That is a summary," writes Gunn—this in "Three Hard Women," a review of H.D, Marianne Moore, and Mina Loy—"of what everybody knows already." Yet, as the context suggests, he's particularly alert to the gendering of hardness, a concept bound to identity and how porous to other people's desires, and other people's voices, any of us wishes to be. His unashamedly phallocentric poetry is aware of how the rigidity of a penis may be premised on an individual or a collaborative denial of the erect organ's in fact surpassing vulnerability. Gunn's persons, as well as his objects, would be invincibly solid, but the tropes of armor, containment, and the bulletproof libido learn to self-scrutinize. "An Amorous Debate" from *Jack Straw's Castle* (1976):

> Then a tremor passed
> through his body, the sheen
> fell from him, he
> became wholly sensitive
> as if his body had
> rolled back its own foreskin.

Wilmer can't help but exclude some of the briefer, lighthearted verse that, in the Faber *Collected*, allow the reader a breathing space. "Courage, a Tale," for example, also appeared in *Jack Straw's Castle*:

> There was a Child
> who heard from another Child
> that if you masturbate 100 times
> it kills you.
>
> This gave him pause;
> he certainly slowed down quite a bit

  and also
    kept count.

  . . .

  The 99th time
  was simply unavoidable.

  Weeks passed.

  And then he thought
  Fuck it
    it's worth dying for,

  and half an hour later
  the score rose from 99 to 105.

I love the paced humor: how the indentations exaggerated by William Carlos Williams into a tendentious philosophy of the "variable foot" appear here as the stand-up comedian's pauses for effect. Keeping "count" gives way, impudently, to keeping "score." Interviewed by Wilmer, Gunn said "stylistic concerns" have to do

> with impulses and decisions in our lives in all aspects. Impulses, of their nature, are kind of open-ended and we have impulses all the time. We also make decisions all the time and those are closed, like closed lines in poetry, they're like metre, they're considered. Our lives are mixtures of those. So I continue to have sympathies with both kinds of poetry. . . . I'm surprised that everybody doesn't.

Gunn is known for oscillating stringently between, as he terms it here, "open-ended" and "closed" forms. He's many-sided and knows others are too: admiring of the hard lines of individual identity, he nevertheless takes out his eraser. Sometimes one feels solid—elsewhere, a series of impulsive mental occasions, or, as Yeats had it, a "bundle of accident." And so Gunn's own "mixture" of poems, both light and heavy (refusing to provide a picture of the major male poet before which to prostrate ourselves), also refutes a voice-led poetics.

Both pair-bonded and promiscuous, Gunn was, in his sexual adventures, formidably and self-endangeringly exposed, all his life, to the other. He died in his seventies of, probably, a drug overdose, having perceived the unjealous open-form lusts and loves of the San Francisco scene as an unrealized utopia, "the community of the carnal heart":

> That's what we were part of, a visionary carnal politics. No wonder Blake was often cited!. . . The 1970s were the time, as I heard someone say later, of a great hedonistic experiment. . . . As hippies were the indirect heirs of the communists between World Wars, so we were the direct heirs of the hippies, drug-visionaries also. At the baths, or in less organized activity, there was a shared sense of adventure, thrilling, hilarious, experimental.

Gunn listed in his notebook, at the end of the sixties, what he took for the stages of "Self-Education." More young man's theorizing, but there's something to it:

1. Nobody watches him, not even himself.
2. He imitates, to be like others.
3. He endows himself with an identity, to be unlike others.
4. He seeks purposes.
5. He seeks to lose identity, to join everyone.

Those stuck at stage three, or four, haven't quite made it. The list is, one assumes, self-addressing, self-critical. Not aloof but agonized. Gunn's verse worries at the matter, inhabiting the question without arrogance or a claim to exemption. "To lose identity" suggests the mystic's hunt for nirvana or T. S. Eliot's catty remark on the desirability of impersonality, at least for those who know what it's like to have a personality.

Gunn wished to write in the "plain style" or, as his essay on Hardy has it, "the reflective mode" that has accreted over centuries of verse in English:

> It does seem to me that the related family lines of the ballad and the reflective lyric, joined by ties of economy and impersonality, have run permanently through English literature as providing in some sense a style that is always available. For their very neutrality and

adaptability to new content, they have remained possible styles for about five hundred years, while other and equally impressive modes have been born, reached maturity, and died. The reflective mode I am speaking of is, as I emphasize, essentially impersonal, essentially non-confessional. It is concerned with its subject to the extent of excluding the speaker's personality, even when his emotion is the subject of the poem (as it often is)—for he sees his emotion as one which anybody in his situation would be able to feel.

In Isherwood he found a "colloquial directness of style" that has "been around since the early eighteenth century. . . . It is in the nature of a bequest to us—like the plain-style of the Elizabethan poets, it is useful for any subject-matter, flexible and all-purpose as it is." But, as August Kleinzahler notes, Gunn's plain style isn't "colloquial," not exactly. Consider "The Miracle," which, published in 1982 in *The Passages of Joy*, doesn't appear in Wilmer's selection:

> "There in the rest room. He pulled down my fly,
> And through his shirt I felt him warm and trim.
> I squeezed his nipples and began to cry
> At losing this, my miracle, so slim
> That I could grip my wrist in back of him.
>
> "Then suddenly he dropped down on one knee
> Right by the urinal in his only suit
> And let it fly, saying Keep it there for me,
> And smiling up. I can still see him shoot.
> Look at that snail-track on the toe of my boot."

The man's speech is denatured — Gunn isn't trying to reproduce the way anyone would actually talk, and this roundly flouts one of the central imperatives of U.S. verse. (For an English person, "rest room," presented here as two words, is a phrase one never quite gets used to: Gunn's poem holds, and tests, the dubious phrase for a moment on its tongue.) The closest one gets to this elsewhere is in verse translation, where another writer might provide a version of Dante, or Ovid, in which people speak with this preternatural transpicuousness.

Gunn is a great poet of the long-term, if not monogamous, relationship. The key poem here—besides "Touch"—is "The Hug," from *The Man with Night Sweats* (1992). Unlike its predecessor, "The Hug" is anecdotal, down-to-earth—told in the past, not the present, tense. Its verse sounds concentrate, rather than dissolve, the feeling of separateness in combination with strong rhymes:

> I dozed, I slept. My sleep broke on a hug,
> Suddenly, from behind,
> In which the full lengths of our bodies pressed:
> Your instep to my heel,
> My shoulder-blades against your chest.

It ends:

> My quick sleep had deleted all
> Of intervening time and place.
> I only knew
> The stay of your secure firm dry embrace.

Yet what intervenes between this poem and "Touch," published twenty-five years earlier, isn't only a change of style—"Rhythmic form and subject matter are locked in a permanent embrace"—but, to speak frankly, AIDS. The deletion of personal limits in the first poem—the snowflake of identity turned to a drop of happily impersonal water in the sea—is replaced by a protective carapace. The men lock together like Roman soldiers in a *testudo*. A cultural shift has occurred, as well as the evolution of a long-term relationship. "The dryness of the embrace," writes Tom Sleigh, "marks the transition from sexual to domestic love, from the physical joy of sex to the physical joy of being held by someone with whom a life has been shared. Now, what heterosexual male poet would celebrate such a transition? Presumably, that poet would say how sexual attraction was attendant on the hug; or else the poet would lament the passing of such passion." A subtle point, relating to the contexts in which gay verse is read, the assumptions a reader makes. Though Gunn surely draws, here, on Jonson's famous translation from Petronius Arbiter—"Doing, a filthy pleasure is, and short; / And done, we straight repent us of the sport"—whose less bleakly postcoital close should be as well known:

> Let us together closely lie, and kiss,
> There is no labour, nor no shame in this;
> This hath pleased, doth please, and long will please; never
> Can this decay, but is beginning ever.

Here the comma-riddled lines aren't "halting", exactly: they linger, wishing the moment to last forever. Defending Jonson's court role, his dependence on patrons and commissions, Gunn insisted that all poetry is "occasional" in its own way, and in *The Man with Night Sweats* AIDS provides the occasion:

> You wrote us messages on a pad, amused
> At one time that you had your nurse confused
> Who, seeing you reconciled after four years
> With your grey father, both of you in tears,
> Asked if this was at last your "special friend"
> (The one you waited for until the end).
> "She sings," you wrote, "a Philippine folk song
> To wake me in the morning . . . It is long
> And very pretty."
> —FROM *LAMENT*

You wouldn't replace a word: the cadences could not be less arbitrary, less idiosyncratic. In a remarkable vindication of Gunn's plain style, the rhyme of "years" with "tears," one of the most hackneyed in the tradition, more than earns its place.

Galway Kinnell, Trying to Become Winged

Galway Kinnell won just about everything in his lifetime: the Pulitzer, a National Book Award, a MacArthur Fellowship. Active in the civil rights movement, a volunteer worker for the Congress of Racial Equality—sentenced to a week in jail—he read against the war in Vietnam and (in the eighties) nuclear weapons. Rilkean, Whitmanian, neoromantic, he cared about nature and was a great poet of family love, though with resolutely unselfish genes (he wasn't one for Edmund Burke's "little platoon"). Here he is in "The Olive Wood Fire," rocking his son Fergus to sleep. Vietnam's on the box:

> One such time, fallen half-asleep myself,
> I thought I heard a scream
> —a flier crying out in horror
> as he dropped fire on he didn't know what or whom,
> or else a child set thus aflame—
> and sat up alert. The olive wood fire
> had burned low. In my arms lay Fergus,
> fast asleep, left cheek glowing, God.

The second and fifth lines are iambic, the diction intimate yet scrupulous. "This vision of a childlike deity who sleeps through human horrors," writes Phoebe Pettingell, "manages to combine Christian iconography with twentieth-century agnosticism." Well, yes—but it's also touching, like W. H. Auden's lullabies, and a poem one wants to share with others. It may be new to them. For who (despite the plaudits I've already listed) reads Galway Kinnell now? And if not, why not?

For one thing, time hasn't been kind to his political and spiritual earnestness: the world-transforming ideas of the sixties have turned commercial (the ending of *Mad Men!*), or naffly new age, in self-help books with rainbows on the cover, and generalizations by the bucketload about Eastern mysticism. Kinnell's stint as a lecturer and journalist in the Shah's Iran (he arrived six years after the CIA's coup in 1953) produced a short novel, *Black Light*, whose clenched protagonist, Jamshid, is ardent for heavenly purity. The narrative touches, a shade pruriently, on Islamic gender politics and discusses feelingly the plight of sex workers suffering under long-standing taboos, as well as culture-corrosive Westernization. Its spiritual-physical concerns make for marvelous descriptions, as, here, of a sky-buried camel: "He paused a moment. He looked up into the sky. Nothing was visible in the glittering air. He knew that in that blueness lived the changed flesh and blood of Hassan. Those strange, bobbing, rubbery motions of the camel had been, all the time, a way of trying to become winged." Yet Jamshid's fixations, however placed, are also Kinnell's. He writes in "The Poetics of the Physical World": "It is through something radiant in our lives that we have been able to dream of paradise, that we have been able to invent the realm of eternity. But there is another kind of glory in our lives which derives precisely from our inability to enter that paradise or to experience eternity."

"Death is the mother of beauty," wrote Wallace Stevens, succinctly: Kinnell goes on wrestling with the problem, and the tussle can seem rote and self-congratulatory. Donald Davie makes the case against him and, by extension, a whole strand of mystically libidinal, willfully and passionately gaseous, posthippie U.S. and British verse (Robert Bly, James Wright, Ted Hughes, Don Paterson)—a case remaining, perhaps, to be answered:

> Galway Kinnell is a man who hungers for the spiritual . . . who has been culturally conditioned moreover to resist the very disciplines that might have opened him up to the spiritual apprehensions he hungers for. By writing poems which thrash in and out of the impasse thus created, Kinnell has made a great reputation—which suggests that there are many readers who are walled up in the same bind, and ask nothing better than to churn and agonize within it.

We might carp at Davie's prissiness, but it's remarkable how well his argument holds up, as he takes the poet to task for overusing the word *mystical* and for annexing without self-awareness the spiritual dramas of other cultures: "He proceeds to declare himself unable to sympathize with the treatment of death by Tennyson . . . or Milton . . .at the same time as he can enter fervently into treatments of the same theme by a Bathurst islander, an Australian aborigine, and a Tamil from two thousand years ago." Asking "what has become of us that we can kill on a vast scale and not even be able to say why," Kinnell would like to recover a primordial wholeness. He blames a spirit of dehumanizing, abstracted, objective-seeming, rational (that is, self-interested, nature-dominating, career-furthering) scrutiny, describing as "fatal" the mind's "knack of detaching itself from what it studied, even when what it studied was itself." Davie, on the other hand, identifies such primitivism, and its prioritizing of emotional response, rather than careful thought, as identical with tyranny. It's Kirk versus Spock—the dissociation of sensibility all over again. Kinnell wishes to escape the unalive processes of cerebration into what are, for him, moments of auroral aseity. Gradually (see the juvenilia) he learned a tonic roughness was called for—a bitty music with space for the discrepant.

Kinnell is one of those poets whose style, though it alters from book to book, maintains a satisfyingly consistent tonal core. I've mentioned the early, unformed, work, but when his first collection, *What a Kingdom It Was*, appeared in 1960, he'd already developed that verbal confidence (how to present large-hearted feelings and ethereal experiences in gripping, dreamy phrases) which never deserted him. "First Song" begins "Then it was dusk in Illi*nois*," and carries the sound of that place name toward a "small *boy*" (my emphasis), who, carting dung, pauses to rest on a fence and listen to the frogs:

> Soon their sound was pleasant for a boy
> Listening in the smoky dusk and the nightfall
> Of Illinois, and from the fields two small
> Boys came bearing cornstalk violins
> And they rubbed the cornstalk bows with resins
> And the three sat there scraping of their joy.
>
> It was now fine music the frogs and the boys
> Did in the towering Illinois twilight make
> And into dark in spite of a shoulder's ache
> A boy's hunched body loved out of a stalk

> The first song of his happiness, and the song woke
> His heart to the darkness and into the sadness of joy.

Kinnell grew up in Rhode Island during the Depression—his father was a carpenter—and while he described this poem as a "pure invention," it does provide a microportrait, however romanticized, and geographically shifted, of the artist as a young man. (It sounds a lot like Delmore Schwartz, whom Kinnell would have been reading). The twilight is "towering," the dusk is "smoky"; these adjectives are unexpected. They make you think. As do the jangling rhymes, suggestive of the cornstalk violins. Kinnell's risky lyricism, bordering on vacuity—"loved out of a stalk," and the closing line—walks that boundary with the impudence of a child who, spotting a wall, simply has to balance along the top. Forgetting, slowly, about his parent's hand, he learns to go it alone. "Religious awe," writes William James, "is the same organic thrill which we feel in a forest at twilight, or in a mountain gorge; only this time it comes over us at the thought of our supernatural relations." Though Kinnell, like James, is no straightforward theist, he too would bridge the natural and supernatural: he seeks a language, littered with crises, to evince invisible powers. But he makes more of that "organic thrill," abandoning James's separation between merely "animal happiness" and something more hyperborean.

Introducing this volume, Edward Hirsch lingers on "The Avenue Bearing the Initial of Christ Into the New World." Set in New York, it depicts the life of immigrants—urban decay, and splendor in decay—resembling T. S. Eliot or Ezra Pound in its high-low registers and its spalled form:

> It is night, and raining. You look down
> Toward Houston in the rain, the living streets,
> Where instants of transcendence
> Drift in oceans of loathing and fear, like lanternfishes,
> Or phosphorous flashings in the sea, or the feverish light
> Skin is said to give off when the swimmer drowns at night.
>
> From the blind gut Pitt to the East River of Fishes
> The Avenue cobbles a swath through the discolored air,
> A roadway of refuse from the teeming shores and ghettos
> And the Caribbean Paradise, into the new ghetto and new paradise,
> This God-forsaken Avenue bearing the initial of Christ

> Through the haste and carelessness of the ages,
> The sea standing in heaps, which keeps on collapsing,
> Where the drowned suffer a C-change,
> And remain the common poor.

Manhattan's Avenue C was renamed, as a historically Puerto Rican neighborhood, Loisaida Avenue in the eighties: for Kinnell it's associated with immigrant poverty. The first sentence—clear as in a novel—plants us firmly in Kinnell territory. He loves to evoke the atmosphere of an extreme moment and combines detail with generalization—embracing a certain "haste," if not "carelessness," himself. "Don't use such an expression," warned Pound, "as 'dim lands of peace.' It dulls the image. It mixes an abstraction with the concrete." Kinnell ignores him: this poem reminds me of Matthew Arnold's "Dover Beach," in how it fastens to abstractions things to hold onto, solidly peculiar: "cobbles a swath"; "the sea standing in heaps, which keeps on collapsing." Kinnell ends with a joke. "Sea change" is from Shakespeare, and *The Tempest*, where Ariel sings, of Alonso, who appears to have drowned: "Full fathom five thy father lies / . . . / Nothing of him that doth fade, / But doth suffer a sea-change / Into something rich and strange." Eliot references this in *The Waste Land*. But though Kinnell risks a superior vantage—looking down, quite literally, on the "living streets" the poor drift down in "oceans of loathing and fear"—he won't, like Eliot, deploy the classics to damn the present.

Perhaps only an adherent of what James calls "the religion of healthy-mindedness" would name his next book *Flower Herding on Mount Monadnock* (1964). The title poem would square Kinnell's celebratory temperament with the evils of the age, but you sense the happy ending coming:

> There is something joyous in the elegies
> Of birds. They seem
> Caught up in a formal delight,
> Though the mourning dove whistles of despair.
>
> But at last in the thousand elegies
> The dead rise in our hearts,
> On the brink of our happiness we stop
> Like someone on a drunk starting to weep.

What this does catch, cannily, is the sentimentality the spiritual poet has always to ward off. Happiness isn't the same thing as sentimentality, but when the poet's recoveries become too reliable, too unfailingly eloquent, such is the danger: Charles Molesworth describes Kinnell's verse as going "beyond descriptive prettiness only by hinting at emotions that would probably be mawkish if further explored," and Robert Peters claims failures of "tact—that poetic sense allowing the poet to know when he has violated formal demands . . . by pushing emotion too far." Here, at least, the final line queries what comes before, though Kinnell is needily fulsome:

> I know
> The birds fly off
> But the hug of the earth wraps
> With moss their graves and the giant boulders.

Is this moment of feel-good optimism excessive, or earned, given the sequence's mood shifts? Mother Earth arrives to "hug" us better, to "wrap" us round. But "I know" is surely (as when the phrase appears in James Wright, for instance) a tad plaintive.

Body Rags, arriving after a four-year gap—like most of Kinnell's books— saw a formal breakthrough. By now, he was writing out-and-out free verse with erratic-seeming line divisions—the capitals disappear from the left margin, and the right zigzags like a lightning bolt. "The Bear" is in seven parts. Each gives us a section of the hunter's quest for the animal, and you'd think it must correspond to the seven days of creation, except there's a leap into the future, and the trek gets weirder and weirder:

> at nightfall I bend down as I knew I would
> at a turd sopped in blood,
> and hesitate, and pick it up,
> and thrust it in my mouth.

Kinnell mentions of his public readings: "When the poem was new, I'd often observe that at the place where the hunter eats the turd, people would look at each other apparently with disgust." The bear is discovered already dead:

> I come up to him
> and stare at the narrow-spaced, petty eyes,
> the dismayed
> face laid back on the shoulder, the nostrils
> flared, catching
> perhaps the first taint of me as he
> died.
>
> I hack
> a ravine in his thigh, and eat and drink,
> and tear him down his whole length
> and open him and climb in
> and close him up after me, against the wind,
> and sleep.

Typing this out, I skipped line breaks—"he / died"—they're counterintuitive, and may feel haphazard, or overly controlling, like Gerard Manley Hopkins turning a sonnet into the equivalent of a musical score, with instructions as to where to place the stresses. But their jolts are more often to the good—intently defamiliarizing, like the adjectives (those "petty" eyes!). Stippled with intervals, persevering, doggedly emphatic—you're either with the poet or infuriated by him and his superintendence.

When you get to writing this way, you lose track of what works and what doesn't. Maybe you write too many poems or spoil some—for lack of a critic outside oneself who would cry halt. Davie connects Kinnell's American sublime with militarism:

> Does . . . the blood-boltered primitivism of "The Bear," show poetry resisting the brutalizing of war, or surrendering to it?
> . . .
> In [Charles] Bell's note on Kinnell in *Contemporary Poets of the English Language*, we learn that already when Kinnell was putting together *What a Kingdom It Was*, ". . . his matter was the reaffirmation of the Promethean and pioneer daring of America, to which I also, after the neo-Augustinian resignations of the war, was committed." This is enough to make one weep. Did it not occur to Bell, nor to Kinnell even as he composed his brave and effective poems protesting the war, that it was precisely "the Promethean and pioneer

daring of America" that was drowning Vietnamese hamlets in a sea of fire?

Fire is indeed an obsessive, unstable trope in Kinnell. Reading his *Collected Poems* straight through, from the mawkish juvenilia:

> The glade catches fire, and where
> The birds build nests they brood at evening
> On burning limbs. Spirit of the wood, dream
> Of all who have ever answered in the glade at dusk—
> And grass, grass, blossom through my feet in flames.

to the war verse:

> *Lieutenant!*
> *This corpse will not stop burning!*

I did wonder if a writer enraptured by (in Richard Calhoun's words) "the flames of a burning world, a destructiveness with which the poet himself has to identify," could write cogently of events to be seen in geopolitical and not flaccidly cosmic terms.

Kinnell's argument is that by descending into ourselves we become kin to everyone: "The Bear" is said to concern (in his interview with Gregory Fitz Gerald) the poet's "sympathetic feelings, our capacity to know the life of another creature by imagining it." He goes further: the poem that is "really a poem . . . goes deeper than personality. It takes on that strange voice, intensely personal yet common to everyone, in which all rituals are spoken." But what does this mean for the actual composition of a poem? "Vapor Trail Reflected in the Frog Pond" contains "an attempt to imagine how it might be for a Vietnamese person to be walking along a road in his own country, just before the American bombers appeared in the sky":

> And by paddies in Asia
> bones
> wearing a few shadows
> walk down a dirt road, smashed
> bloodsuckers on their heel, knowing

> flesh thrown down in the sunshine
> dogs shall eat
> and flesh flung into the air
> shall be seized by birds.

I asked why few read Kinnell now, and we see here how he sidesteps problems of authority and appropriation that, for better or worse, presently engross verse culture. Believing in a universal soul that, more basic than personality, unites everyone, he participates in a U.S. tradition coming out of Emerson, who writes in his essay on "The Poet" of "a great public power, on which he can draw, by unlocking, at all risks, his human doors . . . then . . . his speech is thunder, his thought is law, and his words are universally intelligible." But Emerson's confidence boosting was of its time—just as the country was "beginning to assert itself to the senses and to the imagination of her children"—and Davie's point holds, about a national arrogance that in the twentieth century Kinnell isn't always alert to. Even those who would support his claims on behalf of the imagination may find these lines a bit thin, oblique (defensively so?), hard to understand without his gloss on them.

The Book of Nightmares came next, in 1971, and did succeed by using personal experience as a bridge to large topics. "Under the Maud Moon" and "Little Sleep's-Head Sprouting Hair in the Moonlight" look forward to "The Olive Wood Fire" (Kinnell contemplates his sleeping daughter); in "The Hen Flower," the poet addresses himself—"Listen, Kinnell, / dumped alive / and dying into the old sway bed" —in a, I think, reclaiming of Whitman's big, nation-encompassing ego, excusable in its self-love (because it's striated with uncertainty and undisgusted by others). Then *Mortal Acts, Mortal Words* (1980) has Kinnell return to a cleaner line, which can look complacent, even neophobic. His voice is centered, personal, and no longer disdains, or seeks to cunningly explode, his gift of the gab—that deep, informal, spellbinding persuasiveness that made events of his readings. He wrote of Whitman: "When we come to the lines 'I was the man, I suffered, I was there,' we already understand what it is to disappear into someone else. The final action of the poem, where Whitman dissolves into the air and into the ground, is for me one of the great moments of self-transcendence in poetry." Yet—putting aside this debatable analysis of Whitman—Kinnell's best poems are great with self, not piously emptied of it: alluringly proficient, capacious, seductive, roving, willing to make large claims and risk the equation of a sounding phrase with an immortal sweetness.

James distinguishes (sometimes, inconsistently) mysticism from mundanely "animal" experiences, but Kinnell doesn't, and this makes him one of the twentieth century's finest poets of (heterosexual, male-focalized) eros. "After Making Love We Hear Footsteps" is, again, about Fergus:

> Let there be that heavy breathing
> or a stifled come-cry anywhere in the house
> and he will wrench himself awake
> and make for it on the run—as now, we lie together,
> after making love, quiet, touching along the length of our bodies,
> familiar touch of the long-married,
> and he appears—in his baseball pajamas, it happens,
> the neck opening so small he has to screw them on—
> and flops down between us and hugs us and snuggles himself to sleep,
> his face gleaming with satisfaction at being this very child.

Like Whitman, Kinnell believes touch a conceptual, discussable experience. He broods on its vibrations. The verb "make" repeats, unpunctiliously; "it happens" has, just about, two meanings; the assonances of "stifled," "cry," and "lie" carry forward the passionate wordless utterance that isn't replaced by but crystallized within the succeeding "quiet," and indeed (if you think about it) the life of "this very child"; "screw" appears innocently (not in the context we might expect). Kinnell's verse palpitates with on-the-spot clarifications, tiny explosions of gossip. I even like that biblical "let there be" and suspect the equally famous, and much-anthologized "Saint Francis and the Sow" to also be about making love, though perhaps it's best not to take this comparison too far, given it's about a man and a pig.

Kinnell went on experimenting with—alongside the trademark sequences—ghazals and poems with long, whole-sentence lines. "The Olive Wood Fire" appears in *The Past* (1985), along with the anti–nuclear war poem, "The Fundamental Project of Technology" (arising from his visits to Hiroshima and Nagasaki and the heartbreaking list of exhibits in a museum); also "On the Oregon Coast," an eco-lyric and echo-lyric (Arnold, again) moving from description of the sea seamlessly and essayistically into conversation concerning whether "post-Darwinian" poets should stop anthropomorphizing nature: "We didn't know if pre-Darwinian language would let us." The title sequence of *When One Has Lived a Long Time Alone* (1990) is ten sections, all bookended by the phrase, and written as single, contorted sentences. Life sentences. The speaker (Kinnell himself? The reader?)

> Abandons hope
> of the sweetness of friendship or love,
> before long can barely remember what they are,
> and covets the stillness of inorganic matter,
> in a self-dissolution one may not know how to halt,
> when one has lived a long time alone.

Vishnu spare us from journalists forcing topicality on abstruser matters—but one could leap into politics and that weaponizable male angst issuing in spree shootings and acts of terror. Adrienne Rich diagnosed in Kinnell the "problem of the masculine writer" struggling not only with his stance toward women but also the loudness of his own voice: if he never quite solved this problem, he did turn it into one of his subjects, deconstructing the male ego he no longer aspired to purify in fire. In "Flying Home," he writes of "the airport men's room, seeing"

> the middleaged men my age,
> as they washed their hands after touching
> their penises—when it might have been more in accord
> with the lost order to wash first, then touch—
> peer into the mirror
> and then stand back, as if asking, who is this?

How warmly, unviciously alive this is. Following another frank-seeming repetition—"the middleaged men my age"—the line-end on "touching" suggests, briefly, provokingly, contact between the men, while assonance organizes "more," "accord," and "lost order" into a sacred formality.

This is reminiscent of a passage from *Black Light* where as Jamshid washes his face he feels as if he might disintegrate: "At the pool Jamshid washed his right hand, his left hand, his right foot, his left foot, his face and his teeth. He passed a dripping hand through his hair, from the brow to the back of the neck. As he stood up, he saw in the ripples an image of himself, and even though he shut his eyes he could not keep from seeing himself torn to pieces." Kinnell acknowledges the contemporary stance toward damage and healing. He can, that is, be psychoanalytic, as in "My Mother's R & R," which returns us (like "The Bear," "After Making Love We Hear Footsteps," and "Saint Francis and the Sow") to a scene of primal nurturing. Surreally, these boys are only pretending to be babies:

> Abruptly she took back her breasts
> and sent us from the bed, two small
> hungry boys enflamed and driven off
> by the she-wolf. But we had got our nip,
> and in the empire we would found,
> we would taste all the women and expel them
> one after another as they came to resemble her.

The origin story of supervillains: Romulus and Remus, suckled by a she-wolf. The apologies of men, in verse, for the violence, or grumpiness, central to their heterosexuality (compared here to the founding of Rome!) can seem vain—in both senses—but what can I say, I like the poem: its clear shape, its terminus different to the "glorious, humane, fine-sounding conclusions" (Hank Lazer) we're used to from Kinnell. It reminds me of Wallace Stevens ("Timeless mother, / How is it that your aspic nipples / For once vent honey?"), A. K. Ramanujan ("Mothers smear bitter neem / paste on their nipples / to wean greedy babies // and give them an inexplicable / taste for bitter gourd / late in life") — and seems to me about as durable, as universal, as unequivocally and unironically wholehearted as any twentieth- or twenty-first-century poet could hope to be.

A. R. Ammons and "the political (read, human) world"

A. R. (Archie Randolph) Ammons grew up dirt poor, subsistence farming in North Carolina. At twenty-nine he published his debut, *Ommateum*, with a vanity press. It didn't sell: he claimed the royalty for the first year was four four-cent stamps. Later he won it all, got a teaching job, and was acclaimed by heavyweight critics, including Harold Bloom (for whom he wrote a poem) and Helen Vendler. Her introduction is reprinted in both volumes of the reader-overwhelmingly gargantuan *Complete Poems*—it's as if the poet has been knighted, with a touch of the sword on both shoulders. Lovers of Ammons have had to cobble together, till now, our own box sets, out of reprints, second-hands (my copy of *Garbage*, fittingly, arrived collied and smutched). Here, at long last, all in one package, are the long masterpieces—besides *Garbage*, there's *Sphere*, and my favorite, *Tape for the Turn of the Year*—the genuinely amusing *Really Short Poems* ("Their Sex Life": "One failure on / Top of another"; "Coward": "Bravery runs in my family")—and, glittering like pebbles on the beach, shorter poems totally new to me.

Where to start? With—in my opinion—his most beautiful single lyric: "Hymn," which appeared in Ammons's second book, *Expressions of Sea Level* (1964). He was brought up in the Pentecostal Fire-Baptized Holiness Church (!) and the index to volume 1 lists, besides this poem, "Hymn II," "Hymn III," "Hymn IV," and "Hymn V." Like Walt Whitman, he professes his wide love for all living and even unliving things: "though I have looked everywhere / I can find nothing lowly / in the universe: // . . . moss, beggar, weed, tick, pine, self, magnificent / with being!" "Hymn" is also shaped by the poet's Romantic yearning for both "unity & diversity: how / to have both: must: / it's Coleridge's / definition of a poem":

> I know if I find you I will have to leave the earth
> and go on out
> over the sea marshes and the brant in bays
> and over the hills of tall hickory
> and over the crater lakes and canyons
> and on up through the spheres of diminishing air
>
> . . .
>
> And I know if I find you I will have to stay with the earth
> inspecting with thin tools and ground eyes
> trusting the microvilli sporangia and simplest coelenterates
> and praying for a nerve cell
> with all the soul of my chemical reactions

"And if I find you I must go out deep into your far resolutions / and if I find you I must stay here with the separate leaves." Though Ammons writes poems to a "you" closer to the reader, this one's pitched at a god, or the shadow of one, understood as both transcendent and immanent; the spiritual, or what remains of it, is defined in opposition to the senses, but also (necessarily) evoked in material terms.

Helen Small writes that "an allusion to science in contemporary literature is not simply an allusion to science; it is also an allusion to the authority of science with respect to certain kinds of narrowly defined truth"; Robert Crawford finds in modern poetry "a wish or instinct to extend the range of verse while at the same time acknowledging a certain risked awkwardness in using scientific vocabulary." Ammons took a degree in biology at Wake Forest University, yet these wilfully off-balance Latinisms are also a nod to Milton. The speaker's transit "up through the spheres of diminishing air" recalls the wandering of Satan in *Paradise Lost,* and an adjective from Milton's "On Shakespeare" captures in *Garbage* a vision of "everything / assimilated to star-ypointing song." "I've done what I could," Ammons wrote in 1992, "to wipe out most / some of the western traditions by failing to refer to them . . . I hate all alluding that alludes." Should we believe him? Ammons is full of it—allusion, that is. He mocks, admiringly, Stevens, to whom he was often compared, and "blithering Yeats"; mentions L=A=N=G=U=A=G=E poetry; tells A. E. Housman, or "Housey," that he wishes he'd got what he wanted out of life; parodies Eliot—"sit down by this big rock / and if in a year you're / still not bored, I'll show you // something really interesting"—and I'm sure that "Surfacing Surface Effects" owes something to Hopkins's "Moonrise": "A small moon nearly melted in the almost-morning / night, I arise and thank God I can get up."

Ammons writes very short lines, and very long ones, and uses his trademark colon to establish, at its best, a unique "prosetry" (his word): a parataxis passing, if you squint, for logical argument. "This stanza compels / its way along: a / break will humble it": the colons, line breaks, and stanza breaks preserve in print the poet's defeats of confidence, which are also places a thought may arise. (Elizabeth Bishop worried about the "blank verse moo" of Wallace Stevens, and Ammons also finds in that poet a mode of locomotion to disdain: "Mr. Stevens's lines! // laid like a railbed, tie after tie, / with no sign of integrated // progression but two stiff pieces of / stretched iron.") Ammons can also be stridently, or offhandedly, slangy, irreverent, vulgar—"Confessional Poem": "Let me be honest with you: / in spite of everything I have / a (oh my) penis." Yet he wishes above all to connect the everyday violences of our self-assertion with the epochal "saliences" and "crests" of the biosphere—he cares about the past, seeing it deeply alive in the mutations of the present. "There is / memory enough in the rock, unscriptured history in / the wind, sufficient identity in the curve / of the valley"; "we are dealing with a splintery weave of / surface which contains instances of the / present but also what is ancient and come / again."

This explains his allusiveness, his performance of variations on the old orders. One section of "February Beach," for example, rewards scansion—old-style literary appreciation. "Warm days since / have intervened, / softened // the surface,"

>   evaporated
>   the thaw
>   and let grains loose: now
>
>   x   /   /   / x /   x   /
>   the white grains drift against the dunes
>   x   / x x / x /   x
>   and ripple as if in summer,
>   / x   x   /   /   / x
>   hiding the deep hard marriage

                    x   /   x   /
                    of sand and ice:

A Williamsesque line is allowed to, gently, rhyme: "thaw" and "now" move the verse towards a memory of previous forms. Three-stress sequences combine with iambs; a weave of sound aligns "grains" and "dunes" (internal rhyme); "drift," "dunes," and "deep" (alliteration); and the collocations, with others, of "drift," "ripple," and "as if," and "hiding" and "ice" (assonance). Though Ammons can be cussedly unshapely, even commenting on it—breaking off, say, to remark several lines ending on 'the'—that's just one maneuver within a larger investigation of poetic and perceptual structures.

On the one hand, it's the American experiment in democracy, dramatized by so many writers, in newfangled vernacular; but—I keep coming back to the Romantics—Ammons also inquires into the beautiful and the sublime: "the shapes nearest shapelessness awe us most, suggest / the god." When he wants, he can shape, hew, chisel, with the best of them:

> I sat by a stream in a
> perfect—except for willows—
> emptiness
> and the mountain that
> was around,
>
> scraggly with brush &
> rock
> said
> I see you're scribbling again
> —"CLASSIC"

This would emanate an absolute Zen clarity—were it not for that "scraggly" phrase "was around," and the interjection: "except for willows." Ammons inherits the stances of an inspiration-centered verse, but makes them down-to-earth, lovable, turning his speaker into a naïf who pursues impossible conversations with the elements, trees, animals, brooks, and astral beings. "The mountains said they were / tired of lying down / and wanted to know what / I could do about / getting them off the ground"; "Some nights I go out to piss / among the big black scary shrubs: / the tinkling stars / don't seem to mind." Here, as with that "deep hard marriage" of ice and sand, a language of relationship replaces a lexis of conquest and exploitation.

Ammons may lament "a waste of words, a flattened-down, smoothed- / over mesa of styrofoam verbiage; since words were / introduced here things have gone poorly for the / planet," but he isn't the sort of ecopoet who treats humans as evildoers wild to ruin a primal harmony. We are of nature, part of it, and this is felt throughout the conversation poems I've mentioned. And "Ballad," where Ammons asks a willow "what it wanted to know: the willow said it / wanted to know how to get rid of the wateroak / that was throwing it into shade every afternoon at 4 o'clock." (It also seems to me a fine, cunning poem on the politics of identity: "I can't take you for a friend because while you must / be interested in willowness, which you could find nowhere / better than right here, / I'll bet you're just as interested in wateroakness" . . .) Two of the really short poems provide glimpses of an ideal reciprocity, an unfallen state where competition cannot enter and existence is no longer transactional: "Birds are flowers flying / and flowers perched birds"; "The reeds give / way to the // wind and give / the wind away." The same phrase haunts "Late Romantic"—"how can we give ourselves away if we're not separate / enough to be received"— combining how we talk about ourselves with discussion of global warming: "change the glacier's loneliness and the ice melts." Politics, philosophy, and ecological awareness fuse in a shared, multiform, register-hopping language, which can be highbrow one moment, then nose-thumbing—systematic yet detail-rich.

Ammons's craving for unity in diversity—returning to the beginning of this essay and his mention of Coleridge: "unity & diversity: how / to have both: must: / it's Coleridge's / definition of a poem"—has national as well as literary precedents: he asks in a passage from *Sphere* what his readers "expect from a man born and raised in a country whose motto is *E / pluribus unum?*" The Coleridge allusion is part of a broader political swerve in *Tape for the Turn of the Year*, and according to Robert M. West's useful note, Ammons originally tied the idea to Lyndon Johnson's State of the Union address. Though shorn of this reference, the final poem preserves the association:

>what a celebration! our
>little earth

> united, shining in peace,
>   hate managed,
>   rerouted:
>   the direction thru
>   history is clear:
> unity amassing larger
> & larger territories,
>   till now
> neighborhoods of nations
> meet
> under the name "United Nations"

Ammons steps hearteningly beyond chatter—pressing, sometimes, for a larger view. Reading him can be rather like moving to the side of things at a conference or literary festival ("both in and out of the game," writes Whitman, "and watching and wondering at it") to take a survey of the room. The coteries agitating for power, the condensation of workable intimacies out of gossip: "hate managed, rerouted," "unity amassing larger / & larger territories." But Ammons doesn't desire a superior, maybe snobbish, viewpoint. His increasingly diaristic verse (Ammons improvised *Tape*, from day to day, on a narrow strip of adding machine paper) doesn't omit his own spikes of resentment, grumpy lust, even those periods of insecurity as to the worth of his endeavors—"last night, after / anger & a family tiff, I / suffered a loss & breakage / of spirit, blankness / as of plateaus." A series of poems from the 1972 *Collected* begin with the same phrase: "I can tell you what I need is a good periodontist"; "I can tell you what I need, what I need / is a soft counsellor"; "I can tell you what I need is / money."

Returning to *Tape*, one can't take at face value that po-faced paean to globalization. We also glimpse—part of another description of symbiotic nature—the poet out in the sticks, disparaging urban elites:

> when I stooped to pick
> up the turtle,
> I seen a sight: his back
>   was hazy with
>   mosquitoes, thick
>   as they could
>   stick,

>   bumming a, now mind you,
>   ride on a turtle's back!
>   saving their wings
>   & certain
>   sometime they'd be
>   brought to water:
>   didn't see anything
>   like that in NY:
>   economy, full use
>   of possibility

"Most of our writers live in New York City," writes Ammons, satirically—this is from, to give the full title, 1974's *Sphere: The Form of a Motion*—"there in the abstractions of squares and glassy / floors they cut up and parcel out the nothingness they / think America is." This brings to mind election surprises. Ammons speaks for the heartland, but he also discusses—in a uniquely unmoralizing way—the circulations of global capital and money's power over our lives. I mentioned his childhood poverty: later, he became vice president of his father-in-law's glassware company, and, while we might link him with Wallace Stevens as a philosophical poet, they also both combined the writing and business life. The businessman wants to—ghastly word—*grow* his business at the expense of others; the pure capitalist believes that herein lies the only transition from self-interest to creativity. When Ammons gets to talking about history, or evolution, or nation-states, economics isn't far away—though he's no advocate for Spencer's "survival of the fittest."

"Nucleus" asks—it's the first line—"how you buy a factory," then describes how, in Ammons's language of glimmeringly diagrammed processes:

>   determine the lines of
>   force
>   leading in and out, origins, destinations of lines;
>   determine how
>   from the nexus of crossed and bundled lines
>   the profit is
>   obtained, the
>   forces realized, the cheap made dear,
>   and whether the incoming or outgoing forces are stronger

Is it Ammons's background in the natural sciences that has him use "force" so neutrally—without a whiff of Foucault? (He certainly recognizes power when he sees it, commenting that even "philosophy gives clubs to / everyone, and I prefer disarmament.") *Tape for the Turn of the Year* expands Abraham Maslow's hierarchy of needs, from "get food: / get water: / get sex": to "bank account, nice car, / good address, retirement / plan, investment portfolio"—and I don't think an easy irony is all that's intended. Ammons grants—this in "One: Many":

> how enriching, though unassimilable as a whole
> into art, are the differences: the small-business
> man in
>   Kansas City declares an extra dividend
> and his daughter
>   who teaches school in Duquesne
> buys a Volkswagen, a second car for the family

I'm reminded of Tom Paulin's study of Thomas Hardy—where, analyzing "During Wind and Rain," he remarks, with a candor gone missing from literary criticism, that the lines on family losses, concerning their "clocks and carpets and chairs / On the lawn all day, / And brightest things that are theirs," get into the poem that pride in ownership everybody feels, no matter their politics—especially those who aren't used to having nice things.

Ammons's wife Phyllis is a quiet, repeated, welcome presence in the poems, "as / solid as a jug or judge," and she, too—to reverse a sexist aphorism of Kafka's ("women are traps which lie in wait for men everywhere, in order to drag them down into the Finite")—keeps him grounded: "my wife says there / are so many niches / today where you / can make money." Elsewhere, he grouses, "Why is it that doctors expect to be paid for their / time and lawyers and bowling coaches for their / time but nobody expects to pay a poet," concluding, "I guess poets // are supposed to be so used to poverty they don't need / any money." Born poor, Ammons always remained aware of the demands of what's called, depressingly, and often to shut interesting people up, the real world. But this doesn't mean accepting common sense as the way to go—becoming hard-headed. In Ammons's most famous poem, "Corsons Inlet," he walks by the sea: inspired or just out for a breath of fresh air? Either way,

> the walk liberating, I was released from forms,
> from the perpendiculars,
> straight lines, blocks, boxes, binds
> of thought

Which resembles an ideal freedom, comparable with James Joyce's, or Stephen Dedalus's, imagined flight from the nets of "nationality, language, religion." Ammons touches—it's 1962—on war paranoia: "no arranged terror: no forcing of image, plan, / or thought: / no propaganda, no humbling of reality to precept." Keats said the poet should become a chameleon, even a nobody, a thoroughfare for all possible thoughts—Ammons tries to actually write by this method.

"Saliences" (a key word in his work) states the time paradox we live by and that he returns to over and over: "The reassurance is / that through change / continuities sinuously work / cause and effect / without alarm." ("Local Antiquities": "only / changing with change // stays beyond things / and us, mocks change's / mocking changes.") This would be soupy stuff were it not for the poet's up-close inscapes: "the kept and erased sandcrab trails"; "minnows left high in the tide-deserted pocket, / fiddler crabs / bringing up gray pellets of drying sand, / disappearing from air's faster events." It's the last line there that does it—bouncing from journal-jottings back into the shine of abstraction. (Like Stevens, Ammons knows that philosophical language has its own sensuous appeal.) Ammons excels at these snapshot utterances—peculiarly particular, particularly peculiar, or outright visionary: "a marvelous morning / dull gray aflood with the possibility of light"; "the caterpillar sulls on the hot macadam // but then, risking, ripples to the bush"; "it's April 1 / the willow's yellow's / misting green"; "balloons in inexperienced hands worry / me; I stagger into rushes of loss when they nod upward."

He's a realist: "I knew an old woman who knew when that time / had come and that's what she told me, it's hard to hope / when there is no hope: she, naturally, died." (Those commas, around "naturally!" I'm reminded of how Morrissey tweaks with a sung pause a moment in The Smiths' "Heaven Knows I'm Miserable Now": "*Oh you've been in the house too long*, she said / and I, naturally, fled . . .) But Ammons can also be so clearly and uniironically heartening that I wish his poems were read by those who consume self-help manuals in droves. He speaks, sometimes, often, reassuringly, placing a hand on the reader's shoulder—again resembling Whitman, when that poet breaks with the boasting, and says, quietly, in an alcove, as it were, of the Brobdingnagian yawp: "It is not upon you alone the dark patches fall, / The dark threw its patches down upon me also." "A light catches somewhere," Ammons tells us,

> to find a place to break out elsewhere:
> this light, tendance, neglect
> is human concern working with
> what is: one thing is hardly better
> or worse than another: the
> split hair of possible betterment makes
> dedication reasonable and heroic:
>
> the frail butterfly, a slightly
> guided piece of trash, the wind takes
> ten thousand miles

To isolate these moments from the vast, noisy weather systems of the poet's thinking may be to sentimentalize. Yet Ammons can be as blatant as to announce, in "Loving People," that "people are / losing propositions" until "you decide / to decide to love," and an actual sonnet appears on page 330 of the second volume: "Love surgent, equipped with the direction / of sail, is matchless." Once we had to hunt in out-of-the-way bookshops for this stuff or succumb to Amazon's corporate dominion: the risk, now, is of such frankly touching verse disappearing into the morass of the overall project. Helen Vendler suggests a *Selected* hewn from the newly collated oeuvre—a fine idea.

Postlyric and the Already Known
Dawn Lundy Martin

"Literature makes possible," writes Sandeep Parmar, "a space for *subjectivity*, and for poets of colour that space is always a battleground where expectations of universality (whiteness), authenticity (for whom?), poetic form (lyric or anti-lyric) and voice determine wider subject positions beyond the page"; she notes that "in the past terms like 'innovative' or 'experimental' were determined by . . . almost entirely white and largely male poetic avant-gardes," and finds within Black experimentalism, for one—as analyzed by Anthony Reed—a type of "post-lyric" aware of "the limitations of the speaking subject, the I."

Ours is a golden age of postlyric, minoritized poetries: works often though not always by poets of color, shattering the too smoothly yearning, the only complacently fraught, white-coded "I" who, in more traditional works, wanders through a field or down a street and has a mild-mannered epiphany—into so many drives, velocities, conflictual utterances that surge and seethe beyond the parameters, the consumer-individualist model, of the unified and salable poetic "voice." The postlyric poem is often in prose, or mashes up verse and prose: found prose, endorsed or ironized, placed either way in collision with other discourses; prose redacted, splintered, turned in on itself; prose materializing not as the voice of reason—becalming our misgivings—but as an unceasingly guarded watchfulness asking how one gets from A to B and if such a thing is even desirable; prose written, often, from an entrenched subject position and not bothered if you can't follow or enjoy it: prose encysted, disjoint and intercut, comfortlessly heuristic in its often shocking unreserve—"All that has been spoken. All that threatens the legitimacy of that which is attempting to be said. Phonemic struggle—I'll call it a precursor to blathering. Scintilla. Something dragged in the sand. An ocean of debris. In the instants before arrivals some things happened. What is perpetually almost, spilling off its imagined page, signaling an infinite number of openings, leakages, stuck tongues." This is from "Negrotizing in Five; Or, How to Write a Black Poem"—a poem in five prose parts in Dawn Lundy Martin's first book (winner of the Cave Canem Poetry Prize in 2007), *A Gathering of Matter/A Matter of Gathering*. Both the collection's title and the poem's insist a unitary lyricism—a voice speaking without distortion—isn't possible for this poet. She must juxtapose, accumulate, build self-canceling structures. Her short sentences, or sentence fragments, never cease to provoke—provoke the reader, that is, but also provoke themselves into further bursts of motion, adjacencies that disconcert with suprapersonal, race-historical flashbacks.

You can't learn—the point made by this poem and its title—"how to write a Black poem" as one learns their ABCs: a principle of struggle agitates against codification. In her introduction to the 2018 anthology *Letters to the Future: Black Women/Radical Writing*—which she coedited with Erica Hunt—Martin sets against "the hegemonic desire to ensnare Black art and poetry with language that delimits that art and poetry for its exchange value in the market place" the idea of writing "as anti-doctrine, as future imaginings, as languages with their own rules, as new makings, undisciplined and rebellious." A Black poet might turn against poetic gimmickry perceived as collusive with majority-mandated ways of (inoffensively) appearing and disappearing from view: though to recognize this we should differentiate postlyric from the antilyric writing of white avant-gardes. As M. NourbeSe Philip explains:

> Poets and writers like myself who question and challenge the very ability of the language itself to speak the truth of their memories and engage in what I call practices of dislocation find themselves on the horns of a dilemma. Their poetry can be described as being language based and appears to share a great deal with those poets working within the European aesthetic of language poetry. The language based nature of poetry such as my own starts from a very different place. That of the wasteland between the terror of language and the horror of silence. White or European audiences who do not understand the matrix of this poetry miss what the poetry is all about. They see it as postmodern.

Unlike L=A=N=G=U=A=G=E poetry, the racialized postlyric doesn't cede entirely the idea of the speaking subject to the impersonal mutations of language: people of color need to keep hold of the idea, the possibility, of speaking "the truth of their memories," rather than believing, like white experimenters, that the very idea of subjective interiority is a capitalist fiction. Philip's "Interview with an Empire" appears in *Assembling Alternatives*, edited by Romana Huk and important for understanding this kind of poetry—also in it there's a great, scorching, essay by D. S. Marriott (credited here as David). He too objects to white Language writing as repeating rather than redeeming an erasure of "marginalized voices—black women and men writers for example" who "have had their claims to representation, their positions of performativity, silenced, ignored and oppressed . . . there is a fetishization of the signifier in Language writing which serves to conceal and guard against something else, and that something else is the encroachment of nameless anxieties and displacements associated with knowledge, power and agency."

It is with such "anxieties and displacements" that Martin's poetry is concerned: precisely because she doesn't abandon from the start the idea of agency, or Black spoken truth, she has to fight so hard, so intelligently, to create within a fragmented language the space for it. Lyric is self-expression: this is something else; between "all that has been spoken" (the poetry of social protest risks saying over again, pouring salt in old wounds, things that, though they *must* be said, have *already* been said *ad nauseam* in newspapers and on talk shows and in tweets) and "what is perpetually almost" (utopian hope), what is poem language to do and by what means? Martin writes lineated verse as well: "How many bodies is it," asks "Sunday Lessons," "from the basement / to the church / to singing hallelujah?"—the shot gospel choir in the video for Childish Gambino's "This Is America" comes to mind—but any too-foreseeable (stifling) melos is deflated, historicized; alternatives are sought and begin to be found. "A precise dictation occurs inside the chest. It is a reckoning with a kind of god, a kind of believing." Except this isn't the self-identical voice poets in workshops are tasked to find—a secularized conscience, the Emersonian oversoul stripped of undecidability and risk and commodified—not for someone (moving backward a few lines, in this sequence, "After Drowning") who "travels in articulation, is heavy with language, is hunted, breathes and hears black bitch and black ass in the literal field of the carnivorous."

Martin's poetry emerges from her subject position but is wary of such postures as someone like her, with her history, is expected by today's reader to perform. She intersperses references to slavery, police violence and incarceration, such as our conversations around Blackness justly center, but these moments of recognition operate almost like that trick of the free verse lyric poet, tutored in traditional forms, who slips into regular meter periodically for emphasis, affirmation, to help the reader find her feet. I'm trying to work through Martin's complexly evolving body of work chronologically, but here I must quote ahead of time from her latest, *Good Stock Strange Blood*, where she writes "hurry and / get to the real black bits or no one will care"; and also: "Your tennis shorts or salmon-colored pants will not help you. It's a good idea to have "black" in the title of the "black" book in case there are any questions as to its race. The "black" bits will be excisable, quotable in reviews. The book should be very interested in the thing you know as "blackness," all its clothes, its haberdashery." I've begun my own, inevitably deforming quotation a sentence early to catch Martin's wry riff on Audre Lorde ("Your silence will not protect you"). Also to examine the engineered collision between Black people dressing like prosperous whites to fit in (it won't work) and the "black" poetry collection that—such are the pressures placed on poets of color by their publishing houses, editors, and a review culture shaped by "identity politics" but unable to meaningfully connect those two words—is encouraged not to hide but announce its color except in unthreatening and finally assimilable ways. To protest the excisable is to insist that though this postlyric poet's uninterested in old-style organic or well-wrought forms, her books as wholes (rather than individual poems within them) have to be read and considered as multifaceted and resonating entireties. The reviewer who doesn't know how to analyze postlyric, how to approach the challenging cognitive work done by Martin's sentences—as they align to build arguments, then butt heads, launch in contrary directions—falls back on the "black" bits, reducing her poetics to talking points.

Both the poet and the critic are, then, trying to do justice to large, ungetroundable, much-discussed injustices, while also evading the preinvented language mass culture has designed for supposedly investigating and publicizing such matters but really for exploiting trauma within a money-driven news culture that produces dopamine rushes, not social change. Under these pressures, poetry becomes, as for the High Modernists, difficult (it even becomes prose). This is how I'd describe the motivations behind postlyric, but I should mention also the recent attempt by Virginia Jackson—a key practitioner of what's known in academia as new lyric studies—to tether

her perspective, arising of nineteenth-century poetry, to the Black experimentalism of Claudia Rankine:

> Rankine's trilogy has ceased to pretend that "the lyric speaker" does not (like the president) depend on a White supremacist illusion of collective identity. It does. This is not the place for me to provide a long historical argument about how and why this is true, so it's a good thing I don't have to, because Rankine has come to the same conclusion through her practice as a poet. . . . If I were to fill in the American lyric history and theory I don't have time or space to narrate here, I would say that over the course of the nineteenth and twentieth centuries, American poetry was gradually lyricized—by which I mean that ballads and songs, elegies and odes, hymns and epistles that depended on particular forms of address gradually and unevenly merged into one big genre of address associated with the genre of the person rather than with the genre of the poem. All poetry (or almost all poetry) became lyric poetry. In order for the genre of the represented person to *be* representative, the definite article attached to the concept of "the lyric speaker" erased that speaker's race, gender, and personal history. That erasure amounted to a default whiteness, since that unmarked illusion made it easier for all readers to appropriate the words of the poem as their own.

Applying the terms of lyricization to the furors of contemporary verse culture helps illuminate the trap reactionaries find themselves in when they feel it impossible, designate it impossible, or rage against what they perceive as the externally mandated impossibility of conceiving of minority poetries in any terms except the biographical and identitarian. It is the longstanding evacuation of the lyric "I"—its "default whiteness"—that spurs aggressive reconnection of that disembodied ghost with the life conditions of the author: a move supposed to empower poets of color that may in fact hamstring their creativity—forcing them to stay in their lane. So long as, it would appear, poems sound like a single voice expressing itself, there's no way out of this bind—though I think Jackson's too puritanical about lyric, for the risk here is of conflating the idea of *writing* whiteness with the desire to, even in discrepant lyrics (Gwendolyn Brooks doesn't write white supremacist poetry!), *read* whiteness, deleting alternatives. I also think of the many poets of color who have written and continue to write lyric poetry both inside and outside the U.S. (the absence of "lyricization" from debates around world literature is especially notable) and who have theorized their position: Srikanth Reddy, for instance (who also writes experimental poetry in prose) has shown how fractured selves can express their vulnerabilities and preoccupations through digression within, rather than wholesale disintegration of, the lyric.

Returning to Martin—let's place the power of her writing against what's said here, since the thinking being done within Black poetics exceeds, outruns, theories about it promulgated by white professors. Martin's hybridized poetry is "postlyric," but not in the sense of abandoning lyric entirely (the accents of personal pain are everywhere in her work; she incessantly postulates interiorities; like Rankine, she explores reminiscently pungent moments)—rather, her collisional poetics challenges the very distinction between lyric and nonlyric. Homi Bhabha says that, in Rankine, "short measures of traumatic time, *as the lyric form demonstrates,*"—my emphasis—"have an intense and encrypted existence." Martin's styles—unreconciled, atomic, skeptical of linearity—are residually lyrical. Yes, there's no controlling "I" at the center of things, yet these are experiential, haunting, musical works:

> This is a partial history of fabulously forgetting. We drift inside dreams to escape the dislogic of hunger. Cracked bodies dislodge out of—well, ice cream parlors, telephone booths, husks and fabrics made for shields. Mouths made crisp from drought. A who we are not. My brother's house is hip-deep in the worry of objects. To arrive there is a past death. Is whirring uncontrollably in red night. Is being removed. Is naked canopies.

This appears on page 23 of Martin's second book, *Discipline*, winner this time of the 2009 Nightboat Poetry Prize, and published by that press in 2011 with neither poem titles nor index. The first sentence cites two of prose's traditional tasks. We write "history" in prose and we tell stories—we *fabulate*, a word linked etymologically to "fabulously"—in prose. That is, we record the (supposed) truth and we, writing fiction, invent what never occurred. Except both these activities may be ways of "forgetting" both singular torments—when Martin writes "*we* drift inside dreams," we, who may not be identical with her "we," should recognize that she writes as a Black queer woman—and also of obscuring the visceral moment that is a place of emergence, the doorway through which the new might enter the world.

Violence and deprivation and categorization—"A who we are not"—stalk these sentences. Martin's last five desire to say things point-blankly, yet it's exactly this urgency that shunts her language toward ambiguity and dispersal. Distress isn't melodramatized but explored—including the pain occasioned not by events themselves but subsequently, involuntarily contrived, coping mechanisms. We can pin some of this down. Martin has written in *n+1* about her brother, who, as a child, fired a shotgun through the roof—"That night, my father beat my brother mercilessly with a washing machine hose in the dank basement of our house. . . . The chaos of a violence like that is astonishing"—dropped out of school ("I didn't mind either when my brother failed, because his failure meant my light shone even brighter"), and went missing for two days in 2017. His incarceration illustrates the fate in a racist society of many Black men: "My brother, who is now 55, in jail for the first time, is not singular in his missingness."

Yet Martin, remember, expresses impatience with reviewers who single out the "black bits" in their reviews. So coming to moments mappable onto racial hostility in the U.S.—"A black boy who lives in a corner house already looks like a man. A massive figure with truly apelike features"—we should (the point's worth repeating) bear in mind that the forms of our attentiveness aren't being flattered but oppugned. Bombarded with incitements, inducements, affronts seeming to require an immediate, not a considered, response, we read poems, and the world, aggressively, neurotically, oppositionally. Our society has us (a type of pseudorecognition can be reassuring, a way of not paying deeper attention) respond with reflex outrage to certain things, but could it be that outrage and inaction are in fact secret sharers? Having had our say, we move on, doing nothing to change the situation. Postlyric may encompass a range of affects—rage, terror, yearning—but it's also about exploring these feelings, historicizing them, using them to conceptualize minoritized experience in the twenty-first century. As such, this type of poetry both participates in and profoundly queries the emotional velocities of our moment: "A sick man vomits into a cup at McDonald's in Union Square and it's hard to feel sorry for him because he's so public. Once, when I was a teenager, a friend pointed to a doddering black man on the street and said laughing, What if that guy was your father? It was." The logic of cultural representation—too often slickly equated with political representation—is travestied here. One Black person stands for others, as when Martin discusses her brother, but if this move is sometimes necessary, she's alert to its dangers. Consider how arts culture functions, giving a handful of authors of color a wealth of attention, sometimes actual money, in a show of redress placing upon said writers the demand they don't write creatively, refractively, innovatively, but *represent* their communities in a documentary way that is supposed to, of its own accord, fix, as with a wave of a magic wand, a range of inequalities (this becomes, in exchange for plaudits, the poet's *job*). In this way, the poetry world substitutes constrictive (play by our rules and we'll reward you!) acclaim within a siloed subculture for—what it only pretends to pave the way for—actual reparations for systemic injustices. Empathy has limits ("he's so *public*," a word harshly rescrambling the sounds of *sick* and *cup*); the "Union" has always been riven by race hate.

I'm curious here about connections—sorts that are possible, sorts that aren't. "Once" is a hinge. It takes us, takes the speaker of this poem, the person who comes through with that sardonic "It was," from one incident to another. Is this a painful, involuntary, association, or the poet as cerebral arranger? Like Claudia Rankine, Martin doesn't use quotation marks, so things said blur into events, in fact, are events: to say is to do and to make a racist remark is to injure a Black person; as Rankine and Beth Loffreda write—"to be a person of color in a racist culture is to be always addressable, and to be addressable means one is always within stigma's reach. . . . Literary institutions . . . expect and reward certain predictable performances of race. There can be a comfort, a place to hole up, a place to rest, found in that performance—that is, if the performance conforms." It's therefore important to insist on the difference between the events described in this poem, and also the difference between Martin's essay *about* her brother and her poem into which his presence unpredictably intrudes. It's one thing to write, as she does in her memoir, "my brother was swallowed already—a person trapped within a person. He had ambitions that were entirely unrealistic: architect, golf-course designer, business owner. He had begun to accumulate masses of random objects until his bedroom was so cluttered with things collected from yard sales and traded from friends that he was forced to sleep on a twin mattress on the floor." Another thing to write in a poem:

> My brother's house is hip-deep in the worry of objects.

We can use one paragraph of prose to explain the other, but something different, qualitatively so, occurs here. A poem in prose is where prose begins to analyze itself. We're not told about the brother, but his house: we might sink "hip-deep" into a hoarder's knickknacks, but in this case the domestic space itself, as in the poetry and prose of Gwendolyn Brooks, seems innervated and enervated through emotional transference—an unsafe space. To worry is also to chew over something aggressively, as a dog worries a bone.

Martin's postlyricism positions both the writer and the reader as worriers—teeth bared, clamping on. Trying to make sense of things—to wake up, to see clearly, to attain a moment or two of lucidity—is like struggling out from beneath a scratchy, imprisoning blanket: "Woolen cloth. Unworkable. Hard and scratchy. Doesn't act like much. Not a rug or a blanket. The smell of mold. Covering on walls, the walls, grey and raised, a pattern one can never forget. Fingertips can never forget. A kind of wall that might become you. You might become it—non-intricate weave, a sullen protest, against what, is unknown." To turn into a "wall . . . a sullen protest" is to become harmlessly univocal, as some activist lyrics are. To avoid getting trapped in what Gloria Anzaldúa notes can be an imprisoning, a go-nowhere counteraggressiveness—the petrified (as in turned to stone but also the other sense) rebelliousness of the adolescent position addictively available online, by which one objects to real wrongs but with a shrilly rote querulance only—to avoid this, a poet might write prose. She might ally herself with scraps of utterance refusing coordination into larger programs: she might narrowcast (writing difficult, unwelcoming poems) out of the knowledge that within our money-corrupted and tech-stultified economies of attention to be at-once coherent is to be readily absorbed into rhetorics that, pretending to racial justice, really have disguised agendas. Martin's poem isn't only about being held back by barriers but also about being imprisoned through (another coping mechanism) a merging with said barriers, an identification with their gruesome textures. About losing oneself to a "non-intricate . . . sullen protest" of debatable potency: a social form whose insidiousness Martin suggests through an intrusion of poetic form—"scratch" rhymes, almost, with "much," and this repetition hardens, becomes utter, with the identical rhyme or refrain of "never forget." Fingertips also have patterns, the prints sought at crime scenes and used to put people in police databases, so in several ways ideas of pattern, memory, and constriction come together.

Life in a Box Is a Pretty Life (2015) more explicitly theatricalizes, destabilizes, and emplaces (the two things are possible at the same time) the supposedly universal lyric "I": "the I in dramatic gesticulation, its façade trembling"; "the I radiant in heat, polish. *I am closing my legs now*"; "When they said they'd split me in two, I was overjoyed, wanting to get at the rip of things. . . . When the I speaks, it speaks into an other's speech"; "I was illustrative, an example angled toward proof"; "A dead fawn under machinery. I am the machinery. Am also the end of the sentence." The sort of I-poem that draws a halo around its progressive speaker's head, positioning wholly on the side of the authentic, exemplary, good, and true, Martin wholeheartedly vetoes. "This work incorporates some borrowed and/or manipulated and/or erased language from late 19th-century ideologies and texts including Frederick Starr's 'The Degeneracy of the American Negro'; J. L. M. Curry's 'The Negro Question'; and, Frederick L. Hoffman's *Race Traits and Tendencies of the American Negro*":

It's not the word "body" that's the problem. It's the physical thingness of it, the hump.

For thousands of
years there lies
behind the race one
dreary, unrelieved,
monotonous chapter
of ignorance, nakedness,
superstition, savagery.

When we encounter the savage, we are in reverie. This is precision joy, concomitant stroking. Are you me? Is this our jackal face? O, I love it, I love us. Let me make a comparison. The jackal face akin to my father beating me with a soup spoon, I'm so unruly.

This references the masks of Anubis—jackal god, embalmer—worn by priests in ancient Egypt as they mummified their dead. We know this book has Egypt on its mind because of another piece of interpolated prose ironically lineated (Martin has reversed things, so turning prose into what looks like poetry doesn't, as in a found poem, deify but mock it): "This negro type / is ancient. The / Egyptian monuments / demonstrate its / existence four / thousand years / ago." And Langston Hughes, in "The Negro Speaks of Rivers," explains Black history is far from a "monotonous" chapter of savagery: "My soul has grown deep like the rivers. // I bathed in the Euphrates when dawns were young. / I built my hut near the Congo and it lulled me to sleep. / I looked upon the Nile and raised the pyramids above it." For Martin, a Black woman's body is a historical site striated with both suffering and "joy"—a queer, sexual joy, of "concomitant stroking," where the "jackal face" becomes an "O" face; where "savage" energies in a transvalued way resurface "in reverie." Lovemaking sanctifies the traumatized body through both pleasure and ritualized—mastered, reclaimed, subverted—pain.

Though the body centers Martin's poetics throughout, in this book it really comes to the fore as the locus where thinking unfolds. Aristotle—who was also the father of race science, believing some born to be slaves—wrote that "wonder is the beginning of philosophy"; Martin wonders "how wonder works. When I am squatting to retrieve a cup of vaginal blood, and bearing down, as the instructions say, as in defecation, I am wondering." Is this a specific thought-instance or the idea that one is always thinking, wondering, even unconsciously; that a woman cognizes both herself and the world at such moments even if she doesn't put conclusions into words (to others or in her own head)? "Awareness of being in a female body is a tinge of regret," writes Martin. And in two sections from "25 *Tiny Essays on the Value of Forgetfulness and Sleepiness*":

3.

The I is collecting documents in her body. *Why are you writing me?!*, it bellows.

. . .

11.

If absent from happening, if unbound by discovery. Have coveted dissociation. The body as a construction of miniature vaults. I imagine them to be perfect cubes of thick shiny steel. If the work is an investigation it is an investigation into the horrific, the terrifying, the unknown.

Reclaiming from colonial discourse the notion of a Black prehistory coded in one's very bones, Martin pities her oppressors their amnesia—"The police are so young. They do not hear the wailing." Her poetics of "phonemic struggle" (returning to my first quotation, from "Negrotizing in Five") recalls Fred Moten's theory of Black improvisation, a subsonic wail of anguish made audible through an all-in-the-moment—he relates jazz and literature—yet historical ad hocery: "black performance," he says, "has always been the ongoing improvisation of a kind of lyricism of the surplus—invagination, rupture, collision, augmentation." The depths of bodily experience become, at times, in the interstices of Martin's sentences, hearable. That's as positive as she gets—suggesting it's possible, sometimes, to fathom these matters. "I can't think about how to exist now," she writes in her "Prologue" to 2017's *Good Stock Strange Blood*, "without pressing together big pasts and small pasts. Big pasts (like historical collective trauma) and the narrow self-indulgent past of personal invasion, self-configuration at the hands of another." Sentences that can't straightaway heal or pinpoint or delimit such traumas do at least remain livingly connected to them, so who knows what a scandalously enfleshed phenomenology might recover?

Good Stock Strange Blood reconfigures Martin's—I quote from the acknowledgments—"experimental libretto, *Good Stock on the Dimension Floor*.... The libretto became the bones for this collection, an investigation into the brutality of the raced condition and an embrace toward an AfroFuture outside of recognizable bodies, temporalities, and accessible dimensions." The libretto features three characters, or voices, "Land," "Perpetuus," and "Nave": the Yam Collective had multiple actors portray each; in the book, these characters are no longer named. So we've come a long way from that lyric space I mentioned in which one knows always who's speaking in a poem. What particularly intrigues me—I realize it has become a through line for this essay—is Martin's resistance of the "recognizable": those familiar outrages, talking points, fetishizations of "Blackness" rather than Blackness. It's possible, she suggests, for the recognizable to become so recognizable, so utterly known already, that we don't think about it any longer; it has become familiarized, and we have become, toward it, automatized (and by "we," here, I include myself as a non-Black reader outside the "we" this poem seems to summon):

when the girl died / her body just tangled, you know / they liked to call it strange fruit / the stench and witch of our synchronicity / and how we burden / foreclose the claim / with wells and things / and police / and citizens / and accidents / no one / no one will ever really know the already known

Martin isn't alone in experimenting with this style of prose, which, though it isn't lineated, resembles song lyrics on an insert, or literary-critical prose like the essay you're reading now, in *designating* lineation, alluding to it or ghosting it, with dividing slashes. This poem in prose therefore contains and transforms an alternative version of itself that would look like short lines descending the page surrounded by white space. It's an inherently self-reflective, self-conscious structure, appropriate to a work about what we "know" already and yet will never "really know." This idea emerges out of the conversational speech filler, "you know," as it coincides with a reference most readers will get, to Abel Meeropol's "Strange Fruit," a euphemism for lynched Black bodies that—in Billie Holiday's performance of the song—becomes musically far from (as a euphemism is supposed to be) evasive, taking us painfully into what is "already known," but never as surely as when one more than listens to, but really *hears*, the song.

"*I have been writing all my adult life*," says Martin—or one of the voices floating through this book (this is from a passage of italicized prose, on page 84) "*about the irretrievable. Often the same image appears to me and finds language in the poem resembling the language in some other poem stroking the same wound. . . . I let the repetition occur across writings as layers, minute variations on a writing through time.*" Good Stock returns to and reinvigorates earlier words, motifs, themes: "what is the gesture of the wail but the wail?"; "**I call for my stranger, I long for him**. I look for him in the face of every black ghost on the edge of every piss-stinking park" (the bold text is in the original): would this be the homeless father figure previously mentioned?; "my brother bends away from the hose that beats him"; "feel the hump of our drape. Here: the body, flesh / inevitable, unsatiated hunger like a whip." In her *n+1* essay, Martin says between her and her brother a "chasm emerged . . . me, floating off like some wandering balloon; my brother tethered tightly to a familiar story of trouble and poverty, like most of the kids in our neighbourhood"; and in the Q+A "Prologue" of this collection—"This book is like a long, thin, wavy tendril stretched into the sky from a small spot at the top of my head. At the end of the tendril, somewhere far in the sky where I cannot see, is a mutilated black face. A little me is sitting on the top of my head, holding the tendril like the string to a balloon." This is a book that keeps talking about its status as a book (based on a libretto, refusing to resemble a standard poetry collection): "the book is not writing itself / in the chilled gray day," says one voice, and another—*"The constraints of the book are limiting. We must always consider the bigger book of grief. What I could not know, what no one can ever know is how laden an effect is predicated on an event or a progression of events."* What no one can ever know, again: Martin's book, featuring photographs, also, of the libretto-production, isn't a series of indexable lyrics-as-events: to inquire into trauma is necessarily to inquire into events, but also, for her, to ask if the outlines we draw around events belie further connections, with experiences harder to unproblematically frame—for Martin, that would be a racial history of grief saturating the Black body: "Stare through this window in // my belly where Mother // left her good stock, her pertinent cells, // her matter that matters."

An impossible maternal presence is evoked (that's too strong a word—seen in the distance, harkened to, never embraced) over and over: a Black holding environment, to borrow the parlance of object-relations psychoanalytic theory. "Wanted the swell of black earth, a legacy, *something larger than ourselves to hold us*"; "to be cradled with such fierce gentleness"; and more directly—"*Mother, where are you?*" A beautiful poem (though I doubt Martin would approve of that adjective) called "Faith is hum—" reminds me of a moment in William Blake that Marion Milner, one of those object-relations analysts, linked to the capacity of an unloved child "to set up inside one the fantasy of containing parents who love each other." To, that is, forge inside themselves the loving parents they never had, so they could themselves love others:

> The Angel that presided o'er my birth
> Said, "Little creature, form'd of joy and mirth
> Go, love without the help of anything on earth."

Martin's poem seems to be about self-soothing (when there's no one around to look after you) by humming or rocking. It suggests not self-enclosure within a delusory womb but (this is what reminds me of Blake, who said one might "Hold Infinity in the palm of your hand /And Eternity in an hour") openings onto the infinite. But it ends in apocalypse:

hum is rocking. Rocking is to preserve our black bodies in glass. To hum is to maintain the myth of wholeness. What will we find in heart-cave, pull back sea-rot, the already multiple, the metropolis? *Look what I am holding! Not desire, but infinite multiplicity, the mouth of existence.* On one side waters rise.

Elsewhere glass is imprisonment, is white voyeurism—I think this is Martin's only published couplet (it appears in quotation marks): "What is more frightening than a black face / confronting your gaze from the display case?"—here glass is a gentler, fragile container. Glass and water both flow, are both dangerous and see-through. I think of disaster movies—floods arriving suddenly to crush buildings and kill millions—but also of the unbroken "waters" surrounding a baby in the womb.

In her afterword to Harriet Jacobs' *Incidents in the Life of a Slave Girl* (the Signet Classics anniversary edition published in 2010), Martin explains how through pregnancy Jacobs "acts radically to claim ownership over her own body. . . . In pregnancy, the body reaches out against its own physical limits, temporarily usurping them. . . . In the case of Jacobs, the female body's capability of reproduction is her weapon." It is a mode of rebellion against the chattel system that reduces slave women to things, to only their (exploitable) bodies in a different sense. I've insisted that Martin's poetry (in prose) needs to be read in a different way than her discursive prose, but this essay is notable for how, as she introduces a canonical work and her relation to it, her own central creative theme, that of the Black body, begins to come through in a historicized way—how the very word *body* begins to reverberate, to be recovered from a sheerly metaphorical usage. "There is a whole body of African-American literature within that body of knowledge and inquiry that is 'American' literature," writes Martin; also, "the racial burden of America clings to the black body." Her postlyric verse, though in it utterance is always "already multiple," chooses against disembodied, purely verbal experimentalism, insisting on a poetry of enfleshed interiority: she searches for answers in the Black "heart-cave."

"I am not speaking of or as myself or for any/one"
Vahni (Anthony) Capildeo

Vahni Anthony Capildeo is prolific, and poets so restlessly generative are often animated by a nexus of idea-feelings that they return to and augment. *Skin Can Hold* melds verse (open-form, closed, vernacular, a rondeau, a "sextina") and prose (essayistic, narrative cento, stage directions for performance) inspired by medieval polyphony, Oulipo, Muriel Spark, and with a moment comparing the Guyanese poet-activist Martin Carter to Gerard Manley Hopkins. (Carter's "Sensibility and the Search" mentions Hopkins alongside Dylan Thomas, Edgar Allan Poe, and the French Symbolists, distinguishing from the crapulous mimicry of colonial verse a transnational "family spirit—a kinship—not a relationship between master and slave.") Capildeo's writing (poetry and criticism) transforms into perpetual mental incandescence that which the world's cold eye might otherwise stigmatize as impressionism, eccentricity, hypertrophied outrage. Challenging an Anglo-American verse culture in which, increasingly, people of color have a place, but on the terms of a white commentariat with no language adequate to work both "politically-engaged *and* aesthetically-driven" (as Capildeo writes of Carter's work), this is poetry that enters phenomenologically, with heartbreaking and case-making fidelity, into racial travails. What it's like, for instance, to have someone look at, but not really see you; to nod at your words and spuriously respond, but without hearing what you wish to express. Capildeo also articulates the deep, sometimes self-attacking sadness that comes of seeking, following such encounters, an impossible justice: "Oppression and prejudice are quasi-poetic, pseudo-artful, in their ability to morph, appearing in official bodies, or unthinking social practices; in popular fictions or institutional architecture careless of blood history, or within the convolution of one hateful or self-hating mind." One's face is perceived as always already a scandal, a hurdle to be cleared or a pitfall to be avoided—through ignoring, silencing, drowning out—or, alternatively, an opportunity the white person egotistically seizes to announce themselves to themselves, and others, as not-racist; an invitation to pretend their burgeoning self-pity is of its nature progressive.

Consider, in *Skin Can Hold*, the flayed woman in "Ablutions": "You are ignored by him and knowable to any others as vulnerability in situ, a heap of lines that cannot be crossed out, except deletion by delivery is what his voice does." In "Shame," a performer wears a "coat of mirrors," a "Venetian wire mask" and (visibility, the right and wrong kind, is of the essence) "glow in the dark paint": "I have no shame but fury // I have no shame but weariness // I have no shame but a sense of enclosure // I have no shame but a sense of déjà vu // I have no shame but the knowledge I shall be disbelieved." To be a woman of color is to be erased twice over.

Yet Capildeo's sympathy extends, as George Eliot would have it, beyond their own lot—into the experience of Jewish people, for instance. A reimagining of Shylock's famous speech (which he isn't permitted to even begin) riffs on Clare Quilty's elastic mishearings of Humbert Humbert in *Lolita*:

SHYLOCK: Hath . . .
PERSON A: It is much too hot for June.
SHYLOCK: Hath not . . .
PERSON B: When are you having your holiday?
SHYLOCK: Hath not a . . .
PERSON A: I was booked for Sharm Al Sheikh. I love the sea. They've ruined it.
PERSON B: You were looking forward . . .
PERSON A: Now I'm afraid to fly.
PERSON B: . . . to that.
SHYLOCK: Hath not a . . .
PERSON B: It's the man with the gold chain again.
SHYLOCK: Eyes! Hands! Organs!
PERSON A: Ignore him.

"They've ruined it." In times of resurgent anti-Semitism, Shylock's voice matters—but that "gold chain" also suggests (as often in Capildeo) cross-identifications and solidarities. In Capildeo's debut, *No Traveller*

Returns—published by Salt in 2003—Hindu marriage-wear tropes what we try and fail to get across (in two senses): "What I would say is dripping and knotting, like a gold chain neglected / so the flow of its links sets to fighting and mating." They don't gloss this object, "a thing not for wearing nor for discarding, / to shine light no longer, absorbed in a box," for readers who don't know that culture; nor (sticking with *No Traveller Returns*) does the speaker of "Amulet" deign to elucidate her finery. Let's collate that poem with Capildeo's 2018 collection, *Venus as a Bear*:

"That's an unusual pendant you are wearing."
"Yes, it is rather unusual."
"May I look at it?"
"There is really nothing to see."
"Was it a gift?"
"It is something I chose for myself."
"Do you wear it often?"
"Not all the time."
"Why not? It suits you. Don't you like it?"
"Yes, it is one of those things which you need to feel complete."
—FROM "AMULET," *NO TRAVELLER RETURNS*

There is, too, the amulet
prayed over in front of a thousand-name-chanted fire
by another dead one;
it was like poking my eye or bruising my clit
when the airport guard stared me down
and fingered it as if to pretend
it might be a poison capsule or travestied/radical souvenir bullet,
I felt it hold up my nerves when she grabbed the gold cylinder,
the metal hung in air
clasped externally
yet more internal to me.
So take it off is not an option. Without trying, thinking feelingly,
I am not speaking of or as myself or for any/one.
Damn the subtle body's extension into material, affectively.
—FROM SECTION 4 OF "CROSSING BORDERS: ASSUMING THE HABITS OF THE DAY AND NIGHT," IN *VENUS AS A BEAR*

The person of color is under no obligation to annotate their marginality—to explain themselves—it can be a pleasure to do so, but not when harangued. (This includes the demands of poetry publishers, prize committees, academics, reviewers, and readers.) Rejecting the signifier "pendant," the speaker of "Amulet" withstands the exoticizing gaze that eye-gropes without shame. The power dynamic sharpens in "Crossing Borders" with an experience familiar to those of us routinely delayed at checkpoints—I can't think of another poet who writes so "feelingly" about this except Seamus Heaney (a Catholic in Northern Ireland, stopped at a roadblock, a sten gun in his face). He speaks of "the tightness and the nilness" of that contretemps—Capildeo lambastes the guard's preening exactitude. The rituals—disguising a vast impotence—of airport security compare poorly with those immemorially enacted around a "thousand-name-chanted fire."

"I try," writes Capildeo, "to create changes of modality in one book," which means these collections ask to be listened to as wholes, rather like concept albums (*Venus as a Bear* plays on Bjork's *Venus as a Boy*). But to others, a "shifting of modes, which initially seemed natural, was not universally obvious. . . . Identity politics; the lyrical I; were inadequate to a sense of self evolving from others and their words, accessible or arcane." (Hence the poet's pronoun, "they.") Nettled by these poems, thrust back into painful experiences of my own, I return to a beautiful sentence from Christopher Ricks's *Keats and Embarrassment*: "the deepest feelings are somehow involuntary and yet are our responsibility." Capildeo's poems foreground those who may feel that others are responsible for their deepest feelings. This is part of what it means, repeating Capildeo, to have "a sense of self evolving *from others and their words*." But isn't it a trap, to be positioned or self-position as wholly a victim—passively scorched by one's ordeals? So we'd better reclaim those feelings, seeing ourselves as coauthors, while repudiating that mental-health ideology that has us believe we and we only have the power to make ourselves happy or unhappy. This is a denial of the political world, and Capildeo seems to me peculiarly attuned to the link between that world and the single encounter and to how power self-reproduces through bureaucracies of affect. *Skin Can Hold*'s poem on the Douma Four—activists abducted in Syria—contains the line "*How does that make you feel?*" The language of psychoanalysis drifts into normal conversation—but "make" reeks of compulsion. I'm reminded of the ambiguous power of that same word when it appears twice in one of Terrance Hayes's sonnets: "As if being called *Nigger* never makes you / Disappear.

As if the fear of other people / Never makes you levitate." We are constructed, made, into the people we are by the words and actions of those around us; "fear" may derive from internalized coercion, as well as the awareness that we don't have—as mindfulness advocates insist—total power over our thoughts, but can, in unequal societies, be made to feel things we don't want to.

The U.S. reader may think, reading this essay, of Claudia Rankine. Capildeo discusses in *PN Review* what Rankine "seeks to convey about the predicament of the non-'white'-skinned individual whose daily life cannot be individual, cannot be pure and spontaneous—cannot be *lyric*—in so far as it is subject to the encasements and flayings" (that metaphor again) "of racialized perception." "In line at the drugstore," writes Rankine, "it's finally your turn, and then it's not as he walks in front of you and puts his things on the counter. The cashier says, Sir, she was next. When he turns to you he is truly surprised"; and Capildeo:

> The crystalline aggregation of "microaggressions" in Claudia Rankine's *Citizen*, like a lump of geological fact, fits no human palm without spiking it somewhere. Analysis, witness, lament: the book is seamed with these modes, not composed of any one of them. It amasses its material and shifts points of view without offering settlement.
>
> . . .
>
> Rankine's "then" and "When" slide in like acupuncturist's needles. At the first turn, "you" has, *you* have not been assigned a gender, race or age; nor has the cashier. The microaggression, or pushiness, comes from a "he." The cashier exercises the power to strike the as-yet-unfigured "you" into a "she," a female who is spoken about protectively after a mild outrage has been committed against her. "You," you, have no option but to remain silent. The poem gives no option except witnessing silence. The poem, as an act of language, ruptures that silence, but you, "you," languish in the drama of passivity, petrified by outrage. *Citizen*'s pronouns are not objects of excavation so much as mini-gorgons. They can turn the reader to stone.

Capildeo attends to not only Rankine's much-discussed pronouns but also the duration and sequencing of her sentences. "The drama of passivity," of being "petrified by outrage," diagrams our cultural moment; gorgons are gendered, and in *Measures of Expatriation*—their breakout book of

2016—Capildeo explains that "Medusa's head was co-opted as a weapon, to be brought out of the man's bag when enemies needed to be stopped." Turning-to-stone revives the geological metaphor, where "settlement," in the context of reparations, has two meanings, positioning Rankine's text as position shifting while acclaiming the rebarbativeness with which she leaves unresolved her dealings with her audience. The needles of an acupuncturist are inserted at cardinal points not to injure but to give relief. Capildeo suggests Rankine's power both to disturb and to provide through her art a mode of imaginative remedy: this is criticism alive to work both "politically-engaged and aesthetically-driven."

I've lingered with Capildeo's criticism for two reasons: first, because it can be challenging, and in the end needless, to sift it from the prose in the books of poetry; second, because its perspective on race pulverizes clichés. Returning to "Crossing Borders"—"damn" is ambiguous: it could be a directive to the reader, or from the speaker of the poem to themselves, to repel emplacement. As "thinking feelingly" contravenes a bad "trying," whose voice is it that protests "I am not speaking of or as myself or for any/one?" Speaking directly on the radio, Capildeo damns those restrictions that prevail:

> When I was growing up I had the idea that the poet could be a channel for all languages, for any sort of linguistic phenomenon that any literary work encountered, and then when I came to England I found that marketing and identity politics were combining to crush, like in the Star Wars trash compactor, the body, the voice, the voice on the page, the biography, the history. . . . You had to choose, you had to be a sort of documentary witness wheeled around and exposing your wounds in the marketplace.
> —ON *START THE WEEK*, BBC RADIO 4, FEBRUARY 1, 2016

Measures of Expatriation, which won the Forward Prize in 2016 and was shortlisted for the T. S. Eliot, mocks racialized clichés: "I opened a book and a mango fell out. I opened another, and another mango fell out. . . . Woman doth not live by mango alone." Capildeo complicates those narratives of identity, migration, of self-loss or a self found, which are everywhere and get us, increasingly, nowhere.

Speaking of T. S. Eliot, that dead white anti-Semite (and immortal genius), Capildeo engages deeply with his work, both in the later books, including *Skin Can Hold*—"The end of the poem / The end of the poem happened before / The end of the poem happened before it / The end of the poem happened before it began"—and earlier on. *No Traveller Returns* echoes his phraseology ("Death is the fall of water"), with a note on Dhumavati—"one of the Mahavidyas, aspects of the Hindu understanding of the Absolute as Goddess. . . . She is portrayed as a widow, usually old, ugly, inauspicious, and highly dangerous"—resembling his addenda to *The Waste Land*. It's about reclaiming the Eastern wisdom he appropriates. (My use of *appropriate* hesitates between neutral and pejorative: I agree with Jim Sykes, the scholar of Sri Lankan music, that we require, discussing culture transnationally, an alternative to both the impersonally nonjudgmental language of "circulation" or *flow* some theorists prefer and the language of embattled ownership, *appropriation* in the bad sense, that can go beyond acknowledging local claims and become sterilely perma-outraged thought-policing.) Capildeo takes marginal cultures as an imaginative and conceptual base, just as Eliot presumes the anteriority of Anglo-European texts. Consider "Inscription (Windward Isles)":

> By the light that the absorbed Rastafarian carver
> said to put inside the calabash lantern
> so the pattern comes out
> animal, vegetable, abstract,
> the twenty questions of this habitat
> incised by his mineral edge, to his mind,
>
> I will name them as if you know them,
> name locales as if you ought to know them.

"I will show you fear in a handful of dust": the male poet's vatic imperiousness (I think of Walcott as well as Eliot) is summoned and discarded—"Except that Fort James brings out the suicide in me." When daffodils turn up, they aren't the inspiriting mental possession they were for Wordsworth: "out in the border, some / drooping already, they get / blowzy so quickly, their scent's / pale & powdery. / They remind me / of something I wanted—or / something I want to forget."

The book's prose poems on hybrid monsters recall Carter once again, who in 1974 discovered in axolotls a trope for postcolonial consciousness.

He writes with weary humor, having served in Guyana's first independent government and resigned in frustration after just three years:

> I believe we are somewhat like AXOLOTLS, which is to say that, for some reason or other, something seems to have gone awry with that process of metamorphosis, which, if we are to accept what our leaders tell us, should work to transform us from what we function as—an aggregation of begging, tricking, bluffing, cheating subsistence seekers and assorted hustlers—into a free community of valid persons.

The jokey-earnest tone of the mock-biologist is there in Capildeo too, though another parallel would be with poems, also in prose, by Matthea Harvey and Anne Boyer. These works stage an uncertain, impure, put-upon consciousness that—as Jeremy Noel-Tod writes of Capildeo—"carefully avoids committing itself to unambiguous markers of race and gender" yet invites group identifications: "Monsters have a beaten place inside them. Not 'beaten' as in 'defeated.' Beaten: lacerated, trembling, unbelieving, angry, proud, humiliated. Unable to move out of its own rawness, like a sore or like a song, it weeps. . . . It is dangerous to consort with Monsters." Like Boyer, in her "At Least Two Kinds of People," Capildeo unseats the reader racing to identify with the victim and not the oppressor: "Consider your own motives. Are you, by nature, a Monster hunter?"

Capildeo attacks in literary culture prejudices we prefer to locate outside our coterie rather than confront on our doorstep. The same people, for instance, who leap to disapprove of impoverished communities that feel immigrants are invading their patch, will complain when *their* territory is encroached upon—when, that is, a poet of color achieves publication or is nominated for an award. (Yes, we're here to take your jobs—and your prize money.) The UK, unlike the U.S., is only beginning to see minorities rise to positions of editorial or academic authority, yet tensions are already apparent. In the 2005 pamphlet *Person Animal Figure*, Capildeo analyzes *ressentiment* from within, in a send-up of Molly Bloom's voice from *Ulysses*—a woman's run-on unpunctuated talk, figured as an emotional flood: "Let me say that if I write transcriptions of life as it happens to me this is not out of nervousness I am sure I'm authentic." As Paisley Rekdal revealed within William Logan's review style, the jargon of authenticity continues to shape our responses to minority poets. This goes beyond poetry infighting, displaying in microcosm those forces of reaction which, deforming and degrading public life, have turned racism into the new normal. Capildeo enters into reactionary sentiments so we can know our enemy:

> Being the person who stands up beneath the magazines I am the person who is angry with feminists for putting it into my head that people think the magazines have to do with all women which means with women like me what a load of rubbish ask anyone here right now they would all say no they would think you were mad nobody thinks about my body when I talk when I walk across the park at night with my shopping of course you can't be afraid I'm sure I'm just as good as invisible perfectly safe

Self-protection hardens into conservatism: one accepts the status quo when the alternative would be to feel at risk. Rather than countenance the dangers of walking at night as a woman, the speaker makes a more manageable enemy out of the "feminists"—but they've still got to her; she fends off their insights by inventing a crowd on her side.

Capildeo's working method is to try things out in a chapbook (giving a small publisher a fillip) contained and transfigured—as, within the oyster, a pearl radiantly accretes around a speck of grit or plastic insert—in the next full collection. The poems of *Person Animal Figure* reappear in *The Undraining Sea* (unfortunately out of print) alongside another voice: concise, wisely saddened, epigrammatic—"The people who know how to hear are people who have / something to tell." The sixteenth-century humanist Jacopo Sannazaro provides a glowingly unexpected correlate for the poet sparring to evoke a landscape, or mindscape, their reader finds alien; William Empson could discover (I'll do my best) all seven types of ambiguity in the following—which is far more than skin-deep:

> Skin is ziplocks, skin is feathers,
> skin is over skin.

Skin is closed against the world, protective like a ziplock bag; it's biologically to be expected, like a bird's feathers (which keep in warmth and enable flight, as in both escape and seasonal migration); skin is "over skin" in that one thinness or thickness or shade of skin might hide beneath another in peelable layers like those of an onion; or this could be a carnal snapshot; or a picture of racial hierarchy (white skin trumps the rest, lords it "over" the dark-skinned). Finally, for skin to be "over skin" means to be bored by it, tired, even if temporarily, of talking about it.

One gets trapped, that is, in both a subject position and (as a poet) subject matter, and the escape must be through style. The title of 2011's *Dark and Unaccustomed Words*, from George Puttenham's *Arte of Poesie*, is about challenging received notions concerning good writing and bad—a chance for Capildeo to illuminate and investigate present-day taste strictures. In *PN Review*, after a sentence on sexual violence, with four variations on the word *appropriate* (both pronunciations, both meanings), as well as two parentheses, the poet asks: "Did you find that difficult to read? Badly written? The quibbling, the repetitions, are deliberate." I've consciously foregone the potted biography essay-retrospectives ordinarily commence with. This is because poets of color, and women poets, can be imprisoned this way, within the identity container. But 2013's *Utter* features an unusually long author bio, the start of which may, belatedly, do the job, while outlining Capildeo's own impatience:

> Born in Port of Spain, Vahni Capildeo is the daughter of Leila Bissoondath Capildeo, who told her stories of East Trinidad, and the late Devendranath Capildeo, a poet. Capildeo's other formative influences include Indian diaspora culture (notably a preoccupation with boundaries between the human and the natural), French, and pre-1500 English literature. Capildeo read English Language and Literature at Christ Church, Oxford. Her awards... reflect the intensity, variety and adventure of reading encouraged by the tutorial system. Shortly before her final examinations, she was struck by a speeding police car. During her convalescence, she could not read. At this time, she formed a friendship with medieval musicologist Emma Dillon which led to an enduring interest in the musical possibilities of poetry and prose.

This satire recalls Veronica Forrest Thomson's "Impersonal Statement"— testing the Oxbridge stuff against the experiences of women writing, and living, experimentally. But it's worth noting that the poet of color educated at Oxbridge will have the facts of their education fired at them. Face-to face, in reviews, with sneering tweets, and even (I've experienced much of this myself) in poems themselves. The racist idea here is that the only value poets of color have inheres in a supposed authenticity, an authenticity that one's degree classifications are felt to contradict. This only continues the indignities one remembers, of being the wrong color at these white institutions, and succeeding there *despite* racism. So it's brave for Capildeo to not play by the rules and to explain, however tongue-in-cheekily, that the tutorial system, and a doctorate in Old Norse, has shaped the work.

Utter pools surrealistic zeal—"The cows discovered in the theatre wear / an abject or an absent-minded air . . . / For whom / theatre, if not for cows?"—with references to the canon:

> Moderate tea-drinker. "Water with berries in't?"

The allusion is to *The Tempest* and the drink Caliban receives from Prospero, which may be alcoholic or a potion to make him biddable. A figure of postcolonial resistance, he changes role when Capildeo mentions tea, drunk by English people in vast quantities and grown on once colonial plantations ("moderate," too, plays on centrism—there's a politically uninvolved someone here, sipping tea in his parlour, unconcerned where it comes from or what he might see should he deign to, Shiva forbid, look out the window). Prose poems eviscerate the Woolfian "La Poetessa"— "English her name, English her language, English her absobloomsburylutely witty garments"; Sandeep Parmar close-reads this poem in *Prac Crit*—and "The Critic in His Natural Habitat," a figure who does seem to me a depressingly Oxbridge institution. His voice: "A poet like you could bring a fresh perspective to criticism. People would appreciate that. You needn't worry: they wouldn't expect scholarship. . . . You don't write for the *Times Literary Supplement*, do you? Dorina recently did a brilliant review of Gussie's translations of Brazilian slum poetry composed in Spanish by a French guy who taught on an art history course here, oh, donkeys' years ago." I've met this person before: I wish I hadn't.

With *Measures of Expatriation*, Capildeo moved to Carcanet and a wider readership—but its transnational emphasis, prosimetric myriad-mindedness, duelling subject positions ("men singing about Pakis . . . change their singing to a theme of detailed lust. . . . One of the neighbours must be the woman: I have become the Paki"), wordplay ("I walk about two rooms in spills of exaltation, making no cents"), and counteraccusations ("the staring heterosexuals disembark, / having stared, openly") all build on what came before. "I know your ancestors without researching them," boasts one voice, while another materializes of diasporic experience:

"My child."

The bearded man in the ticket office is calling hardback old women his children. Like the immemorial conversation-killer that Trinidadian parents transmit to their migrant, errant offspring via the newest technologies:

"But you are my child. I can say anything to you. And I can take anything from you. You can say anything to me."

The act of containment (the foreign parent, trying to cancel distance, to tell both themselves and the child that their relationship is permanent and unchanging) has its bad double in the pressure on the migrant to label and package themselves; a pressure the more pernicious because one's own self-feeling, as an "unreal citizen" (I think, and Capildeo may be too, of Eliot again, listing ruined cities and ending "Unreal") suggests the opposite. "Imagine a pointilliste vision given an order of dismissal: the dots of color that vibrate until the eye interlinks them and learns the trick of making sense of the person or the landscape depicted. . . . Being looked at, I was that unmade image."

But the book also has its clear scenes, landscapes, and people; thingy quiddities that won't cede to intellection their leaping concreteness. "The yellow poui is flowering. That means rain. Will that be enough to put out the bush fires on the hills?"; "My voice reverted to a kind of Trinidadian that it had never used in Trinidad: a birdlike screech that would carry over a wrought metal gate (painted orange) across a yard with frizzle fowls and the odd goat":

> Janaki is tall. When she opened the wardrobe and I saw the array of clothes, it seemed right. There is stateliness in her modesty. The formal garments glistering there matched her presence almost weight for weight. She is pure gold.
>
> A statue, moving: does that call up a nightmare scene? Why? A statue, moving: can that instil a sense of peace? It is, is so. Each gesture it makes should be made with consideration: otherwise it risks breaking itself or crushing that which it would reach or touch. Respecting its own range of possible movements, it would respect your space. If it made an approach, it could never be appropriate. It could only approximate you, so wearily, as only stone can be weary, for its way of breathing

is to lose itself: each micropore exhales dust in a tiny brightening of the air, and with each exhalation the stone is less.

I read today of the man in his early forties pierced to death by metal as he dismantled a bridge under government orders.

There are inevitabilities that need not have become inevitable had there been the difference made by thought.

—FROM "TOO SOLID FLESH"

Women and stone, again. Pygmalion sculpted his Galatea; in the Renaissance, the metaphor was everywhere—*The Winter's Tale* sees the statue of Hermione come to life; in Christopher Marlowe's *Tamburlaine*, Olympia "anoints her throat" with an alchemized substance giving it "the essential form of marble stone" (Sharon Stone, in the dire *Catwoman* film, repeats this with her evilly concocted moisturizer). The Victorian poet Christina Rossetti masters the metaphor—"Laura turned as cold as stone / To find her sister heard that cry alone"; "I have no wit, no words, no tears; / My heart within me like a stone"; "White and golden Lizzie stood, / Like a lily in a flood,— / Like a rock of blue-veined stone." Mrs. Dalloway's daughter, in Virginia Woolf's novel, thrill-rides through London by bus, looking ahead "with the staring incredible innocence of sculpture." (Capildeo also praises, in *Measures*, Dante's "stony poems.") If men, looking at women, turn them into objects to be contemplated, then the metaphor also suggests a fortified interiority, a secret life within the woman of stone that she defends against the world.

As Janaki's "stateliness" gives way, then, to that of a "statue," we should keep literary history in mind; Capildeo's timed sensuous prose—"each micropore exhales dust in a tiny brightening of the air"—resubscribes to the monster metaphor but with a new allusiveness. Paragraph breaks scene-switch from a woman to statues to a man who hasn't turned to stone but was killed working with it. The final sentence-paragraph is withering, a dry remark (that is one function of its elegance), but its wording also opposes to fate the ability of thought to intervene in history. These fragile statue-beings, and their neighbors, become in the moment—the advent of difference creates, in conversations, in communities, the need for humane improvisation—responsible for how they behave toward each other. A social ethic: if we could admire others without objectifying them, then disposable labor would be unthinkable. "Pierced to death by metal," in its estranged phrasing, allows the unnamed man a claim on our fast-roaming attention but also sounds like a method of execution.

As Capildeo grows better known, the work—moving now to 2018, and *Venus as a Bear*—has become more approachable, though never cosy: poems about animals and landscapes tease a mainstream decodability. But "Crossing Borders," as I've mentioned, comes from this book, and Capildeo's willful heterogeneousness, a refusal to be evenly opaque or through-shine, or for poem to poem to be spoken by the same kind of voice, is a strength. Each collection performs a life-giving dissensus. It's another form of code-switching or self-alienation, between the roles of experimenter and lyricist, which means the reader also has to become double, or triple, multifarious, able to enter into and live alternatives without taking refuge in one idea of rebellion or conformity: "Any book is a gift, / bringing time; with no time to read it, / the reader has time, unreading the book, / time implicated in its binding, its petals." The angle of attack is always unexpected, as in the sonnet "The Pets of Others" (whose title tousles the expected phrase "the lives of others"):

> Turtle thrashes opposite the dishwasher,
> climbs the water breakline, while the rocks
> wait artificially; what sand is needed
> being supposable only from flippers
> in action, while the chin lifts; she meets the eyes
> of tall and dry onlookers. Her red streaks seem
> so powerful, a punishable woman's!
> Yet compassion flows pointlessly towards her,
> like a sable marram dune shifting to make valleys
> in which some find rest, from which the sea cannot be glimpsed,
> or a way out predicted. Her eggs will come
> unfertilised, after how much compulsive
> thrashing; and she will be saved from eating them
> by her warm-handed keepers, who'd love her wild.

Animals get into poems a whiff of elemental risk (that is, we could say, what they're for; as naked women play their role in men's paintings), licensing a devil-may-care sensuousness that, regretting our exile from the animal world, tries to override this division. So this poem is remarkable for *not* being about D. H. Lawrence's wild thing, which isn't, and could never be, sorry for itself, and for instead evoking a pet amid artificial rocks, a turtle whose "red streaks" suggest a scarlet woman (the letter A stitched on Hester Prynne's dress), trapped for others to gawk at. The language isn't free-flowing, but rather contemplative, with its two semicolons in the octave.

"Yet compassion flows pointlessly towards her": we feel for animals, though they may not understand, and though our goodwill can become cruelly displaced, in this way, from human beings perceived, unlike a passively suffering turtle, as a threat. (The cat-loving old woman in Nissim Ezekiel's "The Old Woman," living on "cornflakes, hate and sweetened milk," or the misanthropic philosopher Arthur Schopenhauer—"one has the impression," writes Darian Leader, who might be talking about poetry reviewers again, "that closeness for this man was ruled out by the exigency to obliterate anyone else who might be king"—announcing he'd rather not live "if dogs did not exist.") Pets are possessions, so does our love for them exceed self-interest? The dune metaphor is metaphysical, in taking us from the turtle, through the shaping of a response, toward an unnamed desert people to whom—one might argue—that compassion should properly flow, like water irrigating the lifeless sand, were it not that compassion, figured as a fount of involuntary feeling, cannot be directed, like water, along artificial canals; though perhaps the project both defended and derided as "political correctness" is an attempt at just this.

They say history is written by the winners. From book to book, Capildeo has tried to do something about that. *Skin Can Hold* contains the "Midnight Robber Monologue," with its echoes of Othello—"When Columbus men landed holding their bright weapons up, I was waiting for them in the form of dew and rust. When the British and the Spanish and the French and the Dutch and the Yankees and the Portuguese took away your language, I grew strong eating your tongues." The amoral energy of this "stranger invader" happens, like love, beyond good and evil, but originates in a specifically Guyanese poem by Martin Carter:

> This is the dark time my love.
> It is the season of oppression, dark metal, and tears.
> It is the festival of guns, the carnival of misery.
> Everywhere the faces of men are strained and anxious.
>
> Who comes walking in the dark night time?
> Whose boot of steel tramps down the slender grass?

> It is the man of death, my love, the strange invader
> Watching you sleep and aiming at your dream.

The political poet writes, with gravity and grace, of their own "dark time" while saving something for posterity—a resonance that speaks to other woe than theirs as well as to a happiness that may yet be collectively realized. Seasons come in cycles; *everywhere* shimmers: the word doesn't seem to me sloppily universal but vital to the contriving of a type of endurance it remains in the poet's power to confer. It may be in this spirit that Capildeo writes, pretends to recover, a "Fragment of a Lost Epic from the Losing Side":

> The dust whispered and skittered under the feet
>   that audibly tried to make no noise.
> The city waited
> The army was on the move
> The women listened from within the darkened windows
> The city would never be so bright again
>
> A shape like crossed forearms held up to shelter the face
> Appeared in the metal of the sky

Bibliography

Mir Taqi Mir

—*Remembrances*, edited and translated by C. M. Naim (Cambridge, MA: Harvard University Press, 2019)
—*Selected Ghazals and Other Poems*, translated by Shamsur Rahman Faruqi (Cambridge, MA: Harvard University Press, 2019)

Ana Blandiana

—*The Hour of Sand: Selected Poems 1969–1989*, translated by Peter Jay and Anca Cristofovici (London: Anvil, 1990)
—*My Native Land A4*, translated by Paul Scott Derrick and Viorica Patea (Tarset: Bloodaxe, 2014)

A. K. Ramanujan

—*Uncollected Poems and Prose*, edited by Molly A. Daniels-Ramanujan and Keith Harrison (New Delhi: Oxford University Press India, 2001)
—*The Collected Poems of A. K. Ramanujan* (New Delhi: Oxford University Press India, 2011)
—*The Interior Landscape: Classical Tamil Love Poems* (New York: New York Review of Books, 2014)
—*Journeys: A Poet's Diary*, edited by Krishna Ramanujan and Guillermo Rodríguez (Gurgaon: Penguin Random House India, 2019)

Marianne Moore

—*Observations*, edited with an introduction by Linda Leavell (New York: Farrar, Straus and Giroux, 2016)
—*New Collected Poems*, edited by Heather Cass White (New York: Farrar, Straus and Giroux, 2020)

Stevie Smith

—*Novel on Yellow Paper* (New York: New Directions, 1994)
—*All the Poems*, edited by Will May (New York: New Directions, 2016)

Eunice de Souza

—*Dangerlok* (Gurgaon: Penguin Random House India, 2001)
—*Dev and Simran* (Gurgaon: Penguin Random House India, 2003)
—*A Necklace of Skulls: Collected Poems* (New Delhi: Penguin India, 2009)

Czesław Miłosz

—*The Issa Valley* (London: Abacus, 1984)
—*New and Collected Poems 1931–2001* (London: Penguin, 2005)
—*Selected and Last Poems, 1931–2004*, edited by Robert Haas and Anthony Milosz (London: Penguin, 2014)

Verse sound

—W. S. Graham, *New Collected Poems*, edited by Matthew Francis (London: Faber, 2005)
—Angela Leighton, *Hearing Things: The Work of Sound in Literature* (Cambridge, MA: Harvard University Press, 2018)

Elizabeth Bishop

—*Poems* (New York: Farrar, Straus and Giroux, 2011)

Robert Penn Warren

—*All the King's Men* (London: Penguin, 2007)

Ted Hughes and Keith Sagar

—*Poet and Critic: The Letters of Ted Hughes and Keith Sagar* (London: British Library, 2012)

Rae Armantrout

—*Partly: New and Selected Poems, 2001–2015* (Middletown, CT: Wesleyan University Press, 2017)

Vinod Kumar Shukla

—*Once it Flowers*, translated by Satti Khanna (New York: HarperCollins, 2014)
—*Moonrise From The Green Grass Roof*, translated by Satti Khanna (New York: HarperCollins, 2017)
—*Blue Is Like Blue: Stories*, translated by Arvind Krishna Mehrotra and Sara Rai (New York: HarperCollins, 2019)

Srinivas Rayaprol

—*Angular Desire: Selected Poems and Prose*, edited by Graziano Krätli and Vidyan Ravinthiran (Manchester: Carcanet, 2020)

Gāmini Salgādo

—*The True Paradise* (Manchester: Carcanet, 1993)

Arvind Krishna Mehrotra

—*Selected Poems and Translations*, edited by Vidyan Ravinthiran and introduced by Amit Chaudhuri (New York: New York Review of Books, 2019)

Thom Gunn

—*Selected Poems*, edited by Clive Wilmer (London: Faber, 2021)
—*Collected Poems* (London: Faber, 1994)

Galway Kinnell

—*Black Light* (Berkeley: Counterpoint, 2015)
—*Collected Poems*, edited by Edward Hirsch (New York: Houghton Mifflin Harcourt, 2019)

A. R. Ammons

—*The Complete Poems of A. R. Ammons*, edited by Robert M. West and introduced by Helen Vendler, 2 vols. (New York: Norton, 2017)

Dawn Lundy Martin

—*A Gathering of Matter / A Matter of Gathering* (Athens: University of Georgia Press, 2007)
—*Discipline* (New York: Nightboat, 2011)
—*Life in a Box is a Pretty Life* (New York: Nightboat, 2015)
—*Good Stock Strange Blood* (Minneapolis: Coffee House, 2017)

Vahni (Anthony Ezekiel) Capildeo

—*No Traveller Returns* (Cambridge: Salt, 2003)
—*Undraining Sea* (Norwich: Egg Box, 2009)
—*Dark and Unaccustomed Words* (Norwich: Egg Box, 2012)
—*Utter* (Leeds: Peepal Tree, 2013)
—*Measures of Expatriation* (Manchester: Carcanet, 2016)
—*Venus As A Bear* (Manchester: Carcanet, 2018)
—*Skin Can Hold* (Manchester: Carcanet, 2019)

Permissions

Quotations from Ana Blandiana's *My Native Land A4* and Martin Carter's *University of Hunger* (in my essay on Vahni [Anthony] Capildeo) are reproduced with permission of Bloodaxe Books. Blandiana's *The Hour of Sand*, Rayaprol's *Angular Desire: Selected Poems and Prose*, and Capildeo's *Measures of Expatriation*, *Venus as a Bear* and *Skin Can Hold* are cited with the permission of Carcanet Press. OUP India provided permission to quote from Ramanujan's books of poetry; Hamish Hamilton and the Estate of A. K. Ramanujan granted the reproduction of passages from *Journeys*.

"Thoughts About the Person from Porlock," "Major Macroo," "Girls!," "Parents," "This Englishwoman," "The English," "Everything Is Swimming," "Not Waving But Drowning," "A Dream of Comparison," "I Remember," "A Soldier Dear to Us," and "Dear Karl" by Stevie Smith, from *All the Poems of Stevie Smith*, copyright © 1953, 1957, 1958, 1961, 1964, 1967, 1985, 1987, 1989, 1994, 1995, 1996, 1997 by Stevie Smith. Copyright © 1985 by Copyright Administration Limited. Reprinted by permission of New Directions Publishing Corp.

Excerpt from *Novel on Yellow Paper* by Stevie Smith, copyright ©1936 by James MacGibbon. Reprinted by permission of New Directions Publishing Corp.

Quotations from Eunice de Souza's novels and poems are reproduced with the permission of Penguin Random House India and Melanie Silgardo.

Excerpt(s) from *Lolita* by Vladimir Nabokov, copyright © 1955 by Vladimir Nabokov, copyright renewed 1983 by the Estate of Vladimir Nabokov. Used by permission of Vintage Books, an imprint of the Knopf Doubleday Publishing Group, a division of Penguin Random House LLC. All rights reserved.

Excerpt(s) from *Pnin* by Vladimir Nabokov, copyright © 1953, 1955, 1957, copyright renewed 1981,1983,1985 by the Estate of Vladimir Nabokov. Used by permission of Vintage Books, an imprint of the Knopf Doubleday Publishing Group, a division of Penguin Random House LLC. All rights reserved.

Quotations from Ted Hughes and Keith Sagar's letters are reproduced with the permission of the British Library.

Quotations from Rae Armantrout's *Collected Prose* are reproduced with the permission of Singing Horse Press.

Reproduced in arrangement with HarperCollins Publishers India Private Limited from book *Once It Flowers* and Moonrise from the *Green Grass Roof* by Vinod Kumar Shukla and Satti Khanna, first published by them. All rights reserved. Unauthorized copying is strictly prohibited.

Excerpts from "The Olive Wood Fire," "First Song," "The Avenue Bearing the Initial of Christ Into the New World," "Flower Herding on Mount Monadnock," "The Bear," "The Dead Shall Be Raised Incorruptible," "Vapor Trail Reflected in the Frog Pond," "After Making Love We Hear Footsteps," "When One Has Lived A Long Time Alone," "Flying Home," and "My Mother's R&R," from *Collected Poems of Galway Kinnell*. Copyright © 2017 by the Literary Estate of Galway Kinnell, LLC. Reprinted by permission of Mariner Books, an imprint of HarperCollins Publishers.

Dawn Lundy Martin, excerpts from *Good Stock Strange Blood*. Copyright © 2017 by Dawn Lundy Martin. Reprinted with the permission of the Permissions Company, LLC on behalf of Coffee House Press, coffeehousepress.org.

Index

"Ablutions" (Capildeo), 244
"Account of a Journey to Tisang" (Mir), 22–23
Advaita, 160
Adventures of Huckleberry Finn (Twain), 172, 176
Aesthetics, 118–119, 121–122
"After Drowning" (Martin), 230
"After Making Love We Hear Footsteps" (Kinnell), 215, 217
"Agglomeration" (Blandiana), 38
AIDS, 204–205
Ali, Agha Shahid, 25, 27, 185
"All Kinds of Love" (Rayaprol), 180–181
"All of These People" (Longley), 39
All the King's Men (Warren), 111–112, 115–116
Ammons, A. R.: "Ballad," 222; "Classic," 221–222; on Coleridge, 218–219, 222; *Complete Poems*, 218; "Confessional Poem," 220; "Corsons Inlet," 225–226; on T. S. Eliot, 219–220; "February Beach," 220–221; *Garbage*, 218–219; "Hymn," 218–219; "Late Romantic," 222; "Local Antiquities," 226; "Loving People," 227; "Nucleus," 224–225; *Ommateum*, 218; "One: Many," 225; "prosetry" of, 220; *Really Short Poems*, 218; "Saliences," 226; *Sphere*, 218, 222, 224; Stevens and, 217, 219–220, 224, 226; "Surfacing Surface Effects," 219–220;
Tape for the Turn of the Year, 218, 222–225; Whitman and, 218, 223, 227–228
"Amorous Debate, An" (Gunn), 200
"Amulet" (Capildeo), 245–246
Animals, 24, 56–57, 66, 256–257
"Ant and Eternity" (Das), 11, 13–14
Antilyric, 229
Anti-Semitism, 244, 248–249
"Anxiety" (Ramanujan), 53
Anzaldúa, Gloria, 236
Arbiter, Petronius, 204–205
Aristotle, 238
Armantrout, Rae, 16; "Assembly," 147; "Canary," 142–143; on cancer, 150–153; "The Creation," 149; "Easily," 146–147; "End Times," 147–149; on Grenier, 144–145; "Haunts," 143; "In Front," 143–144, 151; Keats and, 141–142, 145; "Later," 150–153; Niedecker and, 142, 144; "Once," 149; "Own," 150; *Partly*, 149–150; "Pass," 150; "Prayers," 142–143; "Thing," 142–143; *True*, 146; "Twizzle," 141–142; "Two Three," 145; on U.S. military, 142–143; *Veil*, 149; *Versed*, 150, 152; on voices, in poetry, 145–146
Arnold, Matthew, 210, 215–216
Ars Poetica? (Miłosz), 94
Arte of Poesie (Puttenham), 252
Art of Ted Hughes, The (Sagar), 139

"Arundel Tomb, An" (Larkin), 196–197
Ashbery, John, 189
Assembling Alternatives (Huk), 230
"Assembly" (Armantrout), 147
"At Least Two Kinds of People" (Boyer), 250
"At the Fishhouses" (Bishop), 124
Attridge, Derek, 18
Auden, W. H., 98, 117, 133, 140, 181, 206
"August Midnight, An" (Hardy), 11–14
d'Aurevilly, Jules Barbey, 71–72
Auschwitz, 91–92
Australia, 137–139
Authenticity, 2–3
"Avenue Bearing the Initial of Christ Into the New World, The" (Kinnell), 209–210

Bailey, Benjamin, 147
"Ballad" (Ammons), 222
"Bear, The" (Kinnell), 211–213, 217
"Beast in the Space, The" (Graham), 108
Becker, A. L., 43
Beckett, Tom, 145
Bedient, Calvin, 112
Bell, Charles, 212–213
Beloved (Morrison), 103
Benjamin, Walter, 155–156
"Bequest" (de Souza), 81–82
Betjeman, John, 28
Bhabha, Homi, 233
Bidart, Frank, 124
Birthday Letters (Hughes), 139
Bishop, Elizabeth, 23, 47; on all-women poetry anthologies, 120; Ashbery on, 189; "At the Fishhouses," 124; on beauty, 118–119; on Brazil, 101, 103, 117–118; communication and, 111–114, 116–121, 124–126; communication, conversation and, 118–119, 124–125; Costello on, 121–122; "Crusoe in England," 126; Frost and, 77, 101; *Geography III*, 112; Hopkins and, 102–103; Kalstone on, 123–124; Leighton on, 100–103; Lombardi on, 126; meter of, 114–115; Miller and, 122–126, 128; Moore and, 55–56, 58, 60, 123, 138; "The Moose," 112–114; *North and South*, 121; "Over 2,000 Illustrations and a Complete Concordance," 116–117, 119; *Paris Review* interview, 120, 125–126; "Poem," 117; poetics of communication, 112; "Quai d'Orléans," 120–128; Quinn on, 125; "Sandpiper," 101; "Santarém," 118, 124; to Spires, 120; on Stevens, 220; H. T. Thomas on, 118; "Twelfth Morning; or What You Will," 101–103; Wordsworth and, 117, 122
Björk, 246
Black bodies, 238, 240–242
"Black Earth" (Moore), 56–57
Black experimentalism, 228, 231–232
Black improvisation, 239
Black Light (Kinnell), 207, 216–217
Blackness, 231, 239
Black poetics, 233
Black poets and Black poetry, 229–231, 233
Blake, William, 19, 92, 134, 202, 241
Blandiana, Ana: "Agglomeration," 38; Derrick's and Patea's translations of, 36–37; *The Hour of Sand*, 31–34; Jay's and Cristofovici's translations of, 31–33; *My Native Land A4*, 31, 34–35; "On Roller Skates," 38; "On Tiptoe," 37; "The Owner of the Mill," 35–37; "Perhaps Someone Is Dreaming Me," 34; on Romanian history and Romanian Communism, 32–35, 38; "Season's End," 38; on secret police, 32–33; "Stair Steps," 38–39; "Stele," 36; "You Never See the Butterflies," 31–33, 36
Bloom, Harold, 218
Blue Is Like Blue (Shukla), 154–156
Body Rags (Kinnell), 211
Book of Nightmares, The (Kinnell), 214
Book reviews, 5–6

Borges, Jorge Luis, 156, 187
Bourdieu, Pierre, 103
Bowers, Maggie Ann, 156
"Bowls" (Moore), 60
Boyer, Anne, 250
Brathwaite, Edward Kamau, 174
Brazil, 101, 103, 117–118
Brexit, 112–113, 119
British Empire, 43–44
Brook, Peter, 136
Brooks, Cleanth, 112, 114, 117
Brooks, Gwendolyn, 232, 236
Browning, Robert, 81, 101
Buddhism, 176–178
"Burden, The" (Shukla), 163–164
Burke, Edmund, 206
Burt, Stephanie, 16

Calhoun, Richard, 213
"Canary" (Armantrout), 142–143
Capildeo, Vahni (Anthony): "Ablutions," 244; "Amulet," 245–246; Carter and, 243, 249, 257–258; "The Critic in His Natural Habitat," 7–8, 253; "Crossing Borders," 245–246, 248, 256; *Dark and Unaccustomed Words*, 252; T. S. Eliot and, 248–249, 254; "Fragment of a Lost Epic from the Losing Side," 258; "Inscription (Windward Isles)," 249; Lawrence and, 256–257; on lyric, 247; *Measures of Expatriation*, 247–248, 253–255; Noel-Tod on, 250; *No Traveller Returns*, 244–245, 249–250; *Person Animal Figure*, 250–251; "The Pets of Others," 256; on Rankine, 247–248; "Shame," 244; *Skin Can Hold*, 243–244, 246, 248–249, 257–258; "Too Solid Flesh," 254–255; *The Undraining Sea*, 251–252; *Utter*, 252–253; *Venus as a Bear*, 245–246, 256
Captive Mind, The (Miłosz), 92
Caribbean poets, 13–14
"Carnal Knowledge" (Gunn), 195
Carter, Martin, 243, 249, 257–258

"Catholic Mother" (de Souza), 83–84
Cavell, Stanley, 118
Ceaușescu, Nicolae, 31, 33, 35
Chakrabarti, Paromita, 154
Chattopadhyay, Bankim Chandra, 154–155
Chattopadhyay, Sarat Chandra, 154–155
Chaudhuri, Amit, 16, 178, 187
Chaudhuri, Rosinka, 16
Chicago Tribune, 120
"Chicago Zen" (Ramanujan), 45–47, 53
Christianity, 66, 117
Citizen (Rankine), 247
Clare, John, 77
Class: gender, race, and, 14; Lawrence on, 69–70; Smith on, 67–70
"Classic" (Ammons), 221–222
Clive, Robert, 189–190
Close reading, 15
Coleridge, Samuel Taylor, 3, 44–45, 65–66, 218–219, 222
Collected Poems (Kinnell), 213
Collected Poems (Mehrotra), 188
Collected Poems in English (Kolatkar), 184
"College" (Shukla), 155–157, 159
Colonialism, 7, 80–81, 188–191, 239, 243
Communication: in *All the King's Men*, 115; Bishop and, 111–114, 116–121, 124–126; conversation and, 118–119, 124–125; Hughes and, 129, 132–133; Mir and, 132; poetics of, 105–106, 112; verse sound and, 105–107; Warren and, 115–116
Complete Poems (Ammons), 218
Complete Poems (Moore), 55–58, 60–61, 64
"Confessional Poem" (Ammons), 220
Confessional poetry, 24, 86, 126, 194
"Constructed Space, The" (Graham), 106–109
"Convergence of the Twain" (Hardy), 14
"Conversation Piece" (de Souza), 82–83
Cope, Wendy, 64–66, 87–88
Copplestone, Fenella, 172, 176, 178

Cornish, Ted, 129
"Corsons Inlet" (Ammons), 225–226
Costello, Bonnie, 121–122
"Courage, a Tale" (Gunn), 200–201
"Crabs in the Seine" (Rayaprol), 168–169
Crane, Louise, 122, 125
Crawford, Robert, 219
"Creation, The" (Armantrout), 149
Creative criticism, 4
Creeley, Robert, 198
Cristofovici, Anca, 31–33
"Critic in His Natural Habitat, The" (Capildeo), 7–8, 253
"Crossing Borders" (Capildeo), 245–246, 248, 256
Crow (Hughes), 132
"Crusoe in England" (Bishop), 126
Culler, Jonathan, 5, 47

Dadawala, Vikrant, 157
Dahl, Roald, 68
Dangerlok (de Souza), 79–81, 83, 85, 88–89
Dante, 58–59, 255
Dark and Unaccustomed Words (Capildeo), 252
Das, Mahadai, 11–15
Davie, Donald, 98, 194, 207–208, 212–214
Dawkins, Richard, 133, 149
"Dawn's Rose" (Hughes), 139–140
"Dear Karl" (Smith), 75–76
Deb, Rabindra Nath, 189–190
"Degeneracy of the American Negro, The" (Starr), 237
Delhi, 1211 (Mehrotra), 187
Derrick, Paul Scott, 36–37
Derrida, Jacques, 108
Dev and Simran (de Souza), 85–89
Devotions Upon Emergent Occasions (Donne), 150
Dharwadker, Vinay, 53
Dial, 55

Dickinson, Emily, 116
Dilke, Charles Wentworth, 1–2
Discipline (Martin), 233–234, 236
Distance in Statute Miles (Mehrotra), 185–186, 190
Doniger, Wendy, 40, 43–44
Donne, John, 28, 150, 187, 198–199
Doreski, Carole, 117–118
"Dover Beach" (Arnold), 210
"Dream-Figures in Sunlight" (Mehrotra), 193
"Dream of Comparison, A" (Smith), 74
"During Wind and Rain" (Hardy), 225

"Easily" (Armantrout), 146–147
Eco-aesthetic consciousness, 46
Ecopoems, 62, 215–216
Edwardian verse, 171
"Elegy in a Country Churchyard" (Gray), 113–114
Eliot, George, 244
Eliot, T. S., 46, 78, 101, 119, 169; Ammons on, 219–220; Capildeo and, 248–249, 254; on impersonality, 202; *The Waste Land* by, 38, 92, 210, 249
Emerson, Ralph Waldo, 127, 214, 230
"Emperor Has No Clothes, The" (Mehrotra), 186–187
Empson, William, 105, 113–114, 251
Emre, Merve, 6
"End Times" (Armantrout), 147–149
Endymion (Keats), 15
"English, The" (Smith), 68
English language: Indian poetry and, 78, 80–81, 85, 87, 169–172, 185, 189–190; Mehrotra and, 185–190; Rayaprol and, 169–170, 179–182; reflective verse in, 202–203; Salgādo on, 173–174, 178–179; of Shakespeare, 173–174
Everett, Barbara, 17, 184
"Everything Is Swimming" (Smith), 71–72
"Expression" (Gunn), 194
Ezekiel, Nissim, 16, 257

Faruqi, Shamsur Rahman, 22–24, 27
"February Beach" (Ammons), 220–221
Felski, Rita, 4, 6
Feminism, 66, 120, 165, 251
Ferguson, Frances, 3
Feuer, Donya, 136–137
Fighting Terms (Gunn), 195
"First Song" (Kinnell), 208–209
"Fish, The" (Moore), 60
Fitz Gerald, Gregory, 213
Fitzgerald, Penelope, 104
Fix (de Souza), 83–84
Flower Herding on Mount Monadnock (Kinnell), 210–211
"Flying Home" (Kinnell), 216
"For a Slave King 2" (Mehrotra), 187
Formalism, 15
"For Maria de Borges" (Das), 12–13
"For Signs" (Gunn), 199–200
"For S. Who Wonders If I Get Much Joy Out of Life" (de Souza), 79
Foucault, Michel, 14–15, 225
"Fragment of a Lost Epic from the Losing Side" (Capildeo), 258
Franaszek, Andrzej, 91–94, 96–97
Frog Prince and Other Poems, The (Smith), 71
Frost, Robert, 8, 79, 84, 100, 108; Bishop and, 77, 101; Kendall on, 119
"Fundamental Project of Technology, The" (Kinnell), 215–216

Garbage (Ammons), 218–219
Gathering of Matter/A Matter of Gathering, A (Martin), 229
Gauguin, Paul, 137
Gender, 87–88; Armantrout on, 147; body and, "Quai d'Orléans" on, 126; class, race, and, 14; in English poetry, 64–65; race and, 250; Ramanujan on, 49–51; Smith on, 66–67, 71–72
Geography III (Bishop), 112
Ghazals, 21–22, 24–29
Ghose, Aurobindo, 187
"Girls!" (Smith), 66–68, 71

Gladstone, William Ewart, 104–105
Glissant, Édouard, 19
Global South, 4, 10, 175, 185
Goethe, 117
Goffman, Erving, 28
Golden Treasury of English Songs and Lyrics, The (Palgrave), 171
"Good-Morrow, The" (Donne), 198
Good Stock Strange Blood (Martin), 231, 239–241
Graham, W. S., 103, 106–110
Gray, Thomas, 113–114
Grenier, Bob, 144–145
Greville, Fulke, 200
Griffiths, Eric, 79
Guillory, John, 114
Gunn, Thom: "An Amorous Debate," 200; "Carnal Knowledge," 195; on confessional poetry, 194; "Courage, a Tale," 200–201; "Expression," 194; *Fighting Terms*, 195; "For Signs," 199–200; Hardy and, 196–197, 202–203; homosexuality of, 195–196, 202–204; "The Hug," 204; "In Santa Maria del Popolo," 195, 197; *Jack Straw's Castle*, 200–201; *The Man with Night Sweats*, 204–205; "The Miracle," 203; "Misanthropos," 197–198; *Moly*, 199; "My Life Up to Now," 196; *My Sad Captains*, 195; "On the Move," 196–197; *The Passages of Joy*, 203; *Selected Poems*, 195; *The Sense of Movement*, 196; "Three Hard Women," 200; *Touch*, 197; "Touch," 204; Wilmer on, 194, 196, 198–201, 203
Gurnah, Denise DeCaires Narain, 13–14

Hallam, Arthur, 170–171
Hardy, Thomas, 11–18, 196–197, 202–203, 225
Harper's, 5–6
Harvey, Matthea, 250
"Haunts" (Armantrout), 143
Hawk in the Rain, The (Hughes), 140

Hayes, Terrance, 246–247
Hazlitt, William, 40, 133
"Head, The" (Hughes), 134
Heaney, Seamus, 10, 70–71, 95, 131, 189, 246
"Heaven Knows I'm Miserable Now," 226
Hejinian, Lyn, 142, 149–150
"Hen Flower, The" (Kinnell), 214
Herbert, Zbigniew, 31, 92, 94
"Here It Is Spring Again" (Rayaprol), 170
"Highway Stripper" (Ramanujan), 50–52
Hill, Selima, 87–88
"Hills Heal, The" (de Souza), 86–87
Hindi language, 154, 156–160, 167, 191
Hinduism, 176–178, 244–245, 249
Hindu nationalism, 83, 167
Hiroshima, 215–216
Hirsch, Edward, 209
Hirsh, Elizabeth, 6
Historicism, 5–6, 22
Hoffman, Frederick L., 237
Holiday, Billie, 240
Holub, Miroslav, 31, 92–94
"Hoopoe" (Mehrotra), 186
Hopkins, Gerard Manley, 102–103, 212, 219–220, 243
Hour of Sand, The (Blandiana), 31–34
Housman, A. E., 28, 219–220
"How Cruel Is the Story of Eve" (Smith), 66–67
Howe, Sarah, 2
"Hug, The" (Gunn), 204
Hughes, Langston, 238
Hughes, Olwyn, 139–140
Hughes, Ted, 7, 64–66; on academic prose, 134–135; on Australia, 137–139; *Birthday Letters*, 139; communication and, 129, 132–133; correspondence of, 129–132, 134–140; *Crow*, 132; "Dawn's Rose," 139–140; on father's letters, 135–136; *The Hawk in the Rain*, 140; "The Head," 134; O. Hughes on, 139–140; Larkin and, 129; Lawrence and, 137–138; on literary criticism, 135; "Myths, Metres, Rhythms," 133; *Orghast*, by Brook and, 136; Plath and, 131, 139–140; Reid on, 129–130, 133, 135, 138, 140; reputation in U.S., 130–131; Sagar on, 130–140; on Shakespeare, 132–133, 136; "Shakespeare and Occult Neoplatonism," 132; *Shakespeare and the Goddess of Complete Being*, 129, 134, 136; "Thistles," 136; "Thrushes," 129
"Hugh Selwyn Mauberley" (Pound), 45
Huk, Romana, 230
Hume, David, 3
"Hunger" (Mahapatra), 187
Hunt, Erica, 229
Huxley, Aldous, 174
"Hymn" (Ammons), 218–219

Identity politics, 112, 118, 231, 246, 248
Illustrated History of Indian Literature in English (Mehrotra), 184, 188, 190
"Images" (Ramanujan), 41–42
"I May, I Might, I Must" (Moore), 74
Immigrants, 41–43, 53–54
"Impersonal Statement" (Thomson), 252
"Incantation" (Miłosz), 97–98
Incidents in the Life of a Slave Girl (Jacobs), 242
"In Common" (Miłosz), 95–96
India, 43–46; caste system of, 157; colonialism and, 188–191; Hindu nationalism and, 83, 167; Muslims in, 83; postcolonial, 191; poverty in, 157, 167; Shukla, in history of, 154–155
Indian poets and poetry: English language and, 78, 80–81, 85, 87, 169–172, 185, 189–190; Jussawalla on, 78; Mehrotra on, 184–185; on poetic form, 191; Ramanujan on, 43–44, 46, 53, 78; Shukla on, 154–155; Tamil, 44, 46, 48–49, 78, 186–187
Indian women's writing, 77
"In Front" (Armantrout), 143–144, 151
"Injudicious Gardening" (Moore), 59

"In Memoriam A.H.H." (Tennyson), 170–171
"In Santa Maria del Popolo" (Gunn), 195, 197
"Inscription" (Mehrotra), 191–192
"Inscription (Windward Isles)" (Capildeo), 249
Internet, 42–43; criticism and, 5–6, 10–11; filter bubble of, 113; in political tribalism, 112
"Interview with an Empire" (Philip), 230
"I Remember" (Smith), 74
Isherwood, Christopher, 203
Islam, 117
Islam, Khurshidal, 22, 27–29
Issa Valley, The (Miłosz), 93–94
"It's Time to Find a Place" (de Souza), 82

Jackson, Virginia, 231–232
Jack Straw's Castle (Gunn), 200–201
Jacobs, Harriet, 242
James, Henry, 61
James, William, 209–210, 215
"January" (Mehrotra), 185–187
Jarrell, Randall, 111
Jay, Peter, 31–33
Jejuri (Kolatkar), 47
Jerusalem Poetry Festival, 1990, 46
Johnson, Clifton, 62
Johnson, Lyndon, 222
Johnson, Samuel, 8, 134
Jones, William, 188
Jong, Erica, 120
Jonson, Ben, 195, 204–205
Joyce, James, 51–52, 72–73, 104, 178–179, 226, 250
Jussawalla, Adil, 78
Just So Stories (Kipling), 192

Kabir, 184, 187–188, 192
Kafka, Franz, 225
Kalstone, David, 123–124
Kant, Immanuel, 118, 149
Kaul, Mani, 154

Keats, John, 1–2, 7, 16, 41, 87; Armantrout and, 141–142, 145; *Endymion*, 15; on imagination, 147; on "negative capability," 163; "Ode on a Grecian Urn," 145; on poet as chameleon, 226; on verse sound, 103
Keats and Embarrassment (Ricks), 246
Kendall, Tim, 119, 136
Khanna, Satti, 154, 158–160, 166–167
Kierkegaard, Søren, 106
King Lear (Shakespeare), 27
Kinnell, Galway: "After Making Love We Hear Footsteps," 215, 217; "The Avenue Bearing the Initial of Christ Into the New World," 209–210; "The Bear," 211–213, 217; Bell on, 212–213; *Black Light*, 207, 216–217; *Body Rags*, 211; *The Book of Nightmares*, 214; in civil rights movement, 206; *Collected Poems*, 213; Davie on, 207–208, 212–214; "First Song," 208–209; *Flower Herding on Mount Monadnock*, 210–211; "Flying Home," 216; "The Fundamental Project of Technology," 215–216; "The Hen Flower," 214; W. James and, 209–210, 215; *Mortal Acts, Mortal Words*, 214; "My Mother's R & R," 217; on nuclear weapons, 206, 215–216; "The Olive Wood Fire," 206, 214–216; "On the Oregon Coast," 215–216; *The Past*, 215–216; "The Poetics of the Physical World," 207, 214; "Saint Francis and the Sow," 215, 217; U.S. militarism and, 212–213; "Vapor Trail Reflected in the Frog Pond," 213–214; on Vietnam War, 206, 212–214; *What a Kingdom It Was*, 208–209, 212; *When One Has Lived a Long Time Alone*, 216; on Whitman, 214–215
Kipling, Rudyard, 192–193
Kleinzahler, August, 203
Kolatkar, Arun, 47, 184, 193
Krätli, Graziano, 168–169
"Kubla Khan" (Coleridge), 65–66
Kuṟuntokai, 48

"Labors of Hercules, The" (Moore), 64
"Lady Lazarus" (Plath), 79
La Fontaine, Jean de, 58
Language poetry, 219–220, 229–230
Larkin, Philip, 16, 65, 68, 129, 182, 196–197
"Later" (Armantrout), 150–153
"Late Romantic" (Ammons), 222
Laughter of Foxes, The (Sagar), 130–132, 135, 140
Laurans, Penelope, 114
Lawrence, D. H., 66, 76, 131, 189–190; Capildeo and, 256–257; on class, 69–70; Hughes and, 137–138; "Reading a Letter" by, 178; Salgādo and, 172, 177–178
Lazer, Hank, 217
Leader, Darian, 257
Leavell, Linda, 55–56, 60, 63
Leavis, F. R., 131, 135
Ledbury Emerging Critics, 2, 6
Leighton, Angela, 100–109
Letters to the Future (Hunt and Martin), 229
Levertov, Denise, 146
Life in a Box Is a Pretty Life (Martin), 237–238
"Like This or Die" (Lorentzen), 5–6
"Listeners, The" (de la Mare), 100, 108
Literary criticism: book reviews, 5–6; T. Hughes on, 135; Internet and, 5–6, 10–11; S. Johnson on, 8; by Mehrotra, 186–187; personal, racialized style of, 7; by poet-critics, 16–17; reading, 18; by Salgādo, 168, 172–176
Literary journalism: academic scholarship and, 1, 3–10, 23; book reviews and, 5–6; on nonwhite poets, 2–3
"Local Antiquities" (Ammons), 226
Locke, Alton, 46–47
Loffreda, Beth, 235
Logan, William, 250–251
Lolita (Nabokov), 50–52, 244
Lombardi, Marilyn, 126

Longley, Michael, 39
"Looking Out" (Mehrotra), 186–187
Lorde, Audre, 231
Lorentzen, Christian, 5–6
Love of Tropical Fish, The (Sagar and Swain), 137
"Love Poem for a Wife and Her Trees" (Ramanujan), 49–50
"Lover's Tale, The" (Tennyson), 103–104
"Loving People" (Ammons), 227
Lowell, Robert, 126, 194
Lyricism, 92, 209, 229, 239
Lyricization, 10, 232–233
Lyric poetry, 98; Capildeo on, 247; "I" of, 232, 237; love, 21–22; Martin and, 233, 237, 241; new lyric studies on, 5, 10, 231–232; by poets of color, 232–233; postlyricism and, 228–231, 233–234, 236, 242; Ramanujan's translations of, 49

Macbeth (Shakespeare), 136
MacNeice, Louis, 168
Magical realism, 156
Mahapatra, Jayanta, 187
"Major Macroo" (Smith), 66–67
"Man in the Blue Shirt" (Shukla), 160
Maniu, Iuliu, 31
Man with Night Sweats, The (Gunn), 204–205
Mare, Walter de la, 100, 108
Marlowe, Christopher, 255
Marriott, D. S., 230
Martin, Dawn Lundy: "After Drowning," 230; on Black bodies, 238, 240–242; on the body, 237–239; *Discipline*, 233–234, 236; *A Gathering of Matter/A Matter of Gathering*, 229; *Good Stock Strange Blood*, 231, 239–241; on her brother, 234–236, 240; on Jacobs, 242; *Letters to the Future*, edited by Hunt and, 229; *Life in a Box Is a Pretty Life*, 237–238; lyric poetry and, 233, 237, 241; *n+1* essay, 234, 240; "Negrotizing in Five; Or, How to

Write a Black Poem," 228–229, 239; poetics of, 238–239; postlyricism and, 231, 233–234, 236, 242; on race and racism, 234–235; Rankine and, 233, 235; "Sunday Lessons," 230; "25 Tiny Essays on the Value of Forgetfulness and Sleepiness," 238
Marvell, Andrew, 161
Maslow, Abraham, 225
Maud (Tennyson), 26, 104
May, Will, 65, 68, 72–73
McDonald, Peter D., 4
McLane, Maureen N., 9
Measures of Expatriation (Capildeo), 247–248, 253–255
Meeropol, Abel, 240
Mehrotra, Arvind Krishna, 16, 18, 44, 82, 154–157, 171; American verse and, 186; *Collected Poems*, 188; *Delhi, 1211*, 187; *Distance in Statute Miles*, 185–186, 190; "Dream-Figures in Sunlight," 193; "The Emperor Has No Clothes," 186–187; English language and, 185–190; "For a Slave King 2," 187; "Hoopoe," 186; *Illustrated History of Indian Literature in English* edited by, 184, 188, 190; "Inscription," 191–192; "January," 185–187; on Kabir, 184, 187–188; Kolatkar and, 184, 193; "Looking Out," 186–187; *Nine Enclosures*, 188, 192; "Number 16," 185; "On the Death of a Sunday Painter," 189–190; *Oxford India Anthology of Twelve Modern Poets*, 184–185; *Partial Recall*, 184–185, 188; on Ramanujan, 186–187; *Songs of Kabir*, 184, 187–188; "Songs of the Ganga," 192; "Songs of the Good Surrealist," 188; "The Sting in the Tail," 189; surrealism of, 188–189; *The Transfiguring Places*, 191; Tripathi translation, 191; "Two Lakes," 190–191
Memorial of the Victims of Communism and of the Resistance at Sziget, 30–32, 39

"Men, Women and Saints" (Ramanujan), 49
Microaggressions, 8, 247
"Middle Age" (Ramanujan), 47–48
Migrant perspective, 4
Mill, John Stuart, 89, 105
Miller, Margaret, 122–126, 128
Milner, Marion, 241
Miłosz, Czesław, 31; *Ars Poetica?*, 94; *The Captive Mind*, 92; on forgetting, 98–99; Franaszek on, 91–94, 96–97; "Incantation," 97–98; "In Common," 95–96; *The Issa Valley*, 93–94; Nabokov and, 90–92; "A Ninety-year-old Poet Signing His Books," 92; Nobel prize speech, 97; *Provinces*, 95; "Song on Porcelain," 98; translations, 92; *Treatise on Poetry*, 94–95; U.S. poets and, 98; "A Warsaw Faust," 90, 92; on Warsaw ghetto uprising, 93, 95; on Weil, 93; Western critics on, 98; on Western Europe and the West, 96–97
Milton, John, 15, 208, 219
Mint, 186
"Miracle, The" (Gunn), 203
Mir Muhammad Taqi: "Account of a Journey to Tisang," 22–23; on animals, 24; communication and, 132; Faruqi's translations of, 22–24, 27; ghazals by, 21–22, 24–29; on love and lovers, 25–29; *Remembrances*, 28–29; "Scolding the Rain," 27
"Mirror" (Plath), 147
"Misanthropos" (Gunn), 197–198
"Miss Snooks, Poetess" (Smith), 69
"Miss So-and-So" (Smith), 67
Modern Anglo-American verse, 23, 26, 44, 77–78
Modernism, 171, 178–179, 231
Modi, Narendra, 83, 167
Molesworth, Charles, 211
Moly (Gunn), 199
"Moonrise" (Hopkins), 219–220

Moonrise from the Green Grass Roof (Shukla), 160–166
Moore, Marianne, 140; on animals, 56–57; Bishop and, 55–56, 58, 60, 123, 138; "Black Earth," 56–57; "Bowls," 60; *Complete Poems*, 55–58, 60–61, 64; "The Fish," 60; "I May, I Might, I Must," 74; "Injudicious Gardening," 59; "The Labors of Hercules," 64; Leavell on, 55–56, 60, 63; *Observations*, 55–56, 58, 60–61, 63; "An Octopus," 62–63; "Picking and Choosing," 60–62; "Poetry," 60, 63–64; Ramanujan on, 44; "Reticence and Volubility," 58–59; "Roses Only," 59–60; self-editing, 60–63; Smith and, 70, 72, 74; "To Be Liked by You Would Be a Calamity," 59; use of quotations, 55–56, 58, 62–64, 70
"Moose, The" (Bishop), 112–114
Moraes, Dom, 41
Moretti, Franco, 15
Morrison, Toni, 103
Morrissey, Sinéad, 10
Mortal Acts, Mortal Words (Kinnell), 214
Moten, Fred, 239
Mother, What Is Man? (Smith), 66–67
Mount Rainier, 62–63
Mukherjee, Ankhi, 14
Muktibodh, Gajanan Madhav, 154–155
Murphy, Richard, 138
"My Life Up to Now" (Gunn), 196
"My Mother's R & R" (Kinnell), 217
My Native Land A4 (Blandiana), 31, 34–35
My Sad Captains (Gunn), 195
My Son's Father (Moraes), 41
Mysticism, 19, 29, 82, 207, 215
"My Students" (de Souza), 87
"Myths, Metres, Rhythms" (Hughes), 133

n+1, 234, 240
Nabokov, Vladimir, 50–52, 90–92, 99, 187, 244
Nagasaki, 215–216
Naim, C. M., 21

"Napoleon" (Holub), 93–94
Naukar Ki Kameez (Shukla), 154
Necklace of Skulls, A (de Souza), 79
"Negro Question, The" (Curry), 237
"Negro Speaks of Rivers, The" (Hughes, L.), 238
"Negrotizing in Five; Or, How to Write a Black Poem" (Martin), 228–229, 239
New lyric studies, 5, 10, 231–232
Niedecker, Lorine, 142, 144
Nine Enclosures (Mehrotra), 188, 192
"Ninety-year-old Poet Signing His Books, A" (Miłosz), 92
Nirala, 191
Noel-Tod, Jeremy, 250
North, Joseph, 6
North and South (Bishop), 121
North Central (Niedecker), 144
No Traveller Returns (Capildeo), 244–245, 249–250
"Not Waving but Drowning" (Smith), 72–74
Novel on Yellow Paper (Smith), 70, 104
Nuclear weapons, 206, 215–216
"Nucleus" (Ammons), 224–225
"Number 16" (Mehrotra), 185

Observations (Moore), 55–56, 58, 60–61, 63
"Octopus, An" (Moore), 62–63
"Ode on a Grecian Urn" (Keats), 145
Oedipus myth, 41
"Old Veranda" (Shukla), 154–155
"Old Woman, The" (Ezekiel), 257
"Olive Wood Fire, The" (Kinnell), 206, 214–216
Ommateum (Ammons), 218
"On a Girdle" (Waller), 68
"Once" (Armantrout), 149
Once It Flowers (Shukla), 155, 158–162, 165–167
"One: Many" (Ammons), 225
On Form (Leighton), 100, 103
"On Roller Skates" (Blandiana), 38
"On Shakespeare" (Milton), 219

"On the Death of a Sunday Painter" (Mehrotra), 189–190
"On the Move" (Gunn), 196–197
"On the Oregon Coast" (Kinnell), 215–216
"On Tiptoe" (Blandiana), 37
"Oranges" (Ramanujan), 52
Orghast (Brook and Hughes), 136
Othello (Shakespeare), 180
Oulipo, 243
"Over 2,000 Illustrations and a Complete Concordance" (Bishop), 116–117, 119
Owen, Wilfred, 100
"Own" (Armantrout), 150
"Owner of the Mill, The" (Blandiana), 35–37
Oxford India Anthology of Twelve Modern Poets (Mehrotra), 184–185

Palgrave, Francis Turner, 171
"Paradise Flycatcher" (Mehrotra), 192–193
Paradise Lost (Milton), 219
"Parents" (Smith), 67–68, 71
Paris Review, 120, 125–126
Parmar, Sandeep, 2, 228, 253
Parthasarathy, Rajagopal, 186
Partial Recall (Mehrotra), 184–185, 188
Partly (Armantrout), 149–150
Pascal, Blaise, 93
"Pass" (Armantrout), 150
Passages of Joy, The (Gunn), 203
Past, The (Kinnell), 215–216
"Pastorale" (Rayaprol), 171
Patea, Viorica, 36–37
Pater, Walter, 100
Pather Panchali, 159
Pathetic fallacy, 46–47
Patke, Rajeev, 171
Paulin, Tom, 16–17, 225
People of color, in literary and academic subcultures, 7–8
Perec, Georges, 161–162

"Perhaps Someone Is Dreaming Me" (Blandiana), 34
Perloff, Marjorie, 1–3, 17
Perry, Seamus, 130
Persian literature, 21, 29
Personal criticism, racialized style of, 7
Person Animal Figure (Capildeo), 250–251
Peters, Robert, 211
"Pets of Others, The" (Capildeo), 256
Pettingell, Phoebe, 206
Philip, M. NourbeSe, 229–230
"Picking and Choosing" (Moore), 60–62
Pinsky, Robert, 98
Pite, Ralph, 109
Plath, Sylvia, 79, 86, 131, 139–140, 147, 194
Plato, 160
Pnin (Nabokov), 90–92, 99
PN Review, 10, 247, 252
Poe, Edgar Allan, 243
"Poem" (Bishop), 117
"Poem" (Rayaprol), 182–183
"Poem for a Birthday" (Rayaprol), 181–182
"Poet, The" (Emerson), 127, 214
Poetics: Black, 233; classical, 53; of communication, 105–106, 112; of Martin, 238–239; poetry *versus*, 19; of prose, of Shukla, 160–161; of Ramanujan, 42, 53; Urdu, 26
"Poetics of the Physical World, The" (Kinnell), 207, 214
Poetry, 59, 106
"Poetry" (Moore), 60, 63–64
Poets of color, 2–3, 77–78, 232–233, 243, 252–253
"Policeman's Lot, A" (Cope), 64–65
Polish communism, 92, 97
Politics: in *All the King's Men*, 111–112, 115–116; Brexit and, 112–113, 119; identity politics and, 112, 118, 231, 246, 248; poetry, political crisis and, 117; "Quai d'Orléans" and, 124–125
Pollard, Charles, 78

Pope, Alexander, 100
Populism, 1
Portrait of the Artist as a Young Man, A (Joyce), 179
Postcolonial India, 191
Postcolonialism, 13, 43, 46, 53, 156
Postcolonial literature, 43, 168, 184
Postcolonial studies, 78
Postcriticism, 4, 6
Postlyricism and postlyrics, 228–231, 233–234, 236, 242
Pound, Ezra, 44–45, 78, 114, 210
Powys, Littleton, 74
Prac Crit, 141, 253
"Prayers" (Armantrout), 142–143
Prelude (Wordsworth), 180
Presentation of Self in Everyday Life, The (Goffman), 28
Pritchett, Frances, 24–25, 27–28
"Private Poem to Norman MacLeod" (Graham), 108
Proust, Marcel, 176
Provinces (Miłosz), 95
Przekrój, 93
Psychoanalysis, 49, 246
Puṟam poems, 48
Puttenham, George, 252

"Quai d'Orléans" (Bishop), 120–128
Quinn, Alice, 125

Race: Aristotle on, 238; Bishop on, 103; class, gender and, 14; gender and, 250; Jones on, 188; Martin on, 234–235; Moore on, 64; relations, U.S., 170
Race Traits and Tendencies of the American Negro (Hoffman), 237
Racism and racists, 8, 56, 105, 178, 234–235, 252–253
Radcliffe, Cyril, 192
Radhakrishnan, Rajagopalan, 11
Rai, Sara, 154–157
Ramanujan, A. K., 18, 217; "Anxiety," 53; on British Empire, 43–44; "Chicago Zen," 45–47, 53; on composition and decomposition, 52–53; Dharwadker on, 53; Doniger on, 40, 43–44; "Highway Stripper," 50–52; "Images," 41–42; immigrant experience and, 41–43, 53–54; on India and Indian literature, 43–44, 46, 53, 78; "Love Poem for a Wife and Her Trees," 49–50; Mehrotra on, 186–187; on memory, 42; "Men, Women and Saints," 49; "Middle Age," 47–48; on Moore, 44; on Oedipus myth, 41; on opinions, 42–43; "Oranges," 52; Pound and, 44–45; Rodríguez on, 45–47, 52–53; *Second Sight*, 19, 45; "Self-Portrait," 40–43; "The Striders," 44–45; on Tamil poetry, 44, 46, 48–49, 78, 186–187; translations by, 48–49, 78; as transnational scholar-poet, 40; "Who Needs Folklore," 49
Ramazani, Jahan, 5, 40, 78
Randi, James, 132
Rankine, Claudia, 8, 47, 231–233, 235, 247–248
Ray, Satyajit, 159
Rayaprol, Srinivas: "All Kinds of Love," 180–181; "Crabs in the Seine," 168–169; English language and, 169–170, 179–182; "Here It Is Spring Again," 170; "Pastorale," 171; "Poem," 182–183; "Poem for a Birthday," 181–182; Salgādo and, 168, 179–180; on sexuality, 180–181; "Sometimes," 169–170; "This Poem," 180; Williams and, 170–171, 181; "Yesterday," 170
Reading, 11–12, 15, 18, 23
"Reading a Letter" (Lawrence), 178
"Readings With Parrots and Angels" (Jussawalla), 78
Really Short Poems (Ammons), 218
Reddy, Srikanth, 233
Reed, Anthony, 228
Reid, Christopher, 129–130, 133, 135, 138, 140
Rekdal, Paisley, 6, 250

"Religion for Boys" (Shapcott), 65
Remembrances (Mir), 28–29
"Reticence and Volubility" (Moore), 58–59
Rich, Adrienne, 120, 216
Ricks, Christopher, 65, 74, 98, 246
Ring and the Book, The (Browning), 101
Rodríguez, Guillermo, 45–47, 52–53
Rolle, Richard, 29
Romanian Communism, 30–33, 38–39
"Roses Only" (Moore), 59–60
Rossetti, Christina, 100, 255
Roy, Jamini, 181
Różewicz, Tadeusz, 31
Rushdie, Salman, 185
Ruskin, John, 46–47
Russell, Ralph, 22, 27–29

Sagar, Keith, 130–140
"Saint Francis and the Sow" (Kinnell), 215, 217
Salgādo, Gāmini, 137–138; on Buddhism and Hinduism, 176–178; Copplestone and, 172, 176, 178; on English language, 173–174, 178–179; on Joyce, 178–179; Lawrence and, 172, 177–178; lecture on "Shakespeare and Myself," 172–176; literary criticism by, 168, 172–176; Rayaprol and, 168, 179–180; *The True Paradise*, 168, 171–172, 176–179
"Saliences" (Ammons), 226
Sandburg, Carl, 78
"Sandpiper" (Bishop), 101
Sannazaro, Jacopo, 251
"Santarém" (Bishop), 118, 124
Schopenhauer, Arthur, 257
Schwartz, Delmore, 209
"Scolding the Rain" (Mir), 27
"Season's End" (Blandiana), 38
Second Sight (Ramanujan), 19, 45
Sedgwick, Eve Kosofsky, 6
Selected Poems (Gunn), 195
"Self-Portrait" (Ramanujan), 40–43
Sense of Movement, The (Gunn), 196

"Sensibility and the Search" (Carter), 243
"Seven Letters" (Graham), 109–110
Sexism, 178, 225
Shakespeare, William, 46; English of, 173–174; Hughes on, 132–133, 136; *King Lear*, 27; *Macbeth*, 136; *Othello*, 180; *The Tempest*, 210, 253; *The Winter's Tale*, 255
"Shakespeare and Myself" (Salgādo), 172–176
"Shakespeare and Occult Neoplatonism" (Hughes), 132
Shakespeare and the Goddess of Complete Being (Hughes), 129, 134, 136
"Shame" (Capildeo), 244
Shapcott, Jo, 65
Shore, Jane, 23
Shukla, Vinod Kumar: *Blue Is Like Blue*, 154–156; "The Burden," 163–164; cinema and, 159–160, 163–164; "College," 155–157, 159; in Hindi language, 154, 156–160, 167; in Indian history, 154–155; on Indian people, 166–167; Khanna and, 154, 158–160, 166–167; magical realism and, 156; "Man in the Blue Shirt," 160; *Moonrise from the Green Grass Roof*, 160–166; *Naukar Ki Kameez*, 154; "Old Veranda," 154–155; *Once It Flowers*, 155, 158–162, 165–167; poetics of prose, 160–161; in translation, 157–158
Skin Can Hold (Capildeo), 243–244, 246, 248–249, 257–258
Sleigh, Tom, 204
Small, Helen, 219
Smith, Stevie, 87–88; on class, 67–70; "Dear Karl," 75–76; "A Dream of Comparison," 74; "The English," 68; "Everything Is Swimming," 71–72; *The Frog Prince and Other Poems*, 71; on gender, 66–67, 71–72; "Girls!," 66–68, 71; "How Cruel Is the Story of Eve," 66–67; "I Remember," 74; "Major Macroo," 66–67; May on, 65, 68, 72–73; "Miss Snooks, Poetess," 69; "Miss

Smith, Stevie (*continued*)
So-and-So," 67; Moore and, 70, 72, 74; *Mother, What Is Man?*, 66–67; "Not Waving but Drowning," 72–74; *Novel on Yellow Paper*, 70, 104; "Parents," 67–68, 71; "A Soldier Dear To Us," 75; "This Englishwoman," 68–69, 71; "Thoughts About the Person from Porlock," 65–66; "Too Tired for Words," 73; war poems, 74–75
"Soldier Dear To Us, A" (Smith), 75
"Sometimes" (Rayaprol), 169–170
"Song on Porcelain" (Miłosz), 98
Songs of Kabir (Kabir), 184, 187–188
"Songs of the Ganga" (Mehrotra), 192
"Songs of the Good Surrealist" (Mehrotra), 188
Sonnet 130 (Shakespeare), 27
Sontag, Susan, 184
Sound of sense, 8, 77
Souza, Eunice de, 77; "Bequest," 81–82; "Catholic Mother," 83–84; "Conversation Piece," 82–83; *Dangerlok*, 79–81, 83, 85, 88–89; *Dev and Simran*, 85–89; *Fix*, 83–84; "For S. Who Wonders If I Get Much Joy Out of Life," 79; "The Hills Heal," 86–87; on Indian voices, 80, 84–86; "It's Time to Find a Place," 82; on Muslims, in India, 83; "My Students," 87; *A Necklace of Skulls*, 79; speech sound, in writings of, 79–82, 89; "Sweet Sixteen," 84; "Travelling," 86; voice of, 79; "Women in Dutch Painting," 88–89
Soviet Union, 92
Spark, Muriel, 243
Speech, poetry and, 77–82, 89, 93, 119–121
Spencer, Herbert, 224
Spender, Stephen, 140
Sphere (Ammons), 218, 222, 224
Spires, Elizabeth, 120

Sri Lanka and Sri Lankan literature, 172, 174–179
"Stair Steps" (Blandiana), 38–39
Starr, Frederick, 237
"Stele" (Blandiana), 36
Stephen Dedalus (fictional character), 52, 178–179, 226
Stevens, Wallace, 9, 109, 162, 181, 207; Ammons and, 217, 219–220, 224, 226
Stevenson, Anne, 118
Still the Joy of It (Powys), 74
"Sting in the Tail, The" (Mehrotra), 189
Stonewall, 196
"Strange Fruit" (Meeropol), 240
"Striders, The" (Ramanujan), 44–45
Subjectivity, 6, 9, 175, 228
"Sunday Lessons" (Martin), 230
"Surfacing Surface Effects" (Ammons), 219–220
Surrealism, 188–189
"Sweet Sixteen" (de Souza), 84
Swinburne, Algernon Charles, 114
Sykes, Jim, 249
Symonds, John Addington, 104–105
Szymborska, Wisława, 31

Tagore, Rabindranath, 154–155
Tamburlaine (Marlowe), 255
Tamil poetry, 44, 46, 48–49, 78, 186–187
Tape for the Turn of the Year (Ammons), 218, 222–225
Taylor, John, 141
Taylor, Keith, 43
Tempest, The (Shakespeare), 210, 253
Tennyson, Alfred Lord, 26, 103–105, 170–171, 208
Thayer, Scofield, 55
"Thing" (Armantrout), 142–143
"This Englishwoman" (Smith), 68–69, 71
"This Poem" (Rayaprol), 180
"Thistles" (Hughes), 136
Thomas, Dylan, 243

Thomas, Edward, 100
Thomas, Harriet Tompkins, 118
Thomson, Veronica Forrest, 252
"Thoughts About the Person from Porlock" (Smith), 65–66
"Three Hard Women" (Gunn), 200
"Thrushes" (Hughes), 129
Times Literary Supplement, 1, 253
Tinguely, Jean, 34
"To Be Liked by You Would Be a Calamity" (Moore), 59
"Too Solid Flesh" (Capildeo), 254–255
"Too Tired for Words" (Smith), 73
To the Lighthouse (Woolf), 104
Touch (Gunn), 197
"Touch" (Gunn), 204
Transfiguring Places, The (Mehrotra), 191
Translation, 22–23, 48, 58, 157–158
"Travelling" (de Souza), 86
Travisano, Tom, 123, 126
Treatise on Poetry (Miłosz), 94–95
Tripathi, Suryakant, 191
Trollope, Anthony, 62
True (Armantrout), 146
True Paradise, The (Salgādo), 168, 171–172, 176–179
Twain, Mark, 172, 176
"Twelfth Morning; or What You Will" (Bishop), 101–103
"25 Tiny Essays on the Value of Forgetfulness and Sleepiness" (Martin), 238
"Twizzle" (Armantrout), 141–142
"Two, Three" (Armantrout), 145
"Two Lakes" (Mehrotra), 190–191

Ulysses (Joyce), 51–52, 250
Understanding Poetry (Brooks and Warren), 112, 114
Undraining Sea, The (Capildeo), 251–252
Urdu, 21–22, 26, 29
Utter (Capildeo), 252–253

"Vapor Trail Reflected in the Frog Pond" (Kinnell), 213–214
Veil (Armantrout), 149
Vendler, Helen, 15, 17, 98, 218, 227
Venus as a Bear (Capildeo), 245–246, 256
Versed (Armantrout), 150, 152
Verse sound, 100–109
Victorian verse, 171
Vietnam War, 47, 206, 212–214
Village in the Jungle, The (Woolf, L.), 176
Voices, in poetry, 145–146

Walcott, Derek, 3, 249
Waller, Edmund, 68
Warren, Robert Penn, 111–112, 114–116
"Warsaw Faust, A" (Miłosz), 90, 92
Warsaw ghetto uprising, 93, 95
Warwick Research Collective, 15
Waste Land, The (Eliot, T. S.), 38, 92, 210, 249
Waterman, Rory, 65
Waves, The (Woolf), 85
Weil, Simone, 42, 91, 93
Weird Women (d'Aurevilly), 71–72
Weissbort, Daniel, 140
West, Benjamin, 190
West, Robert M., 222
What a Kingdom It Was (Kinnell), 208–209, 212
What to See in America (Johnson, C.), 62
When One Has Lived a Long Time Alone (Kinnell), 216
Whiteness, 228, 232
Whitman, Walt, 75–76, 78, 129, 192; Ammons and, 218, 223, 227–228; Kinnell on, 214–215
"Who Needs Folklore" (Ramanujan), 49
Williams, William Carlos, 144, 170–171, 181, 201
Wilmer, Clive, 194, 196, 198–201, 203
Winter's Tale, The (Shakespeare), 255
Wittgenstein, Ludwig, 64, 74, 118, 162

"Women in Dutch Painting" (de Souza), 88–89
Woolf, Leonard, 176
Woolf, Virginia, 85, 101, 104, 253, 255
Wordsworth, William, 43–44, 117, 122, 174, 180, 249
"Wordsworth in the Tropics" (Huxley), 174
"World, The" (Creeley), 198
World literature, 156, 187–188
World poetry, 3, 11, 21–22, 77–78

World War I, 45, 136
Wright, James, 199, 211

Yeats, W. B., 43–45, 64, 75, 201, 219–220
"Yesterday" (Rayaprol), 170
"You Never See the Butterflies" (Blandiana), 31–33, 36

Zecchini, Laetitia, 4, 78
Zimbler, Jarad, 3

GPSR Authorized Representative: Easy Access System Europe, Mustamäe tee
50, 10621 Tallinn, Estonia, gpsr.requests@easproject.com

www.ingramcontent.com/pod-product-compliance
Lightning Source LLC
Chambersburg PA
CBHW022040290426
44109CB00014B/921